Global Challenges

A WORLD AT RISK

HARRY CLAY BLANEY III

Global
Challenges

A WORLD AT RISK

New Viewpoints
A Division of Franklin Watts
New York/London/1979

New Viewpoints
A Division of Franklin Watts
730 Fifth Avenue
New York, New York 10019

Library of Congress Cataloging in Publication Data

Blaney, Harry Clay, 1938-
  Global challenges.

  Includes bibliographical references and index.
  1. Twentieth century—Forecasts. 2. Social
prediction. 3. Economic forecasting. I. Title.
CB161.B547   909.82   78-21069
ISBN 0-531-05408-X
ISBN 0-531-05619-8 pbk.

To my parents
and
to my teachers

Preface and Acknowledgments

Intellectual debts are sometimes hard to recognize and harder yet to give proper credit to. When a book attempts to cover wide and complex fields, it is inevitable that some slighting or oversimplification may take place. For these errors of omission and commission, the author takes full responsibility.

Some particular debts and acknowledgments are in order since this book would not have been possible without the special help and work of others. First, I must thank The Woodrow Wilson International Center for Scholars at the Smithsonian Institution in Washington, D.C., for making their excellent facilities available. Both the basic research and some of the writing of this book were done during my delightful time there as a Fellow and later as a Guest Scholar. Very specific appreciation is due to Ben Read, the first director of the Wilson Center, and to his successor, James H. Billington, both of whom created an atmosphere of wide-ranging intellectual inquiry. Special individual thanks must go to Winston Lord, former director of the Policy Planning Staff at the Department of State, who permitted me a period of leave during a very busy time to work at the Center on portions of this book. I should also mention that *Global Challenges* would never have been possible without the opportunity to work on many of the issues explored in the following chapters with Daniel P. Moynihan, while he was counselor to the President, and Russell E. Train, then chairman of the President's Council on Environmental Quality.

A great obligation is owed to those who have read various portions of the text and/or provided me with their helpful advice. Within this group special gratitude is due to Kay Jones of the Council on Environmental

Quality, Gary D. Weatherford of The John Muir Institute, Philander P. Claxton, Jr. of the World Population Society, and William W. Lowrance of Stanford University.

A special word is needed about some of the statistics in this book. Although considerable effort has been made to use the most reliable and up-to-date data available, in many cases there are differences between existing sources, especially over future projections. Because the various sources sometimes use different data assumptions or bases, this results in differing figures, even for the same item. Thus, there will be cases in the text where nonuniform figures are used or wide ranges given. The alternative would simply have been not to provide the information at all. I have assumed that even disputed or less reliable data were usually better than none at all. In addition, one needs to remember that many figures are based on unsophisticated methods or even just broad extrapolations, especially for the developing countries.

All readers should be reminded of the statement of Sir Josiah Stamp of the British Inland Revenue Department (1896–1919): "The Government are very keen on amassing statistics. They collect them, raise them to the nth power, take the cube root and prepare wonderful diagrams. But you must never forget that every one of these figures comes in the first instance from the village watchman, who just puts down what he damn pleases."

Throughout this book there is one prevailing theme—namely, societal risk. This concept contains many complexities with respect to costs, probabilities, and benefits which will influence an individual's or a nation's assessment of what is acceptable and what is not acceptable. I would hope that the reader, in examining the issues raised, will reflect especially on what will be required in the way of education of the oncoming generation and about the capacity and resilience of national and international institutions to cope with a world of high risk. Risk analysis is done in an implicit or intuitive way by all humans, but when the risks become too many or unbearable our ability to assess and cope often breaks down. This in itself may be the most important risk we face.

Needless to say, the views expressed in *Global Challenges* do not necessarily represent those of the Department of State, the United States government, or any other organization with which I may be affiliated. The views herein remain solely those of the author.

Finally, a most personal acknowledgment to my wife, Julia Moore, who did more than anyone to assure the completion of this book through her long hours of editing, helpful critique, and support.

Harry Clay Blaney III
Washington, D.C.

Contents

Introduction:
Our Global Problems

The agenda for our global community for the rest of this century can, in part, be foreseen in the diverse forces at work in the world today. There are problems threatening. We will, it is now clear, have serious food shortages and imbalances and will have to husband our use of scarce natural resources with greater care. The world's population will grow from about 4 billion today to about 6 billion by the year 2000 which will put increasing strains on the world's economic and ecological balances. Fresh unpolluted water will be an increasingly scarce commodity. So, perhaps, will clean air. Our global environment will continue to be threatened by unchecked industrial activity with its dissemination of unknown quantities of toxic substances. More and more nations will have the capability to build and use nuclear weapons, opening up new quantitative and qualitative threats to the security of all the world's people. None can expect to be exempt from this danger, least of all those of us who live in advanced industrialized countries or for that matter those in urban and rural areas in the so-called Third World, only too often caught in religious, ethnic, or regional conflicts.

To cope with these issues all major nations must begin now to develop global policies and programs with a long-term world order perspective. Unless we come to grips soon with these global problems, we shall find ourselves in a short while in a situation where both the severity and the multiplicity of our difficulties will overwhelm the institutions we have created. These institutions were largely created to deal with the problems of the 1950s and not the 1970s, let alone the 1980s. It is for this reason that the United States and other nations must continue their work to provide a framework of world order to contain conflict and establish a measure of justice and progress for all people. Yet it is becoming increasingly apparent that neither the United States alone nor even the world community as now constituted possesses the ability to contain let alone solve the problems of the coming generation.

While forecasting is, at best, an inexact and often dangerous science, nevertheless present trends point to serious discontinuities which could upset the fragile international structure that now holds the world community together. We see this danger time and again as we confront such problems as food scarcity, energy shortfalls, environmental deterioration, population growth, terrorism, and the proliferation of nuclear weapons. The state system and the existing international organizations, created out of the last World War, appear almost anachronistic today. Our international institutions, as presently constituted, are already unable to meet current challenges.

The more serious danger is that the world system will experience a catastrophic collapse if enough of these factors approach a critical level together. Further, they are likely to do so before many more years go by if we take no corrective action now. We are clearly moving into a "high risk" world. The characteristics or signs which point towards this assessment are:

—Growing conflicts between the rich and the poor (the North/South gap);
—The specter of worldwide hunger, despite our efforts to provide food;
—Environmental decay, including fresh water and clean air becoming scarce resources;
—The growing irrelevance of much of the United Nations work as well as other international bodies and thereby the breakdown of a key part of the world's ability to solve its problems;
—The inability of the global system to deal with swiftly moving technology which affects common international areas such as the oceans and outer space;
—The growth of transnational influences such as terrorism and multinational corporations without corresponding effective control or regulation by responsible bodies;
—Rapid population growth and urbanization without adequate social and economic services or infrastructure, bringing enforced poverty to more and more people;
—Increased interdependence of nations without corresponding effective forums for decision-making to deal with the consequences of such interdependence;
—Growing scarcity of essential minerals and commodities;
—Collapse of common reference points (values and accepted legitimate authority) among key actors in the nation-state system;
—Uncontrolled new technology and chemicals run amuck, possibly

creating a number of worldwide calamities with no mechanism to assess
and deal with the consequences;
—Authoritarianism, racism, nationalism, and particularism expanding
in a fragile, dependent world needing cooperation;
—Continued weakening of the world's economic and monetary system;
and
—The growth and spread of nuclear weapons, fissionable materials, and
associated technology.

These and other signs point toward increasing instability and high
risk, threatening global well-being and security. If permitted to continue
unchecked by the collective action of responsible and affected nations,
the cumulative impact of these factors will be devastating not only on
world politics but also upon the personal lives of each of us.

To solve these future challenges we must move beyond mere holding
action or fire fighting. We must be able to do more than just respond to
one crisis after another as each emerges from a modern Pandora's box.
The characteristics of a high risk world are clearly foreseen in everyday
events from the energy crisis to terrorists' attacks or in the conflict over
the use of the oceans.

Nations and global institutions also must move from dependence on
the quick technological fix or temporary solutions and come to grips
with the fundamental forces at work in the world. Our ameliorative
actions must get at root causes and take into consideration the major
trends in contemporary history. We are in a contest not unlike war, but
we have not yet recognized the enemy, who is—in Pogo's unforgettable
phrase—us. The solution of these difficulties rests in large part on our
ability first to analyze our situation and then to seek and find corrective
measures. Above all we need the will and courage to persevere to the
end.

One element however is clear. The world of the late twentieth
century will not be less complex than today. It will probably not be safer
and, very likely, it will be far more dangerous. Can we, therefore, act
effectively now in building a framework and devising policies which can
fully cope with these emerging crises? If America and other responsible
nations were to stand aside from these often maleficent forces and
permit the fabric of international cooperation to be torn apart, then our
own lives and civilizing institutions would surely suffer.

The following pages present some of the main global problems we are
likely to face over the next two or three decades. They attempt to state
our current situation fairly, point towards likely trends, and highlight
the increasing strong interrelationship of each area to others. Finally,
some suggestions are made about possible courses of action which
hopefully will lessen our risks. These views are offered more in the

interest of starting a debate over what needs to be done than in the hope of setting forth any rigid solutions. The nature and the danger of these problems are that they evolve more rapidly than our ability to analyze or tame them. As we explore each challenge or issue, it will become quickly apparent that these are massive problems with complex relationships and antecedents and that there are no simple answers or fast technological solutions. Each risk requires a level of analysis and social response that we as individuals and as institutions have yet to provide. These risks will stretch our capabilities and imaginations.

Global Challenges

A WORLD AT RISK

CHAPTER I

A Technological and Political Overview: Coming to Grips with the Modern Age

Technology . . . creates new possibilities for human choice and action, but leaves their disposition uncertain. What its effects will be and what ends it will serve are not inherent in the technology but depend on what man will do with technology.
Emmanuel G. Mesthene, *Technological Change*

Salient Factors of Our Global System

One of the most significant elements of the transformation of our global system in the last few decades has been technological change. Even the most cursory examination of the salient factors of our time will show that there is hardly a single major political, economic, or social event or trend that does not have a major scientific or technological aspect. This overpowering impact of technology on society is likely to continue into the foreseeable future.

A quick survey of technology's influence on our age will demonstrate this point. First, the development of computers has clearly revolutionized the ability of industry and government to control product quality and output and to assemble a vast array of political, economic, and social data, making possible modern planning and forecasting. Second, food production and distribution has been radically transformed by the so-called "Green Revolution" (the introducton of new high-yielding grain varieties and the application of modern methods of farming). Third, human health and well-being generally have been changed by the introduction of new vaccines and (in a different way) the introduction of new chemicals and drugs. Fourth, population growth and family well-being have been altered by the introduction of new methods of contraception and of preventive medicine which lowers infant mortality. Fifth, television and radio in distant villages are making modern activities widely known and creating possibly a new world mentality. Finally, the combination of modern communications, especially space satellites with computers able to "talk" to each other over vast reaches of the globe, has established a worldwide framework for the dissemination of modern technological know-how which is a prerequisite for an integrated modern world economy. Taken together, the introduction of this new technology has assisted in creating the necessary information and industrial base to modernize a whole society.

Yet, if many of these factors have provided significant means to improve man's control over nature and increased his physical and intellectual productivity, they also have proved to be a mixed blessing in their impact on society. This new technology has brought mankind massive pollution which threatens our very ecosystem. It has created weapons of mass destruction which are already in the hands of irresponsible groups. And it has made possible an all-embracing repression of individual freedoms.

But what can be said about how technological change will influence our future world? Will the main trends that we discern at present continue? Will the technology which now is only in the development stage bring man new hope or bring him new despair? Will there be a growing disparity between the onrush of new technology and man's ability to control that technology and ensure that it does not have serious unforeseen, baneful, or even catastrophic results?

While we do not have definitive answers to these questions, we do know that the impact of such technology on future world political and economic development will be highly significant. From that technology will come new opportunities and new challenges that we only faintly understand at present. Great difficulties will almost certainly test our capacity to manage social and technological change. In any case, we cannot turn the clock back, we cannot purge modern science from the mind of man—nor should we. Given this background, what are some of the specific issues we will have to face over the next several decades?

The Factor of Change

Change is perhaps the most powerful force of present-day international life. In the past change often came at a much slower pace than is the case today. Yet even then the inability of individuals, cities, and nations to adapt to evolving historical trends resulted in a loss of power or even destruction. We have seen over the past centuries massive sweeping historical processes which have brought those on high to the brink of extinction while others have been raised up—often only for a brief period—by forces in technology, the economy, or social organization.

A dangerous element in change is our historical inability to perceive when it takes place and to understand its significance. The Athenians did not understand why their city-state declined, perhaps only the historians did. The same is true of Classical Rome. We usually find it easier to comprehend the social and economic forces of the past than the changes taking place in the present.

In the modern era one reason for our lack of perception is the complexity of the process of global social transformation. So many factors are at work in the global community at any given moment that they defy the ingenuity and the ability of man to examine or even describe them. Yet this capacity is required if we are to avoid dangerous risks threatening our stability and well-being.

We have seen from the past that the inability of a society to understand change resulted often in its decline, usually slowly. Today the results can be cataclysmic. Destruction, sometimes instantaneous, can be one result of our failure to understand the strong forces at work in the present world of high technology and rapid change.

An examination of history and change will show the decisive influence of technology and of increased knowledge. Looking back only little more than a century we find that those who shared in the fruits of the industrial revolution rose swiftly in power and wealth and spread their control beyond their own boundaries to those lands which did not participate in the process. (The same relationship exists with respect to the relative power of the modern sector vis-à-vis traditional society in many developing countries.) More recently the strength of American society has in large part been a result of both the scale of its economy and scientific and technological know-how.

If we were to examine the history of the impact of science and technology on society it would be a story of initially slow, even isolated, individual discoveries which only brought small changes since knowledge spread very slowly from town to town and from country to country. Science was seen as only one learned profession, academic and interesting—but not a major engine of historical change. For example, there was limited application or appreciation of scientific knowledge in the Middle Ages and therefore it was not seen as the main factor requiring adaptation of techniques, values, and social structures.

In contrast we see now how swiftly society has been affected by new technology; for instance the automobile and television are almost universal in urban areas and even in many rural areas in developed and developing countries. Today there are very short lead times between a discovery and its impact. Part of the reason is that science and technology have created a basic modern infrastructure which speeds the subsequent introduction of later discoveries. For example, the utilization of electricity helped the introduction of the telephone and of television. The telephone helped the dissemination of computers and data banks through the use of remote terminals. In modern times we find with the introduction of a new technology comes its almost instantaneous spread—at least within the modern sector. This spread often takes place beyond national boundaries since technology by its very nature does not easily recognize such artificial limits.

Another reason for this instantaneous spread of technology is the immense gain individuals or corporations can derive from its immediate utilization in many faraway locations. Because of the already existing technological infrastructure, there is a ready market to absorb new technology. This is one of the major reasons for the success of the multinational corporation, the repository of so much technical know-how. Even in the developing or poorer world the modern sector desires such innovations or improved methods. Thus we find even in many poor countries color television, expensive automobiles, jet planes, and large modern earth-movers. (However, as we shall see, traditional rural or poorer sectors, without the basic infrastructure, normally do not benefit from much of this know-how, a fact that has created serious imbalances.)

Change also is a function of the mind. Our global communications system makes it possible for many of the people of the world to share vicariously in new scientific and technological change even if it is far removed from their everyday life. For example, many people in remote towns in the developing world watched the landing on the moon. More immediately and of greater benefit, millions in far lands learn about new medical discoveries firsthand. For them new medical discoveries and the changes they bring to remote villages will radically alter their value systems, life patterns, and economy. Consequently, more children will survive to adulthood, they will be stronger and more efficient. This will eventually mean greater demands for food from local farmlands. More schools and teachers will be needed and, subsequently, increased migration to the urban centers will take place. In the end technology will provide family planning techniques so that family size can be predicted and ultimately regulated according to the availability of resources, food, and employment. Can anyone doubt that this will not mean a revolution in the old society? Traditional quickly will become modern. Technological man will rise up even in the remote villages and with him will come a new world.[1]

Another key aspect of change is the tension that it develops in the individual, in his local community, in a nation, and in the larger world system. These tensions can create new risks for the stability of the society or be the driving force for reform or renewal; often they play both roles simultaneously. Specifically, the introduction of technology into a society brings many changes in life-style, employment patterns, and income distribution. Finally, it can affect the fundamental values of the citizens and governments. New leaders emerge along with new needs. In the end the individual will become more dependent on others for their specialized skills and functions. In turn, communities and nations become more dependent on each other. Change thus will bring a growing awareness of the external world and this new consciousness may be the basis of acknowledgment of a wider responsibility.

In working with and trying to examine the nature of change, it is worth keeping in mind that one cannot simply attempt through the use of historical analogy to predict future events. There are insurmountable reasons why the application of historical analysis to the present world system is difficult, if not impossible. First is the fundamental time-gap between the past and the present. Another is the core problem of history: events and people are unique. Conditions are different even if they appear on the surface to be similar. What can be understood about the past is the impact of changing conditions on the action and attitudes of individuals and governments.

If we studied the last century or so, the period of introduction of new technology and communications, we could observe the impact of early and late industrialization on Britain, for example, with its changes in employment, education, mobility, and capital formation. But not least we would have to note also the more recent impact of the external world on this once great world empire and island nation. The two world wars with their destruction of people and resources, the evolution of Empire to Commonwealth, the relative growth of other world powers with their own technology, and finally the integration of Western Europe, initially without Great Britain, were all events with major results. Accompanying these factors were profound changes in the British economy and life: a decline in relative well-being and a decrease in competitiveness in world markets and in technological and business investment. The forces of change were immense but the results of these changes have yet to be fully played out in either Britain's internal society or its role in the world.

The past lingers on in many of Britain's institutions and behavior. The reasons for this are that there always is a time-gap, or "cultural lag," between reality and the institutions of society. The swifter the change the more likely the old institutions will continue to reflect a faded past rather than a complex present. Further, it is more likely that energies and resources will be put to work solving no-longer-existing old or less important problems than directing themselves to the problems of a new age. This is also the case today with many national and international institutions. Some efforts have been made to move these institutions and their activities towards future and present problems, indeed they often put out long studies of many of these global problems. But despite these studies little major reform or effective action takes place.

One of the reasons we have not been as good at understanding change as we might have been is that we are taught about a past world as if it were still existing; we are preparing ourselves for a world we no longer face. Even now our schools teach about the world of past decades and largely ignore the present let alone the future. Most of our present-day decision makers reached adulthood in the era of the cold war or earlier. Their perspective is largely of a world structure and of international relations as they were before the atomic age.

The challenges we faced and "managed" after the last world war are not the problems of the present. The traditional assumptions and techniques of international diplomacy are now inadequate to today's tasks. We will see this in the examination of specific global issues. We can no longer view world affairs simply as managing the balance of power or applying "great power" diplomacy. However relevant these concepts may remain, they cannot encompass the entire range of phenomena which must be understood if we are to avoid world disaster and if we are to shape the key forces at work in the world towards positive ends. We are required therefore to broaden our perspective of world affairs from the schematics of yesterday and move towards new approaches and new concepts.

A fundamental risk, therefore, rests as much in our own mind's rigidity as it does in the objective outside world. There is danger in the lack of adaptability on the part of our societies. To be adaptable means to be "able to adjust oneself easily to new conditions." Adaptability does not mean simply change for the sake of change but rather an ability to design society in such a way so that it can be flexible rather than rigid, without the loss of purpose or fundamental values. Often it is the pliant or bending tree that weathers the storm while the stiff and unyielding one falls. It is not at all certain that modern industrial society will be able in the future to deal with the kinds of global risks we face. There are many indications that we have done a poor job in handling new problems, especially in modifying our old national and international institutions to new realities and their concomitant risks.

We need therefore to recognize those factors or structures in society which prevent adaptability. Clearly there are traditions, institutions, and methods which rigidify people's minds and in turn their society. These can be a stumbling block to recognizing change and to addressing it in effective terms.

Technology and its Global Implications—Panacea or Pandora's Box

It has become poignantly clear that continued technological progress may not always serve mankind's best interest. Our ability to predict the final impact of any single scientific advance on society remains highly problematic. Furthermore, we have discovered in the most recent period that "technological progress" has significantly increased mankind's well-being but has at the same time brought certain risks.

Yet it is the nature of science to discover and invent—at an increasingly furious pace. Little thought often is given by these inventors to the consequences—to the secondary and tertiary impact of these technological advances on man. Some scientists have washed their hands of responsibility for consideration of the normative aspects of man's headlong rush for modernity. But more and more a balanced view is coming forward which holds that man needs innovation but he also needs the ability to control its dangerous consequences.

The interdependent nature of the world indicates we must face the reality that any choice we make which relates to broad-scale technological innovation or change will have an impact not only directly on the matter at hand but also on a whole range of social, political, and economic factors of major consequence for the world community.

A few examples of current issues will suffice to portray this interdependent relationship:

—Can mankind produce more food and other goods to feed growing populations without at the same time bringing increased ecological ravages which can obviate his efforts to achieve a higher quality of life?
—Can we increase the world's energy supply to satisfy growing needs without destroying our countryside, changing global climate patterns, or spreading nuclear weapons technology?
—Can we continue to use the ocean to obtain food and provide resources and transportation without destroying its basic ecology and our primary source of oxygen by treating it as a waste sink?

A start towards a solution to the problem of a sometimes dangerously malevolent technology must be to approach the new technology and its scientific base with qualified skepticism. One must first recognize the limits of technology in solving all of man's problems. Once this is accepted it is more likely that the full fruits of man's mastery over his environment can effectively and positively be utilized for his real benefit and enjoyment.

Science and technology do not, in themselves, provide answers to the major normative questions mankind is likely to face in the near future. They are part of the problem as surely as they are part of the answer.

Governments and their peoples will need to question the directions in which technology is taking them and assess the relative risks and benefits. This skeptical viewpoint is, in the final analysis, a Kantian view of man as he stands before nature with his modern scientific perspective.[2]

A growing debate among decision makers and scientific elites, which will continue into the foreseeable future, is how society will control the unanticipated and unwanted consequences of scientific advances. While one of the major elements of this debate focuses on the question of whether the overall impact of science and technology will bring a new dawn for mankind or let loose upon us unknown disasters, the more difficult issue is how can change be managed for man's benefit and to decrease his risks. The debate, unfortunately, has been too often directed towards either "pro" or "anti" science arguments, which blind us to the real nature of the problem. The public, for example, sometimes links the science of nuclear physics with the development of the destructive hydrogen bomb, the damaging radiation from nuclear power plants, or with the overuse of X rays. Computers are sometimes seen as dangerous repositories of essentially private information. The development of new synthetic plastics and affiliated petrochemical industries is associated with environmental pollution problems.

On the defensive, the scientists have taken the position: "Scientists should advance science. Technologists should continue to apply scientific advances to change the products, services, and processes that support society." Some scientists say that any harmful effects should be prevented through public concern, governmental action, and scientific agreement. Yet this generalized approach provides little help on specific problems of controlling technology which could have undesirable consequences.[3]

There is however increasing perception, at least among some observers of technology and public policy, that we cannot continue to react to problems which come from new scientific discoveries. Rather, we must look to preventing these "problems" before some new scientific discovery is introduced into everyday use. As in medicine, however, the cures for existing scientific problems are given higher priority than the prevention of the possibly harmful side effects.[4] "Preventive medicine" still has not established a strong following either among doctors or within the governmental and private scientific community.

Uncertainty and High Risk

The essence of the technology-control problem was stated by Professor Wolf Hafele: "The magnitude of technological enterprise will be so great that it will not be possible to proceed with the absolute certainty that there will be no negative consequences."[5]

More simply, we are moving into a world in which, while the likelihood of ultimate disaster is very low, the all-embracing consequences of that eventuality are so great that the risk is unacceptable for mankind. We may also be moving into a situation where at any given moment the probability of some disaster is not very high, but over a given period of time it is likely to occur and with costs which are unacceptable. This situation appears to be already existing in a number of areas we shall be examining later. It is enough here to note that we are moving into a world of both high risk catastrophes and high probability. Hopefully, before it's too late, it will be recognized that there needs to be a better approach to global decision making in order to deal with these high risk situations. Toxic wastes, biological experimentation, marine pollution, the spread of nuclear weapons are all in this category today. This list will certainly be expanding in the near future. Further, it is likely that in the future we will be unable to assess the exact dimensions of the risk or even its probability since the nature of the technological enterprise is such that tests to verify risk/probability factors cannot be run without bringing about the catastrophe we wish to avoid. It is also possible that the probability of such risks will become, even without our knowledge, increasingly higher with the passage of time.

In this context, it is important that society examine and reckon with the normative and political implications that flow from technological change and the appearance that science has its own dynamism, which is able to impose its will upon man and his social institutions. If, indeed, science and the utilization of its associated technology are largely the results of impersonal or at least uncontrolled forces, then we certainly have lost a part of our freedom. Man then could become a kind of slave of the very forces that his mind and ingenuity have let loose to conquer nature and expand his choices. Science's purpose was to set him free of "natural forces" but now it could help enslave him. The irony of this is clear but the solution is not. Certainly part of the key to moving towards a resolution of this dilemma is understanding better the interaction between the way technology is used in society and the degree of knowledge and choice achieved by our citizens. Long ago some of our literary predecessors—the writers about utopias and disutopias— described vividly what can become of man if his technology is used to enslave him. Some foresaw this result without the necessity of malicious intent by those who controlled governments. While *Brave New World* or *1984* is not quite here yet, some of their elements have already arrived and we are now living with them uncomfortably.

On the other side, we also know that technology and science can assist in the liberation of man when harnessed by the necessary tools which give to the individual greater choice about his life and his society's future. If technology has proven to have unfortunate secondary effects, it has also proven to have great potential in freeing mankind from many forms of traditional tyranny. But the problem is that technology has not, in practice, fulfilled its potential and for the poorest it remains a largely unknown and even fearful phenomena.

What we are increasingly seeing is a kind of "future shock" on a global institutional scale. Our problems are growing faster than our solutions. The capabilities of national governments to deal with the growth of problems confronting them has, in relative terms, decreased and may decrease further in the coming years. Evidence of this is everywhere—civil strife, global food shortage, massive environmental damage, too rapidly growing populations and increasing urban blight.

With the continued prospect of accelerated technological change, we can foresee over the next twenty-five years not just a "single wave of change but a series of terrible heaves and shudders."[6]

We can imagine whole new technologies which can tear at the basic fabric of national and international communities. There will be gaps between knowledge and action, between institutional capabilities and corresponding new dangers. In these circumstances we increasingly experience the harsh reality of the "crisis syndrome." The analogy between the common man faced with an ever-changing, fast-paced society he does not fully understand or feel at home with and the global community similarly confronted has increasing validity.

Global Risks Without a Global Community

While technology has had its impact, ideology and other factors have greatly influenced the global community. Much has been written about the building of a "Global Society" in the past and in the present, yet we still see great divisions even within national communities—new and old animosities which sap both spirit and resources.[7] In truth, we may be moving towards a divided world. Divided by growing nationalism and other forces. Only in the advanced industrial world, and there among the "elite" who are rich and well-fed, is the concept of one world popular. In the rest of the world, nationalism, regionalism, tribalism, and racism are in the ascendancy. Ideological differences exacerbate these divergent forces. Southern Africa is divided along both racial and tribal lines. Ideological and cultural differences split Western and Eastern Europe. Nationalism and regionalism threaten conflict in Indonesia, Spain, India, Ethiopia, and the Middle East.

The dangerous element in these conflicts is that nationalism is on the rise when the world faces problems which can be dealt with only by a recognition of how interdependent we have become. Henry Kissinger has put it well: "The moral and political cohesion of our world may be eroding just when a sense of community has become indispensable." He stated the problem even more succinctly when he said: "The world has shrunk, but the nations of the world have not come closer together."[8] It is this factor that holds so much risk for the world political system and in the end for each individual. We still do not know whether technology, which has created so many new risks, has also contributed to the development of a cooperative and integrated world community. It will be important in the building of any true global community to refocus the attention of citizens and their leaders from the divisions of the past towards the problems of the future.

Linear Projections and Thinking Global Trends

While there have been many critics of the Club of Rome's *The Limits to Growth* the work has performed one vital and important function.[9] It has raised our collective consciousness about the need to think in global and future-orientated terms about our mutual problems. In particular, in its advocacy of a global model and the development of adequate analysis of quantitative inputs into a global system, it has stimulated (along with other writers and institutions) the necessary process of developing the tools which the world community needs to assess its problems and to act together in solving them. The irony, of course, is that it took a private group, the Club of Rome, to put together many of these long-term issues and attempt (not completely successfully) to provide a computer-based, unified and coherent system of analysis which could be used to make normative judgments and decisions about the pace and direction of modern civilization.[10]

While we have now started the process of thinking about the globe as a single unit, we have not yet moved to the process of acting as such. As more and more research is completed with better empirical data, we should have the necessary tools not only to think about the globe as a single interdependent entity, but also to analyze it systematically as such. But it is still not enough to have only basic data inputs and the analysis of social scientists. The main need is for the political will and the institutional mechanisms that can translate knowledge into purposeful action. That remains, given political circumstances, still a distant prospect.

There are also many other studies showing projections of the world's natural resources and its economic growth.[11] These works often provide linear projections of such future trends as population growth, increased air pollution, depletion of natural resources, consumption patterns, per capita income, etc. Some of these efforts still remain, however, in the category of personal predictions or simply linear projections of the past into the future. Some are more sophisticated and offer all kinds of inputs/outputs with "positive" and "negative" feedback loops, etc. These purport to provide empirical and dynamic models, complicated enough to take into consideration all relevant facts, yet simple enough to give answers which are intelligible to a decision maker. Considerable skepticism must still remain about some of these more or less dynamic models, for few have really taken into consideration *all* or even most relevant and important factors. Fewer still have the necessary *hard* data base which often is required before meaningful conclusions can be drawn and necessary corrective actions taken. It would be very unwise to make massive changes in society based on unsupported conclusions from doubtful data. These kinds of instant quantitative projections (and sometimes doomsday prophecies) have and will give an unnecessarily bad name to the important analytical efforts which must be supported and encouraged to grow. A key element which will influence global decision makers will be the adequacy of information and the degree to which it has been shared, examined, and debated. There will, of course, come a time when decisions will simply have to be taken without firm or certain data because of the nature of the risks faced.

The Information Revolution

In this connection, one of the most salient characteristics of the twentieth century has been the revolution of knowledge and information as a common commodity and as an instrument of change. This affects not only the individual human consciousness but all elements of civilization. Information creates new opportunities and makes what was once inconceivable possible. It can give new strength to old institutions or it can bring old institutions down as swiftly as war or natural disasters.

Knowledge is power. When a person or a society fails to act on the basis of new information it will either destroy itself or be destroyed by others who do understand the meaning of new knowledge. Thus, a very high premium is placed upon the capacity to assimilate new information, analyze its implications, and utilize it in an integrative and effective manner. Empirical knowledge requires disciplined analysis and an organized framework for it to be most useful and least harmful. The rapid dissemination and utilization of knowledge within a society is perhaps the key criterion of its true modernization. It is vital for almost all advanced sectors of society and is the basic prerequisite for continuing technological progress.

Information about changes in society, new technology, and its possible dangers have created a new kind of common awareness and a basic shared storehouse of knowledge which makes possible collective and meaningful decision making in a modern democratic society. Television and radio have made possible a national consciousness, a common language, and a common information base. The political dimensions of instant shared information on the national level are evident. But we have not yet seen their full implications for the global community since a truly worldwide and broadly accessible communications system does not yet exist. Its impact if established, however, will be profound. It is also evident that such a global information system cannot be prevented from ultimately existing unless we wish to turn the clock back on technology and its fruits.

The implications are vast—either countries "plug" into the system, or they fall increasingly behind. But to "plug" into the growing world communications network means maintaining the necessary scientific software and hardware infrastructure so that the data can be effectively used. To be most effective, this global data network will require a certain kind of openness and freedom to communicate which has its own inherent requirements. Such an open system will probably have a vast impact on governmental institutions which wish to be a part of the system. For example, the Soviet Union and Eastern Europe will have to choose between permitting open access to the flow of information or falling even more behind in their efforts to modernize.

Modern mass communications technology also can change the expectations of people and thereby affect both national and international social and political systems in profound ways. Information can and does make slaves masters and masters slaves. Used wrongly, it can help keep some men in servitude. It can be used to perpetuate an existing elite in power or free the suppressed, common man.

Information spread by mass communication technology can provide a whole new world outlook. It could stimulate rising expectations including political unrest. It has and will be the object of much future conflict in the next decades as the global community decides who will control and have access to information. Important decisions will have to be made about the use of the global data systems. Who will control the inputs and outputs of knowledge? Will they be maintained by international bodies or by competing blocs of nations or individual governments? Will only governments have access to this information or will the individual also have access and be able to contribute directly to the system? Will it in effect be a democratic and open information system or a closed and authoritarian one?

The answers to these questions will have an impact on the development of the technology itself and finally on who will benefit from the technology. For example, information from computer-based data banks is now largely accessible to urbanized populations, large corporations, big universities, or governmental bodies. Other groups have less access and thereby relatively less power and ability to "affect" the system. Further, the management of complex information requires, initially, a certain amount of increased centralization and this could influence the concentration of basic information into fewer and fewer centers. The consequences could be a narrowing of the opportunity for individuals to participate meaningfully in decisions about the course of society and perhaps greater alienation of the general public.

This same technology can move in the opposite direction through deliberate efforts to disseminate information widely. Remote, cheap, and small computers, with access to large data banks through telephone lines or linked directly to satellites, can work to assist in the wider distribution of knowledge within an individual society or between nations. The dispersion of information is, perhaps, one of the truly great unsolved problems of the globe. It relates strongly to the need for improved educational opportunities. The combination of modern communications technology and computer-based information can mean new opportunities to expand education into areas and to persons not now reached. In some situations only access to information can bring about substantial improvements in the quality of life and productivity of people in the poorest countries.

Therefore, the challenge to utilize technology fully for this purpose is great. Unfortunately, only limited efforts have been made and even fewer successes have resulted. Time is crucial, since information is growing exponentially and the gap between those with and those without modern knowledge is growing at the same pace. Unless we wish to see a "brave new world" of just "Alphas" and "Deltas," a much greater effort will need to be made to disseminate modern knowledge than has taken place heretofore. Such a gap between individuals and between societies cannot help but create tension and instability.

The Problems of Equity and Oppression

Associated with this special "technological gap" and the realities of who controls technology is the normative problem of equity and the use of technology to oppress. We have just seen some examples of how control over information can lead to authoritarian rule. These problems need greater examination. The general assumption of the modern western spirit has normally been that technology would bring greater benefits to more people and somehow (only implicit in the assumption) a fairer distribution of its largesse. Clearly, this simple assumption has largely been wrong.

The developing countries seem sometimes to be worshipping the scientific-technological idol with blind devotion. Advanced technology for these countries implies automatically a better life—so the rhetoric of some of the leaders of these countries goes. But usually it means only a better life for the already benefited elite. Unfortunately, what we are recognizing more and more is that the new and expensive technology often enlarges the gap between the already rich and modern, and the poor and traditional.

Indeed, technology is seen by some thoughtful observers increasingly as an instrument of oppression in the developing world because of the wide gap between the very rich (possessed of modern scientific knowledge) and the very poor (still living in the pre-scientific age). The temptation is great for the few to continue their predominance over the many through modern technology, thus compensating for their numerical weakness. It is possible that this kind of oppression will be justified in terms of advancing productivity and modernity. It is just as likely that the scientific elite in the developed world (their professional allies and "colleagues") will not only acquiesce in this oppression but will indeed assist it in the holy name of science and "modern civilization" and perhaps economic gain.

We must seriously ask ourselves if this model of an "oppressive technology" and its associated political system are the likely results or even inevitable one. The answer probably is no, but it must be a qualified no. It is qualified by the possibility that progress can be made towards improving ways of giving man and his institutions the ability to control the elements of technology which are likely to be harmful to man's liberty and his natural environment. It probably is not a technological problem but one of adapting man's whole society and especially his institutions so as to maximize his freedom and creativity in the face of rapid change and new possibilities to shape or destroy his natural environment. It is this challenge perhaps more than any other which will be the key to man's survival in the last quarter of the twentieth century and beyond.

Technology and Modern Man

In the final analysis the main question is whether man, having developed the knowledge and technology to destroy both his environment and himself, can refrain from using this power indefinitely for destructive ends. One difficulty is that while some of this technology was developed to be destructive, much of it was created to benefit man and to improve his quality of life. Yet we now have enough experience with the negative consequences of so-called beneficial technology to know that there is a great degree of uncertainty in the introduction of any scientific innovation. We have seen where nuclear technology, itself a by-product of weapons efforts, which once promised to usher in a new age of energy abundance, now has become a major threat in contributing to the proliferation of nations with the capability of manufacturing atomic weapons and the spread of dangerous radioactive waste.

For many the answer to this potential for destruction is the introduction of even more technology to control the earlier technology's unforetold consequences. This approach, however attractive to the supporters of unbounded technological progress, is both simplistic and naive. It does not take into consideration the weakness and imperfect role of social institutions and human beings. It assumes almost perfect knowledge on the part of the introducers and the controllers of technology and the subsequent control mechanisms. It also assumes an unrealistic evaluation of the ability of the human mind and of the unselfishness of the human spirit. In the end it contains a kind of tautology, the answer to technology run amuck is more technology. This is the approach of those who advocate the "quick fix" method of solving the world's problems. This group is numerous. A few years back it was represented by those who pushed nuclear energy to solve the oil crisis. We have had those who advocated "the limits to growth" and called for a radical reduction in the use of natural resources. Each of these viewpoints represents a partial truth and perhaps a partial lie. Indeed, we do need to substitute new energy forms for depleting oil. It is also necessary to conserve more natural resources, to employ recycling methods, etc. But these approaches bring with them their own problems.

Nuclear energy results in proliferation of weapons, thermal pollution, and increasing levels of radioactive waste. A radical shift towards the reduction in the use of minerals, natural resources, and energy could bring a worldwide recession and lower the standard of living for large numbers of people in developed and developing countries. Clearly each isolated "response" to a global problem shares an element of creating an additional risk. The conclusion is that we should be somewhat skeptical of single track grand solutions. This is not to say that new technology or approaches are not better than those that preceded them; often, in fact, they are.

We have learned that each new technology requires great care and planning in its use if it is not to create as many problems for society as its predecessor created. We are now beginning to ask the question of whether it is not possible to do a better job in managing our new inventions than has been the case in the past. We have seen this in the number of critical books and articles that have been written over the last decade about the problem of technology management or assessment. Further, a few countries have started to establish central governmental focuses for weighing the costs and benefits of technology. These are at least a beginning.

Even as we move towards a more planned approach to the introduction of new methods there have been voices from the scientific community warning of the dangers of too much control over science. A debate has been joined about the relationship between man and nature, between society and its handiwork. Modern man is being forced to come to terms with his own inventions. It has not been a very pleasant confrontation. It has been filled with contradictions and compromises. But what was implicit always between man's creation and the limits and the laws of nature is now being made explicit. In the end it will result in a greater respect for both nature and science.

The control of technology has not yet become a vital element of immediate public concern in many countries, but for some countries pressing issues have brought sharp debate. The question of control has started to reach into the everyday life and politics of modern society. The issue is found when a new nuclear plant is sited, when a new dam is proposed, or when the public demands some control over pollutants from a factory or automobiles. It exists over SST flights and over the use of aerosols.

The public in most free, industrialized countries is aware that the modern environment is polluted by a growing number of new technological and chemical hazards. Together and individually these hazards are making ordinary living more and more dangerous. The public is learning about a world of high risk not from turgid academic tomes, but from their daily newspaper and from immediate experience: from smog-filled air, dirty oceans, toxics in drinking water, and contaminated food. This experience brings reality to the debate and this, in the long run, will create the basis for reform.

One problem is that the "common man" does not see the issues in the same way as the scientist. What the average citizen desires is to be free of unexpected hazards. He realizes that he must depend upon the knowledge, experience, goodwill, and ability of those who control technology and of the public institutions that are created to act in his interests. There is an analogy between the relationship of an individual and his government in dealing with specific environmental and social risks and that of a nation and the global system in dealing with global challenges. The global community needs to act in those areas where an individual nation cannot protect its citizens. The citizen today acknowledges the need to depend on the acts of government to protect him from dangerous technology. He does not yet recognize that the global situation is in many ways similar.

The issue of man's control over change and new technology, over his environment and choice, is being debated in professional groups, prestigious academies, and governmental circles. While more sophisticated than its public counterpart, the debate contains some common elements but it also has important differences. A most important difference is that many scientists see in the airing of the question of public regulation of technology a danger to freedom of scientific inquiry and experimentation.

Science, a profession that in the past has been seen as the vanguard of progress and human well-being, is now under attack for helping bring upon society a number of man-made disasters or at least serious nuisances. This has caused some individuals or groups within the scientific community to respond in a defensive way, citing the many goods that science has brought and arguing the case for unfettered freedom of experimentation and, by inference, for a "free marketplace" approach to the introduction of science's end product, technology.

In the same way we also see industrial groups, entrepreneurs, and other institutions with an interest in the selling of technology take an equally defensive posture against almost any kind of governmental or public oversight of new technology and its utilization. The arguments made by this group reflect and draw upon the views of certain segments of the scientific community which support unlimited freedom of experimentation. The point is made that "progress" can only continue in the context of maximum freedom of scientific inquiry and innovation.

The authoritarian countries, like the Soviet Union, are cited as examples of where the dead hand of the bureaucracy and its control over science and entrepreneurship has destroyed growth and retarded man's progress. There is a great degree of truth in this but it does not meet the main issue of the need to provide a better means of reducing the high level of risk. The advocates of unfettered technology are as unrealistic and as myopic as were the nineteenth-century robber barons in their advocacy of pure *laissez faire* in business. We now realize the many benefits of some regulation and the harm that the application of Social Darwinism to industrial business behavior did to our environment, to social justice, and to competition in economic affairs. In the end we will need to come to terms with both the requirements of advancing man's scientific knowledge and the need to protect society from unacceptable risks.

The challenge is almost of Daedalian or Icarian proportions: of man who reaches too far and fast with his own technology. How can society ensure that dangerous risks are minimized while preserving freedom of inquiry and stimulating creative and entrepreneurial talents for beneficial purposes? This will become an increasingly major topic of examination and debate within nations and ultimately within the international community. This will be especially the case if existing institutions show they are ill-equipped to provide necessary answers and carry out remedial action.

This larger issue exists in many different forms and places such as the control of weapons of mass destruction, the protection of life-sustaining ecological systems, the food/population equation, and in the use of scientific knowledge to control and manipulate individuals and societies. It also is raised by the question that is being asked by many: why has not man's extensive scientific and technological know-how been more effectively employed in alleviating man's sickness, his poverty, and his ignorance?

CHAPTER II

Human Needs-
Human Dangers

THE POPULATION CHALLENGE

Global Facts and Their Consequences

The world now faces an unprecedented growth in population. We have the fastest growth rate in human experience along with the highest population base ever known. To the current base of more than 4 billion we are now adding some 76 million additional people annually. These absolute figures may increase even if the growth rate itself is somewhat reduced. Currently the developing countries constitute some 70 percent of the world's population and account for some 86 percent of the annual increase.

Current estimates are that the world's population is increasing at about 1.8 to 2.0 percent per year.[1] Projections, using the United Nations' "medium variant," now predict a world population at the end of the century of about 6.26 billion. The present estimates reflect new population totals and new assumptions about fertility and mortality in various parts of the globe. Also some fertility rates have recently declined due, in part, to family planning programs and legalization of abortion. However, the world's population will still grow by the end of the century some 58–60 percent larger than it is now. Unless greater and more effective efforts to slow population growth are undertaken, it is possible that the present rate of increase of about 1.8–2.0 percent per year will grow slightly during the next ten years before it gradually slackens off by the end of the century. (See Figure II-1.[2])

In examining the problem of how to deal with population growth one must recognize a key factor, namely that a large proportion of the

Figure II-1.   World population growth

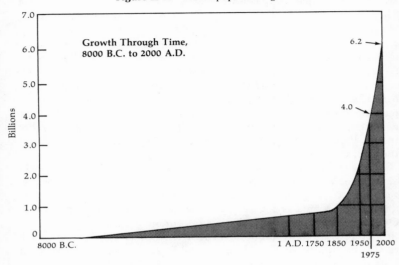

population of most developing countries consists of children and very young people. These young people are entering the reproductive ages far more rapidly than older people are leaving them. The number of people in the age span of human reproductivity is constantly increasing. Unless the fertility of the individual is decreased, there is a potential for many more births each year. This momentum of population growth is built in and the problem cannot be solved over the short term only. Yet, it is extremely important that an early start be made to reduce the rates of population growth. A great deal of difference exists between achieving "replacement" levels by the year 1985 or by 2000 and achieving them by 2020. In a typical developing country, a ten-year delay in reaching a two-child family average will result in about a 20 percent increase in the population size when it levels off. No matter how much present rates are eventually reduced, most large developing countries will experience very substantial population increases due to this built-in momentum. This is, however, an argument for rapid action, not for delay in dealing with this question.[3]

Population growth rates themselves vary greatly from region to region, country to country, and from area to area. In nations the population growth rate ranges from 3.5 percent in Honduras, 3.2 percent in Mexico, and 2.4 percent (possibly somewhat lower) in India to a 0.6 percent natural increase in the United States. The two Germanys, however, have a negative growth rate. The greatest rates of growth by far are in the developing countries of Asia, Africa, and Latin America. These rapid growth rates in most developing countries are a heavy burden on the health, welfare, and quality of life of individual families and on the economic and social development of countries. In practical terms, in most of these countries, it absorbs a half, two-thirds—in some cases all—of their per capita economic growth.

Many of these countries already recognize the problem and have official population growth limitation policies and programs. However, most of these programs are new and reach only a very small part of the needy population. The danger continues in many of these countries that the food/population equation will continue to deteriorate seriously over the next decades.

While many countries at least permit private family planning services to be made available to their citizens, some countries actively oppose birth control programs. Among the Communist countries, the People's Republic of China and Cuba have rigorous birth control programs. Others, including the Soviet Union, encourage population growth, but they do provide contraception and abortion and have, in fact, low birth rates. Still others, such as Hungary and Rumania, have revoked their laws allowing abortion. Many African leaders believe their countries are underpopulated and that economic development will make family planning programs unnecessary. There are exceptions to this viewpoint, notably Kenya and Ghana. Nigeria has also recently adopted a national family planning policy and other countries are considering steps in that direction.

In Latin America there are mixed attitudes. Argentina, Peru, and Uruguay are pronatalist. All Central American countries and a number of others have, in fact, official family planning programs. Mexico recently has undertaken a massive national program. The Catholic Church hierarchy has acted as a restraining influence in several countries, but national leaders have cautiously moved forward. Marxists, following their traditional anti-Malthusian viewpoint, are aggressively opposed to national support for birth control programs even though the great Marxist countries, the Soviet Union and China, and most of the Marxist countries of Eastern Europe have them.

In the Middle East, Egypt has a strong population program; Tunisia, Morocco, and Turkey less vigorous ones. Others in this area are less concerned about population problems. The Islamic League has taken a position against family planning. In Asia almost all countries (except Burma) have national population growth control programs. The most vigorously followed and successful program in the area is in Mainland China.

The United Nations World Population Conference at Bucharest in August, 1974, helped to focus world opinion on this topic and produced a World Population Plan of Action agreed to by 136 countries. On its face it promotes recommendations that, if followed, could lead to effective population control programs and rapid reduction of birthrates. The debate at Bucharest reflected strong differences among the Marxist nations and most others about the nature of the world's population growth problem and how to deal with it. The Marxist countries and a few other countries emphasized the importance of social and economic development, some asserting it as a precondition for the reduction of high fertility, and attempted to reduce the emphasis on population/family planning programs. Essentially, all non-Marxist industrialized countries, nearly all of the countries of Asia (except China), and many other countries urged greater recognition of the importance of these latter programs as necessary elements in a comprehensive development program. Quantitative goals or time frames for reduction of birthrates or population growth were not included in the World Population Plan of Action but the option of individual countries to set goals and undertake policies and programs to attain them was affirmed.[4]

The nations of Asia and the Pacific (except China), meeting in a Post-Bucharest Consultation in Bangladesh in January, 1975, adopted the goal of making available family planning services to all of their people by 1980 or 1985 and for affirming replacement levels of fertility in two or three decades (1995 to 2005). Such reduction would mean a total of 500 million fewer people below the United Nations medium projection for world population by the year 2000. By 2050 the reduction would be approximately 3 billion. The World Population Plan and the nature of the debate at the Bucharest Conference indicate that continued national and international action in the population field is required to develop the recognition among national leaders of the necessity for major population programs with clear goals.

The Food/Population Growth Imbalance

Perhaps the most serious challenge of rapid population growth from a humanitarian viewpoint will be the adequacy of world food supplies for the developing countries as their populations press against limits of available land, water, capital, and other resources.

The most obvious and compelling aspect of interdependence and linkage today is that between food and population. Population growth is a principal cause of the ever-growing global demand for food. In developing countries it accounts for at least 80 percent of the annual increase in food requirements. Whether millions face starvation in the coming decades will depend not only on the ability of those countries to raise food production but also on their success in limiting population growth to manageable levels.

There are now 1.3 billion more people to be fed today than in 1954, and over 400 million people are already suffering from protein-energy malnutrition. Rural underemployment and mounting urban unemployment—fed by despairing millions who migrate to the cities—have already reached alarming proportions. (See Figures II-2 and II-3.) Crop failures anywhere will raise the possibility of massive famines in parts of the developing world. The lack of resources, discussed in the section on food problems, means that there is a very great need not only to make important strides towards increasing the world's food production but also towards controlling population growth rates, especially in the poorest, fastest-growing countries.

Food import requirements of all less developed countries in 1970 were 25 million tons of cereal grains. In 1974 they were 37 million tons. The United Nations Food and Agriculture Organization estimates that by 1985 import requirements could increase to about 100 million tons. Although some United States experts are more optimistic, many others estimate that if the populations of developing countries increase at the rate of the United Nations medium projection to the year 2000 (6.4 billion people), and if by great efforts they also increase their indigenous food production by the amounts considered by some experts likely, their annual import requirement for cereals will nevertheless rise to more than 100 million tons by the end of this century. Whatever surplus food the world may be able to raise to meet these requirements will be produced primarily in the United States and Canada. It will be well beyond the financial ability of the developing countries to purchase this vast quantity of imports and it will probably exceed any practicable capacity to transport them from North America and distribute them within the needy countries of South and Southeast Asia and Africa. The only option of these countries will be to abandon any improvement in nutrition over present levels, to accept a marked rise in death rates (particularly of infants and children), to increase their food production by amounts greater than now believed practical, or to reduce their population growth more rapidly than the United Nations medium projection. These are hard choices but they constitute the realistic elements of a very difficult situation.

The alternative of reducing population growth more rapidly than the United Nations medium projection has some important advantages for the developing countries. Achieving a global replacement level of fertility (a two-child family on the average) by the year 2000 would hold developing country populations 500 million below the original United Nations medium projection by 2000 and 3 billion below it in 2050. The

Figure II-2. Population Change. The changing size and proportion of urban population in more developing and less developed countries: for the years 1950, 1975, and 2000.

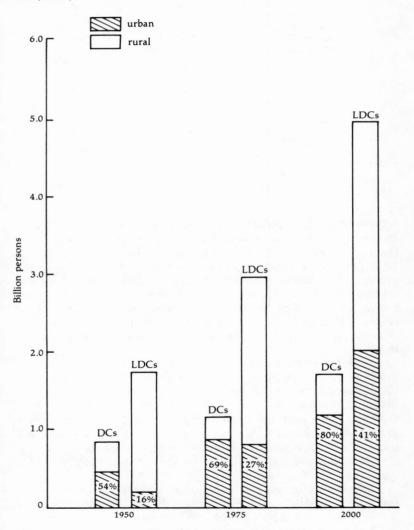

Source: Based on the United Nations estimates and U.N. "medium" variant projections, and U.N. Document E/CN.9/XIX/CRP.2, Oct. 21, 1976, *Orders of Magnitude of the World's Urban Population in History* and *The 4th World Food Survey*, U.N. Food and Agriculture Organization, Rome, 1977.

Figure II-3.   Growing Cities. Estimates and rough projections of selected
Urban Agglomerations in developing countries (millions of persons).

	1960	1970	1975	2000
Calcutta	5.5	6.9	8.1	19.7
Mexico City	4.9	8.6	10.9	31.6
Greater Bombay	4.1	5.8	7.1	19.1
Greater Cairo	3.7	5.7	6.9	16.4
Jakarta	2.7	4.3	5.6	16.9
Seoul	2.4	5.4	7.3	18.7
Delhi	2.3	3.5	4.5	13.2
Manila	2.2	3.5	4.4	12.7
Tehran	1.9	3.4	4.4	13.8
Karachi	1.8	3.3	4.5	15.9
Bogota	1.7	2.6	3.4	9.5
Lagos	0.8	1.4	2.1	9.4

Source: Based on U.N. estimates and medium variant projections.

500 million smaller population in the year 2000 would reduce developing
country food import requirements by roughly 100 million tons, enabling
them to approximate overall self-sufficiency in food. Some limited
recognition of the need to make progress towards a greater population
growth rate reduction has been achieved already. As noted above, the
countries of Asia and the Pacific, meeting in a Post-Bucharest
Consultation to adapt the World Population Plan of Action to their
region, recognized the pressures of population growth on food
availabilities and agreed to set the goal of replacement level fertility for
themselves.

Another important factor in the food/population equation is that
people in the developing countries spend about 50 percent or more of
their income on food as compared with roughly 20 percent for those in
industrialized countries. The "poorest of the poor" spend even more. In
the Third World overall demand for food is related more to population
growth than to incomes. As incomes rise in the developing countries,
there is an increased demand for grain for direct consumption. As
incomes rise in industrialized countries, there is increased demand for
grain indirectly via meat products.

The focus for solving the food/population equation rests largely in
the developing nations since two-thirds of the world's people live in low
income countries and have the highest birthrates. Also countries with
the highest birthrates are usually those with the least productive
economies, the fastest rates of urbanization, the greatest illiteracy, and
the worst medical facilities. Most experts now believe that these factors

are interrelated and require coordinated and concerted action by governments and by the appropriate international organizations. More attention to developmental strategies which are comprehensive in their approach to population and economic growth is required both by national donor countries and by the various international organizations which work in these areas.

The Population and Development Equation

It has become increasingly clear that in a large number of countries population growth has outpaced, and is still outpacing, their otherwise respectable levels of economic growth. Many imaginative development programs have not resulted in an improved standard of living. Due to population rises the per capita increases in income for many countries remains less than 2 percent per year. In some nations each year actually brings a lower standard of living. The new and drastically higher price of oil has generated an additional balance of payments cost for developing countries of some $20 billion annually, significantly more than all the aid they receive from all outside sources. It is possible that by the 1980s the poorest 500 million people in developing countries may be living at levels of poverty even worse than those at which they live today. The gap between the aspirations and achievements of these people could continue to widen, with incalculable consequences for their nation's social and political structures and for the peace of the entire world.

We know that poverty often leads to excessive population growth and we know that excessive population growth ensures continued poverty. Such a destructive economic spiral can be corrected only by simultaneous efforts on both sides of the equation. Reductions in excessive population growth can speed development and more rapid development can slow population growth.

The Population and Environment Equation

There is a very important link between population and environment. Population growth and increasing affluence have led to urban concentration and industrial expansion which can endanger the environment and the health of the inhabitants. However, environmental damage is not only a scourge of the rich. The relationship between man and his environment will fundamentally influence the quality of life at any stage of development. In many countries population pressures have gone beyond the limited arable lands and denuded the hillsides of trees. The result is that the soil has been eroded away and the lowlands swept by destructive floods. Also in the areas where there is an increasing concentration of pastoral population with their flocks living on the edge of deserts, herbage and trees have been destroyed, opening the way to an advance of the sands. Dense and growing populations contaminate the soil, water, and air and sometimes spread disease. There is the ever-present danger that the need to expand food production to feed a growing population will, in the end, further damage the land. The evidence indicates that intensified use of fertilizers could imperil the life of lakes and streams, and that the widened use of pesticides could threaten birds and other wildlife.

A Strategy for Global Population Growth Stabilization

It must be acknowledged in any relevant strategy to solve the problem of population growth that this phenomenon is not the only source of the difficulties which beset the developing world. Disease, poverty, authoritarianism, gross inequalities in wealth and opportunity have many origins of which population growth is only one, albeit a major aspect. No single "solution" which seeks to achieve population growth control exclusively through, for example, the provision of family planning services will ever adequately solve the problem of overpopulation let alone the other important problems of the poorest countries. The answer to these larger needs must rest with basic social and economic development of the poor countries and regions of this globe. Progress in this fundamental area will not be cheap and it will not be accomplished by some single simple panacea or "technological fix."

On the other hand, without coming to serious grips with the population growth problem we also will not be able to deal with the other factors affecting the well-being of two-thirds of mankind. Solving the population crisis is a necessary part of any successful effort to remedy the other broad problems which beset the poorest countries and peoples. We must recognize that the "population problem" is *not* a single uniform phenomenon throughout the world. It cannot be characterized with simplicity for all countries or even all areas in a given country.

As stated above, a two-part, worldwide strategy seems inevitable to bring food production and population growth into reasonable balance within the foreseeable future. One part of this strategy is to hold world population growth by the year 2000 to about 6 billion people by achieving a two-child family average by that time. The second part is to undertake programs to assure the production and distribution of enough food for some 6 billion people by the end of the century, particularly by increases in production in developing countries.

The following actions appear to be essential if there is to be any chance of success in slowing population growth by the needed amounts:

—Concerted global cooperation, individually and through international

organizations, to create an understanding and commitment on the part
of political leaders to set and attain specific population growth rate
reductions;
—The concentration of donor country assistance efforts on countries
which are most severely hampered by population growth, which
contribute most to the general population problem, and which show the
most serious determination to act;
—Countries with high population growth rates should integrate
population factors and programs into their regular development
strategies;
—The establishment and accomplishment of the goal of providing
family planning information and services as rapidly as possible—to
reach all who are interested no later than 1985; and
—Having donor countries and international organizations coordinate
their total programs to emphasize fertility reduction and to give priority
to assistance for development programs conducive to lower birthrates.

We need to remember that the population problem is not equally
serious or all pervasive in all countries even in the developing world.[5] In
some countries the population is already much too large for its food
production and available resources, while in others there remains room
for further moderate and planned growth. However, there now appears
to be some question whether we can continue past growth rates in food
production given reversals in world grain yields in the 1970s. This factor
puts even more emphasis on efforts to reduce population growth rates.

Another important factor in examining the impact of population
growth is the distribution of people between rural and urban areas and
the role of migration between these two areas. This last factor is closely
related to agricultural productivity, the provision of services for the
urban poor, and unemployment and underemployment of concentrated
groups in cities.

Statistics provide some idea of the growing problem of urban
migration: we had only 701 million people in urban areas in 1950, today
we have about 1.5 billion, while in the year 2000 we will have 3.1 billion.
There is little hope, if these projections hold true, for the developing
countries to provide a decent life for the vast majority of their urban
population.[6]

Finally, rapid population growth deeply affects political stability and
the possibility of meaningful economic growth. We see this political
instability most clearly in urban unrest but it also manifests itself in
rural food riots and in violence against various authorities. Above all,
rapid population growth means fewer social services to an ever-smaller
segment of the total population.[7]

We must recognize that the population of the world and especially of
the developing areas will increase dramatically no matter what is done to

slow population growth, and thus we must now plan to deal with the impact of these additional people on the earth's environment, resources, and economy. This growth cannot be escaped, particularly by the developed countries which will be deeply affected by the possible or even probable catastrophe of a massive food/population equation breakdown. The industrialized countries alone have the technological and economic wherewithal to provide assistance to help solve the problems the developing countries will face in the coming decades. There is a need, in the final analysis, on the part of both the developing countries and the industrialized world to recognize that an effective population program is an essential component of any development program. Regardless of what can be done in the population area, it will be necessary for the richer countries over the next three decades to assist the poorer countries in carrying out massive and innovative approaches to economic and social development.

The requirements of an effective population strategy include focusing on general social and economic development programs which are most conducive to reducing fertility as well as improving overall quality of life. While population programs are necessary elements of development programs, alone they are not sufficient. Evidence suggests strongly that accelerating social and economic development has itself an impact on population growth. The overall level of social and economic development has effects on fertility levels which are in some measure independent of and distinct from the effects of family planning programs.[8]

The difficulty, however, is that in many, perhaps most, developing countries, overall development is not likely to move fast enough to have a substantial effect on slowing population growth. It is important, therefore, to try to identify those elements of development that have the greatest effect on slowing population growth and give priority to them.

Probably the most important elements within the social structure which affect population growth rates are those that affect the basic motivation for smaller or larger families. These elements seem to include per capita income, infant mortality, general health conditions, female education, and the general status of women in the society. The implications of these socioeconomic indicators for a future comprehensive development program strategy to deal with population growth problems indicate that first greater emphasis should be placed upon economic assistance programs which can directly impact on elements in a society which are conducive for reduction in fertility rates; second, in addition to such directed and specific programs which can affect motivation, there remains a need for strong family planning services;

and third, each of these programs are and can be made mutually supportive of each other.[9]

The development assistance programs of donor countries and of the involved international organizations now include only a very small share for family planning or direct population programs—something less than 2 percent. For example, the World Bank had in its 1972–76 plan a goal of using only about 1 percent of its total available funds for population programs. Thus, in the overall picture population programs are very small. They will probably be too small by the time the added motivation and information about choice of family size are disseminated to the very large segment of the population not now reached by current programs. Also as the leaders of more governments become increasingly aware of the drag on economic growth that high population rates represent, there should be a sharp increase in national requests for assistance to help them provide family planning services and commodities in the coming decades.

Yet in the final analysis the ultimate decision about population growth rests with the national government and with the people themselves. Already most large developing countries are attempting to act on this problem. Here new technology can serve the larger needs of mankind in both developed and developing countries. Science and technology can provide a useful and indeed necessary tool, assisting mankind both to maintain freedom of choice and to help improve the quality of life in overpopulated countries.

There is a vital need for a major worldwide effort to research the whole problem of human reproduction and to seek the development of low-cost, effective, safe, and acceptable fertility control methods. The developing countries in particular need methods which do not require physicians and are suitable for primitive and remote rural areas. Major breakthroughs in this field are possible; for example, the development of a male "pill," the reversible sterilization of both males and females, or injectable contraceptives effective for a long period of time—three months or more. The United States should be in the forefront of this activity, given the depth and breadth of its medical research. Such discoveries would benefit not only the developing countries but the developed world as well.

In addition to the above approaches traditionally utilized in economic development programs there is the vital need to reach the very large numbers of people who do not now have family planning assistance available to them. These people are largely in the rural and small urban areas of developing countries. On the average in these countries less than 15 percent of the people now have access to elementary health, family planning, and nutrition services. Further, many countries believe that family planning services cannot be effectively delivered and will not be well received except as part of a general basic health and child care service. Unfortunately, few countries maintain such a service outside of major urban areas.

Within this context the establishment of a comprehensive system for the delivery of basic preventive and curative health service and family planning assistance to rural and urban areas is essential to meet both population growth and humanitarian quality of life goals. Such a system should be based upon local paramedical personnel, and of a nature that the developing countries could soon support it on their own over the long term. It will initially require the support of United Nations agencies and donor countries.[10]

As programs to slow population growth in many countries develop, even with substantial self-help, they will require increasing assistance from outside. Donor nations, including the newly rich countries, should be prepared to provide greatly enlarged assistance to population programs of developing countries. The United States should support increases of $35 to $50 million per year for several years in appropriations for assistance to such programs. These are not small sums, but they are small indeed compared to the human and economic losses that will occur unless they are available and wisely used.

On an institutional basis, there is need for better integration of the efforts of individual donor countries and of the varied international organizations which work in relevant fields. The World Health Organization (WHO), the Food and Agricultural Organization (FAO), the World Bank (International Bank for Reconstruction and Development—IBRD), and the United Nations Fund for Population Activities (UNFPA) all need to work more closely together in integrated, interrelated programs to ensure a systems approach to economic development and population growth problems. A more forceful and effective program and policy "integration" mechanism is required in the United Nations system to carry out this task. Too many of these organizations act as totally independent entities and often with programs which are duplicative or even contrary to programs supported by other groups. The need is too great to permit this disorganization to continue any longer. As we see the world's problems as interconnected we need strategies that reflect this understanding if we are to solve our difficulties and emerge from this century without a catastrophe.

The population explosion has a long head start on efforts to bring it under control. Such efforts are having visible successes, but the momentum of growth is immense. Unless it is controlled, unspeakable tragedies lie ahead. They can be avoided, but only by the most determined and urgent combined efforts of international agencies, national governments, private organizations, and concerned individuals.

THE FOOD AND NUTRITION CHALLENGE

Introduction

There are few areas which so clearly show the increased risks of a breakdown in the world community than the problems of how to deal with its food, nutrition, and health needs. While food production worldwide is increasing a little faster than population, its distribution is uneven and reserves are low. More than two-thirds of the world's population produce only one-third of the world's food. The gap between what the developing countries produce and what they need is growing and will continue to do so into the next decades. Some 400 million people experience hunger and malnutrition. Despite the Green Revolution and other agricultural improvements more people suffer from starvation or malnutrition than receive adequate diets in the developing world. Various kinds of calamities such as a few years of bad weather conditions could lead to major famines.

The world lives under the ever-present threat of widespread crop failures which could set into motion a serious global food crisis. Even normal variations in harvests will require the carrying over of sufficient reserves to deal with local or regional shortages. Yet in the early 1970s grain stocks in the major food exporting countries declined. For hundreds of millions the crisis was real and not just potential.

Another important aspect of food is nutrition, the quality of food intake. Special groups, such as children, are particularly vulnerable to the effects of malnutrition. There is a close relationship between nutrition and health and thus to overall well-being. Further, good or bad nutrition can also affect individual productivity and intelligence, and thereby the ability of the poorest sectors to improve their condition.

The goal of providing all people with an adequate diet and health services remains unfulfilled. Food aid from the developed countries can be only a partial solution. The long-term answer must be increased agricultural production by the developing countries themselves and controlled population growth. Greater equity in food distribution also is required if we are not to face one day two incompatible worlds—one of starvation and the other indifferent in its affluence and gluttony.

In addition, unless population growth diminishes there could be less or the same amount of food which could mean continued poor health or even a decline in general well-being. Poor harvests, increased population, poor distribution of income, and continued malnutrition can bring only major calamities, including starvation and even war. (For comparison of grain production and population, see Figure II-4.)

The World Food and Nutritional Challenge

World population growth and increased economic development are putting continuing pressures on world agricultural production. This condition is likely to continue into the last decades of this century unless significant improvements are made in both reducing population growth rates and increasing global food production and distribution. Millions are now suffering and will continue to suffer from chronic malnutrition and recurrent famine in the developing world, especially populations in the poorest and fastest growing countries. This condition for the next decade or two cannot be escaped or evaded.

We have already seen in the recent past severe crop shortfalls in some key regions. These regional famines indicate in a very painful way the thin margin that exists between world food supply and demand. Much of the world's population and its food supply are and will remain for several decades vulnerable to slight changes in climate, to flooding and drought, to availability of fertilizers, and to economic dislocations. Thus we can expect a world which will see protracted suffering for very large and growing segments of people. The World Bank estimates that 75 percent of all people in the developing world have deficient diets. In India alone about half a million children die every year from diseases caused by malnutrition and 70 percent of children from poor families suffer from growth retardation due to mild and moderate malnutrition.[11] At present about 400 to 500 million persons are suffering severe malnutrition or are near starvation. Some experts estimate that this figure will increase to approximately 600 million by 1985.

The production of food has not expanded much beyond the rate of population increase. The reasons for this are varied and include especially the continuing high birthrates in the developing countries combined with lower infant mortality and longer life expectancy. Also there has been increasing consumption of more and higher quality food by people in the developed countries. Further, the Communist countries have not been able to expand their food production at a rapid pace and have experienced recurring shortfalls requiring them to import large amounts of food that would otherwise be available to poorer nations. Also some industrialized countries have from time to time restrained agricultural production in order to reduce surplus food stocks and maintain or increase prices paid farmers. Together, these factors have limited the amount of food available especially to the poorer countries.

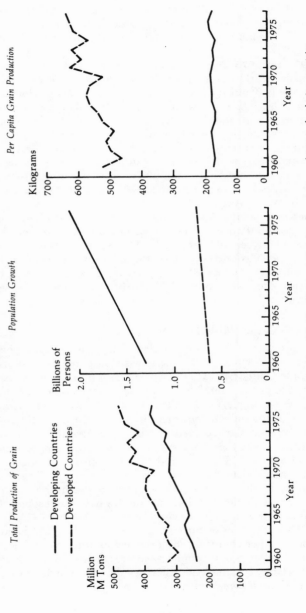

Figure II-4. Grain Production (1960-77)

Note: Grain production comprises on the average 35% of total food production in developed countries and 64% in developing countries.

The greater variations in total and per capita grain production in developed than in developing countries are attributable to greater weather variations in temperate than in tropical farming zones and to more extensive policy interventions by developed than developing country governments in farm acreage and production levels.

*Excludes centrally-planned economies.

Source of data: U.S. Department of Agriculture.

The next few decades will see little progress without major changes in the world's economic system and unless significant structural reforms are made in the production, transportation, and marketing of food resources.

During 1972 and 1973, despite population increases of a little over 2 percent annually, worldwide food production declined. This was the first such decline in about twenty years. The world's food production, which needed at least an increase of about 24–25 million tons just to cover population growth and rising living standards, declined by about 33 million tons, resulting in a 74 million-ton deficiency. Such gaps could recur in the future and place global food stocks at historically low levels. Under these circumstances there would be little carry-over available to make up for such a large gap. In fact, while stocks are now growing, world grain reserves have in recent times fallen to their lowest levels since the end of World War II.

The global economic situation also contributes to our food problems. For example, global inflation has raised world food prices sharply, by some 34 percent between 1972 and 1974. The result has been pricing some of the poorest countries out of the grain-import market. In addition, the high cost of imported energy has decreased the capacity of poorer countries to afford greater food imports or to finance increased domestic agricultural production.

The United States in World Food Production

In this overall equation the role of the United States is crucial. Beyond being a major contributor of financial assistance for agricultural development, the United States is the world's largest producer of food supplies. The role of the United States in the world's grain market is overpowering. For example, in 1972 the United States sold to the Soviet Union alone some 400 million tons or nearly a quarter of its 1972–73 production. This resulted in a depletion of United States grain reserves which led in turn to very high domestic and global prices for grain and associated food products. This had a serious impact on the price and availability of other imported food.

To understand further the role of the United States in the world's food system one must remember that this country has been responsible for 85 percent of all international food aid between 1965 and 1972. The United States has given away through grants more than $10 billion worth of food to other countries and provided another $12.6 billion worth of food at low prices or through low-interest loans. The dominant position of the United States and other developed countries can be further seen in the following figures for 1973:

—Developed countries constituted only 20 percent of the world's population but produced 75 percent of the world's total food production.
—These developed countries accounted for 75 percent of the increase in the world's food production since 1954.

The influence of United States agricultural production on the world food market is further illustrated by the following figures: Overall, the United States accounts for about 20 percent of exported agricultural commodities. During the 1974–75 crop year United States food exports consisted of the following percentages of total world food exports: soybeans about 90 percent, feedgrains about 50 percent, wheat nearly 50 percent, and rice more than 20 percent.[12] Total United States grain production (wheat and feedgrains) during the period 1970 to 1974 ranged between roughly 170 to more than 250 million metric tons. The United States is the largest food producer and exporter in the world and is likely to remain for many years the world's main breadbasket.[13]

The other side of the picture is that this growth of worldwide demand also represents an expanding economic and humanitarian opportunity for the very efficient agriculture of the United States. These exports are vital for the American balance of payments and earn for the United States approximately $20 billion annually or about 25 percent of total earnings from all exports. With such a large impact upon international trade the role of the United States in the future of the world's agricultural structure implies a very special responsibility. It can, for example, serve as the resource of "last resort" in case of severe shortfalls in global production by maintaining large reserves which would be committed in advance to international uses under fixed internationally agreed-upon objective definitions of shortages. But the world cannot count on the United States doubling its grain exports in the next decade as it did in the last one. Even national reserves such as those of the United States are not sufficient, demonstrating again that we are living in a global context where one nation—even the strongest and most productive—cannot entirely provide the necessary resources or power to overcome serious global challenges.

The real key to future food production remains in the capacity of the developing countries themselves over the next decades to greatly augment their own food production with the United States holding a reserve for years of shortage.

Global Food Policies and Problems

Another factor in the world food equation is the possibility of competition between the rich and middle income poor countries that can pay for imported food and the very poor nations that cannot and need to depend upon grant assistance to import food. In years of shortage, there could be a serious scramble for limited reserves which are available largely in North America. If the need for food imports should continue to expand during the coming decade as fast as in the last few years, the gap between demand for North American food supplies and their availability would grow and could cause serious economic and political problems for all countries concerned. The rich countries (Japan and the Soviet Union) already are trying to tie down their future food supplies through multi-year contracts but the food-deficit developing countries are not as able to ensure their future supplies, especially as more of their foreign exchange goes for high priced imported oil.

We might therefore face a future situation in which the exporting countries or even some kind of international organization would have to operate a global food-rationing program. To deal with this kind of problem requires international cooperation on the part of all groups of countries: the richer exporting group, the richer importers, and the poorer deficit nations. Clearly, the costs of cooperation to deal with global food problems must be shared by all.

In focusing on the objective of increasing food production faster than world population growth we must see the problem in its entirety and recognize that it has a number of interlinking parts. Each part must be considered in forming a strategy with any chance of success in providing adequate food and nutrition for the world's growing population. First, we must understand the capacity of the less developed countries to produce more of their own food. Second, we need to examine the ability of the developed countries, especially the United States, not only to increase their own domestic production but to provide additional exports of food to the developing countries, at prices they can afford or through grants or long-term concessionary loans. Third, we must add to this equation the likelihood that the developing countries can reduce their population growth rates. Fourth, we must look at the possibilities which new technology, increased global fertilizer capacity, new land for cultivation, new nutritional information, the development of better methods of preservation and transportation, and changes in dietary patterns can contribute to an overall increase in world food supplies and nutritional levels.

Developing Countries and Food Production

In the recent past many developing countries have made important gains in increasing food production through the discoveries and implementation of the Green Revolution. This "revolution" was the utilization of fertilizers and high-yielding varieties of grains, especially wheat and rice, which had been developed through an international effort of concerted agricultural research. In the decade ending in 1971 the developing countries had shown major gains in crop yields and overall food production. At that time fertilizer supplies were plentiful and inexpensive. The developing countries increased their grain production from the period of the late forties to the period of the late sixties about 80 percent. The developed countries during the same period increased their grain production by about 60 percent. Part of this latter figure, however, resulted from policies to cut down on surplus food stocks.

The Green Revolution depended on new technologies as well as the introduction of high-yielding varieties of grain. The new dwarf wheats required ample fertilizer and water, and the results were yields about double earlier ones. In particular, India gained greatly as a result of the new yields. By 1973 some 80 million acres were planted in high-yielding rices and wheats in Asia and Africa. A fifth of the rice area and about a third of the wheat fields in non-Communist Asia are now planted with the new varieties. However, these new gains are proving difficult since the yields are dependent on a high input of fertilizer, the price of which has risen to a point where severe shortages are taking place. There is also some question of the long-run future availability of fresh water which is required for most of these new varieties of grain. There have been some indications that the benefits of the Green Revolution are slowing down. There may be limits to the extent of future gains, as an increasing population and urbanization take more and more land from productive uses. The increased use of fertilizers has resulted in serious environmental problems likely to put new limits on future increases in food production.

The Green Revolution in the developing world looks impressive only because it is compared with abnormally low yields previously. Even with the use of new varieties, the yields in India and other developing countries average only one-third those achieved in Japan. This holds true for other crops. For example, the developing countries have 35 percent more land in grain production than the developed nations, but they produce about 20 percent less grain. The most significant factor is that these rapid production gains only kept pace with population growth in the Third World. Take the case of Mexico. After the introduction of the production gains from the Green Revolution, Mexico became a net exporter of cereals in the late 1960s, but due to a high population growth rate, the country was forced to be a net food importer in the 1970s.

The next few years will be crucial for developing a sound approach to future world food problems. We have not yet, despite the Green

Revolution and the 1974 Rome World Food Conference, provided a sound basic structure for solving the problem of persistent food insecurity for a large proportion of the world's population. For example, in 1971, per capita food production was only 6 percent greater than ten years earlier, while production rose 19 percent in the developed countries. The saddest figure however was that for 1972 when per capita food production in the developing countries remained the same as a decade earlier; in 1973 it was up only 3 percent.

Real improvements in worldwide nutritional levels took place from the 1950s to the 1970s as per capita consumption of grain moved from about 582 pounds annually in 1960 to 681 pounds in 1973. But, the annual average decreased at that point by some 35 pounds.[14] We are not yet sure that this downward trend is only temporary. There are many factors for this decline, including the high cost of energy and fertilizer.

Developing countries imported 500 thousand tons of grain in the three years spanning 1969-71. These same countries are now importing some 29 million tons annually. Official projections for 1985 foresee imports up to the 50-75 million ton range. Some experts say that with accelerated domestic agricultural efforts this import requirement might only amount to about 22.5 million tons.[15] Other experts estimate that with very high population growth rates even larger food deficits by developing countries are possible, ranging up to 120-130 million tons by 1985 and nearly 280 million metric tons by the end of the century.[16] A generally used figure of the gap between food supplies and the needs of the developing world in 1985 is 100 million tons of grain. It is, however, doubtful that population growth rates will indeed increase in the face of such shortages. We can, in any case, foresee food deficits for the developing countries beyond 1985 even under favorable conditions.

Another indication of the problem is the decline of grain reserves. In 1961 grain reserves (reserve stocks and cropland idle under United States farm programs) equaled 105 days of world grain consumption. In 1972 it equaled 69 days and in 1976 it was only 31 days of consumption. These figures present us with some difficult dilemmas in formulating a strategy that can be adequate to the dimensions of the food problem. Population growth then is an important additional element governing whether we will see a major food crisis with accompanying starvation for large numbers of people or whether we can get through the period with at least minimal nutritional levels for the poorest elements of the world's population.

While the earlier momentum of the Green Revolution has slowed due to limitations of available fertilizer, the effects of inflation, etc., other factors could cause serious problems. Some of these problems are due to conditions in nature—environmental limitations. Other factors are man-made—the basic economic structure of national and international food markets and the policy decisions of governments and international organizations.

One of the major "natural" limitations on future food production will be simply the problem of land availability. In some parts of the world there is a net loss of arable land. In the Middle East, Sub-Saharan Africa, the Indian subcontinent, and some parts of Latin America severe erosion is taking land away from food production. In the Sahara Desert regional pressures from increased human and livestock population have resulted in overgrazing, deforestation, and denudation of large land areas. Thus we see expansions of desert areas in the Sahara at a rate of several miles per year. Also increased cultivation can bring ultimate ecological disaster and finally food production losses. The clearing of trees in mountain areas for the planting of crops can mean floods and loss of topsoil in the inundated areas.

There is a major debate now going on about how much land areas can be expanded for the production of food. Many experts believe there exist enormous reserves of unused but potentially arable land. They cite vast tracts of potentially usable land in Brazil's Amazon River Basin, massive open areas in central Africa, and large areas of such countries as Burma, Malaysia and Thailand. The optimists in this debate say that only half of the land in the world that has food production potential is actually farmed. They argue that if all potentially arable land could be farmed, even with present technology, the world could feed a population of some 8 billion or about twice the present level. These same optimists also note that yields could be increased substantially with the full application of fertilizer. The difference between yields in developed and developing countries is cited as proof of the added potential of increasing factors of production in the agricultural sector. Further, the oceans can provide much needed food—if exploited to their full potential. (We will examine this latter question in Chapter IV.) It is enough here to say that the strawman "optimist" is probably right on this last point, but the problem is that so far we have made little progress in the development of our oceans' food resources, and trends in utilization of the oceans' living resources to feed mankind show a pessimistic rather than optimistic turn. We are, in short, at a very primitive stage on ocean food production and we are likely to remain in this condition for a considerable number of years unless very major decisions are made by the world community on the development and sharing of the potential food supplies from the seas. At present, fish are often being depleted below their best levels for maximum sustainable yield while we are doing very little about the cultivation of ocean-based food resources which are feasible and proven to some extent. New technologies and distribution systems are, however, required if this area is to be in the future a major source of food for a growing population.

The argument that fertilizers can provide the needed additional food is supported by statistics showing that nations that use the most fertilizers also produce the highest agricultural yields. We have seen in the recent past a cycle of fertilizer boom and bust which resulted in first a major expansion of fertilizer capacity and then lower prices and finally a contracting of capacity and a decrease in new plant construction. The oil crisis of 1972–76 also resulted in hydrocarbon-based fertilizer (nitrogenous) increasing in price and decreasing in availability. There was little increase in new capacity during this period. Some foresee the growth of new capacity, however, as the oil-producing countries themselves invest in new nitrogen fertilizer plants based on their desire to utilize now wasted natural gas. With this development we may see sufficient fertilizer production by 1980 but at vastly increased prices. The quadrupling of world petroleum prices meant that the cost of nitrogen fertilizer rose from 11 cents to 25 cents a pound in the 1972–74 period. Many countries cannot afford such prices even though they need fertilizer for vital food production.[17] In the future the poorer countries might again not be able to pay the costs which would cause a new cycle of boom and bust all over.

Another problem with the argument of the optimists is that a point of diminishing returns sets in. Fertilizers applied too liberally can burn out the soil. Heavy fertilizer use can produce serious zinc and phosphorous deficiencies which are already apparent in the soils of some developing countries. Thus while initial use produces dramatically higher yields, increasing use results in proportionately smaller yields and decreased economic gains per unit applied. Over the short run the Third World still can utilize fertilizers profitably with major increases in yields but over the long run there will be upper limits. A major part of these limits will be environmental costs since fertilizers introduced in large quantities into the environment can, through runoffs into water systems, bring severe ecological problems. We are already seeing the result of this situation in the United States with the eutrophication of lakes and rivers resulting in serious oxygen deficiency in these freshwater sources. A similar situation exists with respect to the utilization of pesticides and herbicides when they are used extensively to increase food production.

One major problem in the food production system is the loss of food due to rot, rodents, insects, and other pests. The largest proportion of this loss takes place in the developing countries. For example, the Food and Agriculture Organization estimated that 55 million Africans could be fed for a year from the grain lost due to the impact of spoilage and pests on crops of that continent. Also about 4.25 million square miles of available land cannot be used for grazing because of the tsetse fly in Africa. The wise use of technology to reduce such losses can increase considerably future food production in the developing countries. Herbicides and pesticides, which are often petroleum based, are expensive and they have, as noted, serious negative environmental and health impacts which must be taken into consideration in their use.

Another major element in the food production system is the problem of internal and external distribution of food that is produced or imported. Often large amounts of food are subject to spoilage due to poor distribution and storage. This means that any future improvement of food systems in the developing world must look at ways of improving domestic storage of perishable foods, efficient transportation, and other related activities and the economic factors affecting the market system down to the local level. This is especially true for the rural areas which often still utilize very primitive methods of storage and distribution. The market mechanism also may be a disincentive for sound practices when it forces a farmer to sell his crop after the harvest when prices are low. He does not earn enough to expand his output while the speculator hoards his low-priced stock to sell only after a food shortage and after much of the consequent human nutritional damage has already been done. The development and use of better food processing technology can bring significant gains in total nutritional availability to the people. Unfortunately, improvements due to the application of the techniques of heat sterilization, freeze drying, and refrigeration are not utilized efficiently and widely or even at all in some areas. The availability of such food technology could result in food resource additions especially in hot climates and it would strengthen the whole market mechanism and the incentives for increased food production. But such improvements are costly and require increased electricity or other energy and training of skilled personnel.

The availability of electricity and other forms of energy would bring major benefits to the agricultural sector of developing countries, including the enrichment of the soil, the availability of irrigation, use of food preservation, utilization of farm machinery, availability of information, and speedier transportation to markets. The energy demand of the developing countries is projected to increase to about 8.5 percent yearly as against a worldwide increase of 5.5 percent, yet the ability of developing countries to pay for their additional requirements remains in doubt and their food deficits will only increase this inability.

Another factor affecting future food production will be availability of the required water. The increased use of irrigation is important to the expansion of yields and the extension of land for agricultural use. For example, the introduction of a simple technology, fuel-powered water pumps, has had a significant impact on yields when they have been used in developing countries. Unfortunately for purposes of bringing new areas under irrigation many river systems unsuitable for irrigational use have been developed. There is, in fact, a growing worldwide shortage of fresh water due to increased population, industrialization, and other demands on water resources. We may have to look to new technology such as the diversion of rivers or, more likely, desalinization of seawater as the source of additional water for food production. Yet some expansion in the use of naturally available water in the developing countries is possible and often existing facilities are underutilized or inadequately operated.

Another debate is taking place among the world's experts about long-term climate changes and their impact on food production. The final answers will provide significant information about the possibility of increased crop failures and need for major investments in food production. For example, monsoon rains and their changing patterns can greatly affect Asian rice crops. Other weather factors can devastate whole crops and bring major shortages for millions of people, especially but not only in the developing world. Some experts also are talking about major long-term changes in climate patterns which they maintain we are now going through. While climatic changes are poorly understood, some experts hold that a persistent atmospheric cooling trend has been established since 1940 which could portend a period of much wider annual frosts, and possibly a long-term lowering of rainfall in the monsoon areas of Asia and Africa. In the developed world drought and early frost, brought on possibly by such long-term meteorological changes, can reduce food production by large amounts. If this affects, for example, food production in the United States, it could result in a disaster of worldwide proportions. Some experts believe that the southward advance of the Sahara Desert results from climatic change in addition to the impact of man in the Saharan area.

We shall likely see an increased sensitivity to climatic changes due to present trends in global agricultural production. Such trends which increase climatic vulnerability include: more intensive land use (which exposes more production to local climate extremes), expansion of cultivation to marginal lands, tailoring of crops, especially grains, to narrow climatic ranges, and large areas of single crop culture (which increases vulnerability to massive failures).[18] While our knowledge of long-term climatic trends remains rather rudimentary, its possible devastating effect on global food production must be taken into consideration by national and international decision makers as they plan for future expansion of agricultural production and analyze long-term needs and possible shortfalls.[19]

Future Global Food Problems

Based on the foregoing facts the question of the world food situation for 1985 and beyond contains a number of complex and not entirely known factors with short- and long-term implications. First, population growth rates in excess of food production increases are expected to continue for large parts of the globe until at least 1985. The result will be severe food imbalances regionally and perhaps even globally. Second, the distribution of world food supplies will remain a serious problem, perhaps more so than the total world crop and animal production. There may even be some short-term regional surpluses. Third, the developing countries using only their own earnings and normal credit facilities, will have a most difficult problem in affording the purchase of the substantial food imports they will require for the next several decades. Fourth, there will continue to be malnutrition and starvation in many countries and regions, sometimes even in the face of surpluses, but particularly in times of crop failure due to natural and perhaps manmade calamity.

The food shortages will be focused in the developing countries of Asia and Africa with human suffering impacting on the whole world, resulting in unrest and conflict affecting all. The solutions to these problems are known but whether the necessary actions will be taken in time remains very much in doubt. It will be increasingly difficult to develop the necessary institutional, economic, and human resources rapidly enough to ensure that food production keeps pace with food demand especially in critically poor countries with high population growth rates.

An even greater uncertainty will be the application of science and technology to food production, particularly in the period beyond 1985. There already exists yield-increasing technology and its impact has been taken into consideration in most forecasts for increased productivity. But the accelerated adoption of these existing technologies or ones in advanced stages of development is not assured by any means. Probable food needs for the last decade or so of this century will depend not only on the accelerated utilization of known advanced methods but also on some new unknown technology. Thus it is imperative that we make a major effort towards an international cooperative undertaking to accelerate new planning and increase research and technology innovation to meet these future needs. The task is huge but the cost of failure will be far greater.

The Institutional and Political Challenge

Despite the many influences of nature and limitations of the global environment, probably the greatest influence on world food availability rests in man's own hands. Food production decisions are often primarily made with domestic considerations in mind and only secondarily are global needs given any consideration. It is this factor which needs to be drastically changed if progress is to be made.

One major element which has influenced food production has been governmental decisions or policies designed to maintain a lower food price in order to combat domestic inflation and keep the cost of living down. Often such policies, which include price controls or subsidized imports, influence the farmer's decision in the direction of less production. Such policies often result in weakening domestic agricultural infrastructure by reducing the incentive for the farmer to expand production or use new technologies. The final result often is higher prices since the decision of the farmer to produce less will bring new scarcities and increases in price.

In addition, many developing countries have given primary priority to industrialization and thereby the agricultural sector has been given short shrift. Another aspect of this problem has been the emphasis on urban population which often is the focus of political pressure and social discontent at the expense of the often larger rural sector which cannot effectively mobilize itself as a political force but which nevertheless is the main source of food for the entire population. Neglect of the rural sector only increases the migration to the cities and assists in the decline in agricultural productivity in some areas. Lack of modern facilities and technology, especially electricity, also perpetuates the backwardness of the food-producing rural sector. Lack of financing in the rural sector holds back innovation and introduction of new technologies.

One of the major future issues in developing a global food system which will truly serve mankind's needs is the existing national and international institutional and economic patterns which shape the supply and consumption of food. Perhaps the most important single need for increasing the food supply of the developing countries is influencing the relative levels of farm and nonfarm incomes.[20] In the developed countries this is an important factor and it is associated with increased efficiency both technological and managerial. For the developing countries' experience has already demonstrated that use of modern technology and know-how can be made available to small farmers with the result of increasing production despite many natural limiting factors. An effective food production and marketing system is the prime future requirement for most developing countries. Farmers must move from primarily subsistence farming to growing cash, especially food, crops. Sometimes a switch to nonfood cash crops from food production can cause domestic food availability problems.[21] A market system must be simultaneously developed. Major social changes are also needed including provisions for education, health, family planning, and an opportunity to expand the poorer farmer's sense of well-being. Major incentives must be given to the farmer to produce not only more crops but crops which are able to provide more added nutritional value than those now utilized. Traditional social patterns may also have to change to realize these goals.

The world is now standing on the edge of a major disaster in food supply. Only recently the world's grain reserves available for immediate shipment to meet emergencies could be measured in days, not weeks or months. Further, global grain reserves could generally remain on the low side for an extended period due to large sales to the Soviet Union and China and fluctuations in crops due to weather, etc. This thin margin offers little safety for those countries faced with imminent famine. It also is highly destabilizing in world commodity markets.

The world's growing dependence on North American food production and reserves places the rest of the world in a highly vulnerable position in the event of crop failures. The United States has averaged serious droughts in roughly a twenty-year cycle going back to mid-nineteenth century, when rainfall data was first collected. Recently, in 1974, heavy spring rains, a dry summer, and early frosts produced sharp declines in the corn and soybean crops. Even sharper declines in United States crops could trigger not only intense world competition for available exports but, combined with serious crop failures in the developing countries, a major worldwide famine and millions of additional deaths.

That we have come so close to this situation without ameliorative action by responsible governments and international organizations indicates that reforms are necessary in governmental decision making. A wider perception by citizens of the developed world of their larger responsibilities and better understanding of how the global economic and political process works are vitally needed.

The Struggle for a Global Food Strategy

High food production growth rates, after the significant gains in the 1950s and 1960s, ended with stagnation in the early 1970s. This was due to simultaneous inclement weather in Africa, Asia, Australia, and the Soviet Union. Another important factor was the extraordinary rate of population growth. Together these factors produced widespread food shortages, with famine and starvation in some areas. Food prices skyrocketed with food-deficit developing countries especially hard hit.

Additional forces came into play including the rapid increase in energy costs resulting from the oil exporters pushing prices up several-fold. High prices, low stocks, and the widening of the food import gap of the developing countries created a new common perception of possible disaster among concerned countries, which resulted in the calling of the World Food Conference (WFC) in Rome in November, 1974. The recommendations of that conference included the following:

—Higher priority to agricultural development, particularly increased investment in developing countries through an international agricultural development fund;
—A global food early-warning system to share information on harvests and any projected changes in supply and demand;
—An internationally coordinated system of nationally held grain reserves;
—A global annual food aid target of 10 million tons, beginning in 1975; and
—An institutional framework for focusing on long-term food problems, including a World Food Council, a Consultative Group on Food Production and Investment, and reorganization of existing institutions to better deal with problems of food aid and world food security.

The record to date on implementing these major World Food Conference proposals has been mixed. What has been accomplished includes the establishment of the United Nations Food and Agricultural Organization of the Global Information and Early Warning System on Food and Agriculture and the establishment of a ministerial-level body of thirty-six nations called the World Food Council. This latter organization is charged with general oversight of international food problems and institutional arrangements to deal with global food problems. Despite these moves the major substantive need to establish a fully adequate global food reserve remains unsatisfied. The United States made a formal proposal to create a "coordinated system of national grain reserves" within the International Wheat Council. The hope is that a new wheat agreement will be negotiated to include a reserves component. This was far short of the goal of major internationally managed food stockpiles that many experts thought were needed to ensure against serious shortfalls. Also in 1975 the United States and fifty-nine other nations declared their acceptance of the International Undertaking in Food Security which outlines principles to be applied to reserve stock building. This system, however, remains incomplete and has not been fully implemented.

The first goal of the WFC was to establish an International Fund for Agricultural Development to mobilize additional financial assistance on a concessional basis for agricultural development in the developing countries. The fund's aim is to raise $1 billion from pledges by individual countries. The United States pledged $200 million on condition that other countries contributed their fair share. The fund will only come into operation once the full amount is raised.

As stated, another proposal of the WFC was to achieve an annual goal of 10 million tons of food aid. This should be achieved. The United States plans to ship about 60 percent of the target. However, to meet the need fully, additional pledges from traditional donors and future contributions from new donors will be necessary.

The continued goal of creating an effective global food reserve system has been one of the most difficult tasks of the international community. So far the World Food Council has only been a forum for debate but has not been effective in establishing a grains reserve. The United States wishes to utilize the International Wheat Council as the focus for bargaining over a new world food reserve system. So far, acceptance of a new International Wheat Agreement has been blocked by most members' rejection of the United States proposal to establish grain reserves based on just quantities. Other Wheat Council members favor reserve provisions based on prices and quantities.

Recently the United States has proposed a domestic, farmer-held reserve system for wheat and rice due to depressed prices resulting from oversupply. This effort could enhance the development of an international reserve system. But the United States has insisted that such a system not be based upon this country acting alone as the granary for the world.

Another factor which may help the establishment of the food reserve has been the recent increase in world crops and thereby reserves. Due to good crops in recent years, world grain reserves were estimated to be about 171.8 million metric tons in July, 1977. Should the 1977–78 crop reach 1.087 billion metric tons, reserves in July, 1978, could total a record of 202.1 million tons. With these large reserves, the irony is that they may help forward the present grain reserve negotiations. Such a reserve, in addition to helping poorer countries in need, could also help support the world and domestic price of grains—something greatly desired by the farmer. Again we see a situation where domestic economic factors can greatly affect global problems—in this case hunger. We must remember that the recent abundance of grain will not ward off the danger of hunger which still is a reality for millions.

Further, we must keep in mind the great cycles of shortage and abundance which characterize world food problems. The Soviet crops continue to be a disappointment, and poor weather continues to affect farming in many parts of the United States. Further, world stocks have not been rebuilt sufficiently to deal with a number of poor consecutive growing seasons and future increased demand due to population growth.

The Nutritional Challenge

In addition to just providing more food for a growing population, there is a critical need to improve the world's overall nutritional levels. This is more than a question of pure quantity. The United Nations estimates that some 460 million people in the world are malnourished. Currently, the means exist to improve nutritional standards significantly in the poorer countries without major changes in the provision of food or altering the fundamental economic structure in these countries. Yet when we talk about improving nutrition, we are very much talking about changing peoples' ideas and sometimes their value systems.

An idea of the nature of the problem can be gotten by noting that children are the key group who need good nutrition to ward off infectious diseases. More than 10 million children under five years of age in the developing countries suffer from severe protein/calorie deficiency; while another 80 million suffer only slightly less grievously. Yet another group—numbering into the hundreds of millions—do not have the minimum diet prescribed for the developed countries. Many particularly suffer from vitamin deficiency diseases.

One major problem in the developing countries has been the inequalities of economic distribution which result in important gains for the upper and middle classes while the poor, especially the rural poor, gain very little.[22] As examined elsewhere, new technologies and techniques which could improve the nutrition and well-being of lower-income peoples are not being fully utilized, if at all, in many developing countries.[23] Most writers on the subject agree that improvements can be made just through better planning and management by governments of the resources presently available in a given country. The first stage would be to undertake a comprehensive diagnosis of the nature and immediate causes of existing malnutrition, including identification of specific deficiencies.

Nutrition must be seen in a special light since it affects all elements of social and economic life, but especially human health and development. Many of the world's major nutritional problems or deficiencies have been identified and include:

—Vitamin A deficiency;
—poor protein/calorie levels;
—poor nutrition among 0 to two-year-olds; and
—nutritional deficiencies in the diets of pregnant and lactating women.

Some experts believe that if any major improvement in correcting these dietary deficiencies is to take place, it is important to increase the real purchasing power of lower-income groups, in addition to providing nutritional education and other assistance. Thus, this school of experts believes that only through major changes in the structure of the economic system will nutrition be improved for the most needy. Changes must be made so as to focus economic growth on increasing food production, new employment opportunities, and generally increasing the income of the poorest. Some experts hold that nutrition improvement can take place through modest intervention in the system, while others believe major long-term improvements can only be accomplished through new economic systems and radical changes in the societies' institutions and economic benefits.[24]

On the other hand, an important case has been made that economic factors alone cannot provide good nutrition and that direct intervention by governments may be needed.[25]

While the debate on the degree of radical social change required for markedly improved incomes, food, and nutrition will continue, certain specific actions can make a difference in improving nutritional levels in the developing countries and elsewhere. A comprehensive approach to dealing with malnutrition is required and there are a number of specific efforts which could improve the quality of nutrition.

One important factor is nutritional education. Through information people can better use the already existing resources. In many societies there are various practices and beliefs which are detrimental to good nutrition and health. How much improvement can be expected through only education is debatable; most investigators believe education must be combined with other factors to increase overall nutritional values.

Another factor in improving diets is to provide food fortification. One can, through the use of new techniques, increase food values, sometimes at lower costs than from standard food staples. One problem that can be addressed by these methods is overcoming specific vitamin, protein, or mineral deficiencies. The basic theory of formulated foods or diet fortification is to provide more nutritional value for about the same cost or to decrease overall cost. The use of new genetic varieties of plants can also give higher nutritional value than standard seed types. Generally, food fortification cannot solve all the problems of diets which are fundamentally inadequate in general food value or calorie consumption. There is great value in the fortification of foods with vitamins, but the problem is getting the cost of such fortification down to a level that even very poor societies can afford. Further, there are major management, processing, and transportation problems which must be overcome to get fortified food to the mass of the population. Some experts have held that it is basic caloric limitations in a diet which must be improved and not just protein malnutrition. There now appears to be a consensus among nutritional experts that overall energy or caloric deficiency is the problem to solve and it cannot be cured by concentrating on individual specific food deficiencies. However, these specific deficiencies are serious and must also be solved along with vital calorie requirements.[26]

Yet another focus for improving nutrition has been the introduction of child feeding programs, particularly school lunches. These programs in the developing countries represent the largest single national intervention program, totaling up to 90 percent of all funds expended in this sector. The problem with these programs is they often do not reach the very poorest group of children—the rural poor—who do not attend school or other institutions which run feeding programs. Better use of local social structures which do relate to the poorest groups probably would increase the reach of such feeding programs.

Finally programs directed at special deficiencies should not be ignored. This is especially the case with young children. For example, very young children experience nutrition loss due to frequent infections and require additional protein. Fairly inexpensive nutritional programs can control specific problems such as vitamin A deficiency, which is a major cause of blindness. With such programs vitamin A deficiency blindness could be almost eliminated in a decade or so.[27]

Relation of Nutrition to Health and Population

There is clear evidence that poor health, especially gastrointestinal infection among children, can lower nutritional capabilities and precipitate malnutrition by reducing appetites or decreasing the capacity of individuals to absorb nutrients. Thus efforts to improve health and sanitation services and standards among the most vulnerable sectors could also contribute to reductions in the incidence of malnutriton. The provision of integrated services including immunization, better sanitation facilities, and medical services and family planning assistance through community health centers or clinics can contribute to the overall well-being of the poorest sector where these services generally are not now accessible.[28]

One key study undertaken in the town of Marangwal in the Punjab demonstrated the value of concentrating nutritional services and health care into one program. One group of children were given dietary supplements and health care, while another only health services, and yet another only dietary help. A final control group received no assistance. The combined treatment provided the best results with nutritional supplementation alone still providing a major impact. Medical care by itself did not help the group's nutritional status.[29]

Clearly, to deal with these diverse problems a number of different approaches are required. To gain the full benefit of these individual measures there must be major national and international efforts to provide a comprehensive attack on malnutrition. Thus nutritional education must be combined with increased health and sanitation services and improved marketing systems, etc.[30] The key to success is not just combining these services together but in each country identifying those initiatives and social structure which can bring these services to the poorest people. The use of paramedical personnel and local community leaders is required for long-lasting impact. The problem then becomes not just technical but also political and economic.

Population growth has seriously cut into prospects for significant per capita income growth especially among the poorest. A concerted global effort to reach these people with basic health, family planning, and nutritional services will assist our goal of increasing overall well-being. Evidence is accumulating that reduced population growth and improved nutrition are linked far more closely than it was once thought. In some poor areas a good way to lower birthrates is to provide a better chance of survival to children of a family. Many families have more children in order to ensure there will be two or more surviving sons. So through increasing the health of children societies can provide inducements to decrease the desire for large families.

Knowledge about nutrition can be important. Though the people in the Indian state of Kerala have the lowest income in India, they have the highest literacy rate. A majority of the women are educated, and there is a substantially higher awareness of the importance of nutrition. The result is that the Keralans enjoy India's highest per capita consumption of nutritionally rich foods such as vegetables, fruits, fish, and eggs. They have the highest percentage of villages with sanitary water supplies and the lowest infant mortality rate in the country. The state also has experienced a drop in its birthrate over the last ten years, from 37 per thousand to 27 per thousand, the Indian average being about 37.2. This example provides sufficient justification to increase or continue programs which link health, population planning, and nutrition. In the final analysis it is the poor countries themselves that must provide the will or commitment through increased priorities and provision of resources that will enable the majority of the population to enjoy improved well-being. Once a nation is willing to undertake a major effort to attack these interrelated problems and even to change basic social and economic structure, the richer countries need to provide assistance, given the lack of adequate resources in most of these countries to carry out such far-reaching programs.

GLOBAL HEALTH

While great strides have been made in the last decade to improve global health conditions, there still exist widespread and often unchecked diseases in the developing countries. In Asia, Latin America, Africa, and the Middle East, some 2 billion people continue to live with the threat of malaria, schistosomiasis, yaws, measles, leprosy, and other diseases. As noted earlier, malnutrition contributes to their poor health, with the chief sufferers being children.

Specifically, in some African countries mortality among children under five is close to 50 percent. The World Health Organization estimates that fewer than 10 percent of the 80 million children born each year in developing countries are immunized against the six common childhood killer diseases: diphtheria, whooping cough, tetanus, measles, poliomyelitis, and tuberculosis.[31] Only 6.6 percent of children under five are vaccinated against diphtheria and tetanus. In Colombia, only 5 percent of the children have been vaccinated against polio. Measles vaccination is nearly unheard of even though this disease is a major cause of death among children in many poorer countries.

One example of the need to examine the total impact of every new technology on the environment is the way the building of irrigation systems in tropical and subtropical areas, while expanding the production of foods, also created the means for the spread of schistosomiasis. This water-borne disease, carried by a freshwater snail, is rapidly spreading and infecting more than an estimated 200 million people. The impact on an infected person is recurrent fever and diarrhea which results in debilitation and sometimes death. It is the world's leading infectious disease—concentrated mostly in Africa, Asia, and some parts of Latin America. The aquatic parasite (a tiny worm) penetrates the human skin on contact after having left its snail host, then enters the blood and migrates to the liver where it reproduces. Its eggs are excreted with body wastes to enter again into the cycle.

Another serious disease is malaria. In the 1950s, as a result of a World Health Organization control program, malaria was reduced globally from about 300 million cases a year to about 125 million cases. Recently, there has been an alarming resurgence of this disease. In tropical Africa alone, about 90 million cases of malaria occur each year and about one million children under age fourteen die every year. Southeast and South Asian countries, along with some Latin American countries, also have reported increases in malaria cases. Present techniques have proved less effective in controlling malaria and now the main aim is to find a safe and efficacious vaccine.

For the majority of people in the Third World the greatest risk is the ever-present reality of sickness or disease which often is exacerbated by malnutrition. The threat of malaria, schistosomiasis, yaws, intestinal parasites, and a number of other diseases is faced by hundreds of millions of persons. The results include early death, the weakening of the body, and lower productivity. For example, the prevalence of river blindness (onchocerciasis) has severely inhibited economic development of the rich Cotta River areas. Worldwide, 30 million people are affected with river blindness.

The most serious problem is among the children who experience the highest risk of death due to illness. In the Third World the major cause of sickness and death in the five-and-under age group is the pneumonia-diarrhea complex. This disease group accounts for an estimated 750 million cases of gastritis, 125–350 million of pneumonia, 90 million of measles, 70 million of whooping cough, and 50 million of dysentery each year. While many of these diseases are not normally fatal, infants and the elderly are now dying of severe colds and stomach disorders because inadequate diets have weakened their resistance.

Here again we see how different elements come together to affect a complex natural and social order. With high population growth rates there is less food, with less food there is poor nutrition which leads to increased infant mortality, which in turn brings us back to the desire to have more children and thus the vicious cycle comes full circle.

Economic Impact

Poor health, like poor nutrition, is a serious barrier to economic development. The worker with malaria or a parasitic infection is less productive than a healthy person. The cost of disease in early life can be a burden forever to the affected person. The loss of productivity through death or disability in developing countries cannot be measured but must be significant.

There is also the danger of the spread of diseases throughout the world if they are left unchecked. Increased international travel hastens the spread of disease, and no country is safe from this risk. The contribution of new technology and increased volume of world trade also contributes to increased risks.

New Global Health Risks

There are a growing number of new human health risks as a result of spreading industrialization and the introduction of new chemicals and technologies into the environment. The expansion of the auto and electricity has brought increases in emphysema and other lung diseases. Mercury poisoning results from the use of pesticides and from industrial wastes. Lead and cadmium poisoning are increasing. Lung cancer is on the rise due, according to most experts, to air pollution and other environmental factors. There appears to be an increase in the overall amount of toxic chemicals in the environment. We do not know what the long-term impact of the accumulation of these persistent compounds on human health will be. Contamination of drinking water has proved to be a serious hazard in both developing and developed countries. Carcinogens have been found in the water of a number of heavily populated areas in the United States including Ohio and Louisiana.[32]

Food Contamination

A growing problem for the exporting-importing countries of the world is food contamination. With growing interdependence in world trade and especially in food goods, there is greater need to ensure that food is healthy and not toxic to humans or animals. Thus attention should be given to new and more effective means to develop basic food standards, uniform inspection methods, and the eventual adoption of international standards for food that is shipped in international trade. With the growth of food additives the need for this kind of approach grows daily. Also the presence of pesticide residues, a growing phenomenon, must be controlled if we are all to be safe from serious health problems. What is needed here is international adoption of criteria for acceptable intake and residue tolerance limits of commonly used pesticides. The United Nations Food and Agricultural Organization (FAO) is looking into this but more attention and effort are needed if action is to be taken before we have a crisis on our hands.

There exists a joint FAO/WHO Expert Committee on Food Additives, which periodically carries out evaluations of international and non-international activities in food from the viewpoint of its safety. The committee is supposed to establish the acceptable daily intake standards (ADIS) for various additives including contaminants, and prepare for these standards specifications of identity, purity, and methods of analysis. It is quite clear that if this group is to be effective it needs to be strengthened considerably and given wider powers or else a new group established with more resources and powers. This should be related to the efforts of the Codex Alimentarious Commission which was set up to look at food standards in international trade to better protect the consumer. Doubt about the effectiveness of present activities grows, and an examination of this area is needed to see if a superior mechanism could be established. Hopefully, consumer groups should have a major role in strengthening existing efforts or establishing new mechanisms.

Future Risks

Major elements of our changing environment and their impact on global health indicate increasingly the danger of exposure to toxic substances, food contamination, and pollution. This exposure increases chances of sickness or even death on the part of a large number of persons. We are already too familiar with the introduction of toxic or carcinogenic substances into the environment. These pose serious health risks for people in all regions but especially to those living in industrial areas or in cities. The result of new environmental health hazards could be a decline in life expectancy. For example, the United States, with the highest per capita expenditure on health—more than $70 billion annually—ranks only thirteenth among industrialized nations in infant mortality, eighteenth in life expectancy for men, and eleventh in life expectancy for women. By all measures Americans are less healthy now than they were twenty years ago. Some of this decrease could be caused by increased work-place and environmental risks.

Clearly we have not adequately utilized the full potential of modern technology and analysis to deal with major death-dealing diseases. We can go to the moon but can't solve the riddle of cancer. Automated health-screening methods are available and can save many lives but are only accessible to a few—often those who need them least.

In the future there may be other health risks which all mankind would share. For example, one could be exposure to atomic radiation— i.e., contamination of the environment by radioactive materials. These could come from global contamination by radionuclides released by atmospheric nuclear explosions or from leaks in atomic plants near population centers. While the Test Ban Treaty prohibits release of nuclear materials into the atmosphere, there are countries which conduct atomic tests in the air—France, China, and India. With the increased use of nuclear power we can expect increased danger from atomic radiation coming from fuel manufacturing, reprocessing plants, nuclear power reactors, etc. Thus in our quest for more energy we could be adversely affecting human health.

Problems of Health Care

As with the great disparity in income between the very rich and the very poor, the disparity in health care is a mirror of the existing economic inequalities. In the poorest countries, annual expenditures for all health services range from $.50 to $1.00 per person, compared to $441.00 per person in the United States. The poorest in the developing countries are especially hurt by the unavailability of adequate health services since they are the group in the most need. They have the poorest nutrition. They have the largest families and the lowest levels of education.

Yet the poorest receive the worst health care—whether it is in rural America, the villages of Africa, or the Indian subcontinent. For example, in Kenya there is only one doctor for every 50,000 people, with most of them concentrated in Nairobi. In most African and Asian countries few people in a given year ever visit a public health facility, let alone a doctor. Even in Latin America, the situation is not much better; in Guatemala, the average citizen visits a hospital or dispensary only once in about every five years. Further, there are six times as many doctors in Guatemalan urban areas as in rural villages.[33] Most countries also have decided to give lower priority and funds to health care as against other needs such as housing and education. With the increase in population, the prospect is that rural areas will not see much of an improvement in the coming decades even if greater efforts were made to reach this poor segment of society.

The need of the majority of people is not being met by the showcase urban medical facilities which serve only a very limited group of the population. This is essentially the same problem as with other governmental programs—concentrated on the vocal (and possibly dangerous) urban groups with the rural poor left out entirely from any meaningful assistance. In some countries almost all the health care budget goes to expensive modern facilities, sometimes catering only to the modern-sector elite. In Thailand, for example, 60 percent of the doctors live in Bangkok, which contains 8 percent of the country's population.

The developing countries are very short of medical and health personnel. It is not uncommon for many areas to be served by one doctor per 20,000 or even 30,000 persons. (The United Nations has recommended that the basic standard should be one doctor per 10,000.) In the United States, the ratio is one doctor per 610 persons, the United Kingdom has one doctor per 750 persons, and Japan one doctor per 870 persons. Upper Volta has one doctor for 59,000 people. To reach the standard recommended by the United Nations would require training an additional 3.5 million doctors at a cost of at least $100 million. Yet only about 12,000 new African medical doctors are graduating yearly when African births are over 10 million—or just one doctor to take care of over 8,000 new children let alone the existing underserved population. Another problem for the poorest countries has been the severe drain of trained medical personnel to industrialized countries. Often the poor countries pay for expensive medical training for their prospective doctors, only to have them leave and work in the richer countries. In 1972, 46 percent of newly licensed physicians in the United States were graduates of foreign medical schools. Colombia, which has been graduating 600 new doctors a year to serve its population of about 22 million, has been losing sixty to eighty doctors annually to the United States.

Relatively simple and inexpensive preventive medical techniques are not being fully utilized in the developing countries. As noted, widely available vaccines against major diseases are not utilized. Above all, preventive medicine is not practiced or provided for the most poor and most vulnerable sectors of the population. Greater efforts are also needed to produce medicines and hospital equipment more cheaply and simply for use in the developing world.

Health and Population Growth

Some experts believe there is a correlation, as we have mentioned, between high infant mortality rates and high birthrates. In many poor countries, surviving children are looked upon as a source of labor and a form of social security for parents in their old age. Thus, in areas with high infant mortality, having numerous children provides a measure of insurance that enough offspring will survive to maturity to fulfill their "function" to assist the parents. In some societies, such as China, when there has been a decrease in infant mortality rates through improved health care, there also has been a decrease in birthrates.

The problem for the developing countries is especially great since they are experiencing an infant mortality rate of from 60–200 per 1,000 live births, contrasted to China's 15–20 per 1,000 live births, and much less for the developed countries. Infant mortality is one of the most formidable problems since out of 60 million annual deaths in the world, 30 million occur in children under the age of five.

If a major change in the population trend in the poorer countries is to be achieved, the demographic factors and the disease factors must be seen as inseparable. Adequate food will reduce infant mortality, which together with good health services and economic opportunity will contribute towards motivation for smaller families. Initially, however, better nutrition and health services will increase life expectancies and thereby the size of the population in less developed countries. In the long run, though, high quality life will lead to reduced population growth rates and better productivity.

Health Services for the Poorest

A new approach to health care has been to try to provide very basic health care and other services to the poorest groups especially in the rural areas. This has been done through the use of small clinics operated by paramedical personnel. Local inhabitants are given basic training and materials which can support a program that provides simple but vital health care, public sanitation, and family planning services to rural villages. China, with its so-called "barefoot doctors," is an example of a country using this approach. Through the provision of low cost health services, accessible to everyone, death and infant mortality rates have been lowered. In addition, through the provision of family planning services as an integrated element in this basic approach, there has been a reduction in the birthrate.

One modification of the Chinese "barefoot doctor" approach is the establishment in Sava, Bangladesh, of the People's Health Center which tries to reach the 95 percent of the population in the rural areas that is not reached by modern health care. The doctors involved in the program train paraprofessionals, like "barefoot doctors," who are part of the social fabric of the villages and who are content to work in rural areas. The People's Health Center has a health insurance plan whereby a family pays about 30 cents to join and the monthly fee is about 12 cents with a 6-cent daily charge for treatment (yearly per capita income is between $50 and $70). Four thousand families have enrolled, and the village itself pays for those who cannot afford these fees. The center has a staff of forty-two, only four of them physicians. Most of the paramedics are village women with minimal education. It takes about a year for the doctors to train the paramedics. The center has established six subcenters, each open one or two days a week. The main center contains a small hospital ward, outpatient facilities, laboratories, and an operating room. The paramedics provide emergency care, family planning, hygiene, public health, and nutritional information services.[34]

One way that the richer countries can contribute to the spread of basic health and associated services to the poor is to provide for the original training of paramedical teachers—the teachers that teach the local paramedical personnel. Another important cost item that developed countries can pay is the expense of needed supplies including family planning materials.

Clearly, by combining public health efforts, provision of pure water supplies, better waste disposal, improved diets, and the wider use of immunization, we will have made an important contribution to the overall well-being of the poorest and the highest risk sector of the world's people.

Health Assistance—A Global Effort

International cooperation in the health field centers now on the World Health Organization (WHO) and its related regional bodies. In addition minor health related activities are undertaken from time to time by groups other than those sponsored by the United Nations. One such group is the Organization for Economic Cooperation and

Development (OECD). A new entry into this field is NATO's Committee on the Challenges of Modern Society which has a pilot project in the field of advanced health care delivery systems.

WHO, with an annual budget of about $150 million, is by far the largest organization and has been occupied traditionally with providing technical assistance to Less Developed Countries (LDCs) and preventing diseases which are endemic in the Third World. If the organization is to be effective worldwide it will need to be strengthened.

Certainly, no area of international cooperation deserves greater support by the world community. In particular we need to strengthen the ability of both the more advanced industrialized countries and the Third World nations to utilize more effectively the technology available for bettering health conditions. Increasingly this will require international cooperative efforts at levels not yet contemplated. Further, WHO, while organizationally strong in terms of manpower and broad membership, still is methodologically backward in terms of long-term planning, systems analysis, and technological know-how.

One very useful program of WHO is its epidemiological reporting service. By monitoring the evidence of disease worldwide, it can reduce the risk of an international spread of dangerous infectious diseases. In addition, WHO establishes international biological standards to ensure the efficacy, safety, and potency of pharmaceuticals. WHO is related to the ten-nation International Agency for Research on Cancer, a still-small, multinational, scientific body engaged in basic cancer research. Much more needs to be done in the area of international cooperation against cancer. We have not even started to mobilize the world's potential resources against this disease.

Further, WHO has been very weak in supporting population/family planning programs. Most work in this area is funded by the United Nations Fund for Population Activities (UNFPA). The major aim has been to introduce family planning services as a component of maternity, maternal-child, and general health services.

One important concept in the delivery of health, family planning, and nutritional services is the better utilization of indigenous cultural and social structures in each country. These local networks can be utilized to provide these important services to more people, especially the poorest. By combining modern technology and skill with traditional institutions, it is possible to achieve low-cost delivery of integrated services. While the social structures that are best for this purpose will differ from country to country, the concept clearly needs greater exploration testing and expansion.

A broad strategy to attack health and related problems must include all of the following approaches:

—A program of comprehensive vaccinations against the major diseases such as smallpox and measles.

—Special control programs against infectious endemic diseases such as malaria, onchocerciasis, and schistosomiasis.

—Special community water and sanitation programs against water-borne diseases.

—Preventive medicine programs including nutrition, family planning, and hygiene including the training of paramedical personnel to assist the rural and poorest sectors.

A major common problem in improving the world's health has been that of cost. Without development of low cost delivery systems, neither family planning nor better health will be available to the poorest who need these services the most. Until such programs are developed, the results of excess human reproduction, disease, and malnutrition will present formidable barriers to improving the quality of human life and increase the high risks that the majority of mankind experiences every day.

CHAPTER III

The Environmental Challenge

Introduction

A vast diversity of problems challenge our world ecological system. They reach into every geographical area, into all natural realms, and make their impact on people everywhere. Man's activities have reached the very depths of the oceans and the highest levels of our globe's atmosphere. Man's untowardly effect has left deposits of toxic metals in the ice of the polar regions, in the flesh of far-ranging birds and animals, has upset the ocean's life chain, and has brought blight to distant forests and plants.

The impact of pollution is felt not only in the already overcrowded industrial centers of the rich "North" but in the rural areas in the poorer "South." If smog and sulphur oxide are the bane of auto-infested cities, soil deterioration and overgrazing are endemic in the developing-country agricultural areas. All, however, will share in the possible devastation of major climate change.

Each problem area has its own unique aspects but each shares in common an essential transboundary characteristic, going beyond the frontiers of an individual country. Each, therefore, requires international cooperation.

AIR POLLUTION

Air pollution can have a number of serious impacts upon the natural environment, global climate, and human and other life forms. There are many forms of pollutants. Some are transformed by sunlight or other materials in the atmosphere and in their changed form may become more dangerous. A large number of these pollutants come from the production or conversion of energy.

The most important basic pollutants include the following:

—the *oxides of sulphur* (called SOxs)
—the *particulates* (these consist mostly of fine ashes, airborne soot, and droplets)
—*carbon monoxide* (CO)
—the *oxides of nitrogen* (called NOxs)
—the various *hydrocarbons* (HC)
—the various *heavy metals* which find their way into the atmosphere, especially lead from gasoline
—*carbon dioxide*, which, while not normally a pollutant, when found in excessive quantities can affect the globe's climate in ways that are potentially harmful.

In general, air pollution can harm human health and cause an increase in sickness and even death. Localized impact, mostly in urban areas, can be very serious. Studies indicate a strong statistical correlation between high levels of pollution and deaths. The London "killer smog" in December, 1952, is one example, and high levels of pollution in New York City from 1963 to 1968 offer another model of the relation between pollution and human death rates. Air pollution in New York City during that period may have led to 10,000 pollution-related deaths a year. Another important element in human effects of air pollution is that it is most serious for those persons who are older, have heart trouble or respiratory diseases. Air pollution is an added stress to those in the population who are most vulnerable to getting sick.

Many of these health impact factors work together. For example, smokers from urban areas are more likely to get lung cancer than smokers from non-urban areas.[1]

What is known in this equation is that cancer-causing elements are found in polluted air. One important element to remember about the impact of air pollution on human health is that the combination of elements together can be more serious than if each element existed alone. The best example of this is the combination of particulate matter and sulphur dioxide. While sulphur dioxide alone can be removed by the human upper respiratory system, if it is combined with particulate matter, and then combined with water, the result is an absorbed coating of sulphuric acid on the individual particle. Once drawn into the lungs, such particulates can cause very serious damage.[2] These effects also mean that governments cannot just set standards for pollutants in isolation but must examine the full range of synergistic reactions and their health impacts.

Some of the properties of air pollution are the particulates, which include smaller pieces of material of all kinds including particles of tar, soot, and fly ash. Also serious are the droplets of sulphuric acid which are formed from sulphur dioxide. These particulates can have an effect on the weather. These particulates in the air form nuclei for the creation of rain droplets and this may be affecting the amount of the world's rainfall. By affecting the incoming solar radiation, they may be changing the heat balance of the atmosphere.[3] We should note here that some particles are naturally formed from such sources as volcanoes, which provide a kind of minimum background measurement to which we must add those particles man creates.

Another form of pollution comes from sulphur compounds that are released from the combustion of fuels and from smelters for copper, lead, and zinc. Much of the sulphur dioxide comes from the burning of coal. About 98 percent of the air's sulphur content comes from the burning of fuels which form with oxygen to obtain sulphur dioxide which then comes in contact with air to form sulphur trioxide (SO_3) which, in turn, reacts with water, forming sulphuric acid. This sulphuric acid is the dangerous element in the classic smog. It is dangerous to both material structures and to man, producing irritation in the upper respiratory system and in the lungs.

One of the major environmental impacts of sulphuric acid in the atmosphere is the phenomenon of acid rain. The sulphuric aerosols are in the atmosphere but are washed out by rain which becomes more and more acidic. Because of the distances that are covered by the sulphuric substances, the pollution created in one country comes down many hundreds of miles away in another country. The very acid rain (sometimes with a pH value of 3) that falls on Scandinavia comes largely from the United Kingdom and Northern Europe. We now have evidence of increasing acidity of rain over North America.[4] The impact is on both plant and animal life. Aquatic life, for example, is hurt since acidity can destroy both salmon and trout, resulting in serious impacts on fish life in Norwegian fresh waters.[5] Also soils are damaged, hurting the growth of plants which require a relatively neutral pH value.

Acid rain can also cause damage to buildings made of various stones and concrete, especially limestone and marble. For example, the art works in Italy have seriously deteriorated as a result of acid in the rain and air. In strong enough concentrations, sulphuric acid will corrode metal and discolor paint. The loss to all of mankind of great art works cannot be estimated but it is very real and will affect many generations. This phenomenon can be caused by both local and distant pollution sources.

Another form of air pollution in industrialized countries and in urban areas comes from the automobile and sometimes from electric power plants. The condition is often called photochemical smog; it causes eye irritation, respiratory problems, and plant damage. The major components of this form of pollution are the various compounds of nitrogen and oxygen (nitrogen oxides), hydrocarbons, and carbon. Often it is the secondary pollutants from this kind of smog that are the most dangerous. Sunlight affects NOx and the hydrocarbons which then together interact to form new compounds. The relatively toxic nitrogen dioxide (NO_2) gives the typical brownish color to this type of smog. Also, sunlight breaks nitrogen dioxide apart, forming nitrogen oxide and oxygen, but the oxygen atom joins with an oxygen molecule producing ozone. Ozone is a powerful oxidizing agent damaging to plants and buildings.

Hydrocarbons, another major component of photochemical smog, are oxidized in the air and smog to form various types of HCO, which, in turn, are very reactive and form other dangerous compounds. There are a number of health impacts from this kind of pollution on the eyes and on the capacity to breathe and it is very damaging to plants. The exact impact on man of photochemical smog is not yet known and needs more study.

Another substance coming from the auto is carbon monoxide. It results from the incomplete burning of fuel. It is odorless, and in high concentrations it is poisonous. When in the body it puts the red blood cells out of action by various chemical reactions preventing the use of oxygen in the normal oxidizing functions of blood.

Whenever leaded gas is used in automobiles, we will find lead atoms in the atmosphere. It is now found almost everywhere, even in the annual ice layers in northern Greenland. There has been a steep growth in such lead content from the 1950s which clearly indicates that the lead comes from leaded gas introduced in the late 1930s and early 1940s.[6] Lead also builds up not only in snow layers in Greenland but also in man. The lead in persons working in auto tunnels is far greater than that, for example, found in farmers.

The average body takes in about 20 to 30 micrograms of lead per day by breathing, drinking, and eating.[7] We are still not sure of the impact on man of this low-level exposure. Lead is deposited in the bone tissue and impairs the action of the bone marrow. Since it is cumulative, it can be especially dangerous over time. Since the 1920s more than 6 billion pounds of lead have been released into the atmosphere. With the move towards lead-free gasoline the hope is that this form of pollution eventually will be greatly reduced. The United States has already made this change, but some foreign countries still use lead in their automobiles. We need to remember that lead is just one of a number of toxic elements which are daily being introduced into our environment by our activities.

The sources of these different pollutants are mainly from transportation (hydrocarbon emission and carbon monoxide) and the combustion of fuels for electricity and heat (sulphur oxides and particulates). In urban areas and industrialized countries the automobile is the key source of the nitrogen oxides and the hydrocarbons of photochemical smog.[8] The impact of each of these pollutants differs and thus one pollutant can be dangerous at very low levels while another pollutant has an adverse effect only at much higher levels. In the majority of urban areas the hydrocarbons are the most dangerous to humans with particulates and nitrogen oxides next.[9]

On the international scale the main problem is that while a country has control over the air space above its land, pollutants are transported over long distances and have their adverse impact far from their point of origin. With the growth of nationalism worldwide there is also a tendency of many countries to believe that whatever they do within their own boundaries, including their air space, is their sovereign right. But it has also been established that a country is responsible for the harm its polluting does to another nation.

The main and continuing difficulty has been how to develop the necessary international mechanisms that can analyze the problem, encourage cooperation between countries, and establish ways to control air pollution that might create damage to other countries.

To a degree the industrial countries have acknowledged responsibility for dealing with the problem of transboundary air pollution. First, the Organization for Economic Cooperation and Development (OECD) Environmental Committee established the "polluter pays" principle both as a mechanism to try to ensure a fair competitive position between countries and as a means of internalizing the costs of pollution control on the part of the polluting industry. The principle was agreed to among the industrialized countries since it was realized that by failing to control the pollution in one country they would thereby put themselves in a disadvantageous competitive position.

Pollution of the Upper Atmosphere

We have already seen the potential for environmental damage including climatic changes from the "man-made" release of carbon dioxide and from concentrations of aerosol particulates. There is yet another serious impact from man's activities which affects the upper atmosphere. Both agricultural chemicals and a group of chemicals sometimes called chlorofluorocarbons (CFCs), halocarbons, "Freons," or simply fluorocarbons are now suspected as the key elements affecting the upper reaches of our earth's air cover and in particular the ozone layer. A number of scientific reports have indicated that a danger may exist to the ozone layer. They called at a minimum for further research and, as a prudent measure against possible long-term catastrophe, immediate cessation of all unnecessary fluorocarbon production.

The National Research Council (NRC) report in 1976 held that the release of chlorofluorocarbons into the atmosphere presented a definite hazard to the Earth's ozone layer and entailed a threat of "drastic" climatic changes. The NRC's Committee on Impacts of Stratospheric Change recommends that unless new findings emerge to mitigate the threat, nonessential uses of this group of chemicals should be drastically curtailed. The committee recommended specifically that halocarbons not be used in aerosol cans after January, 1978. It also recommended that important uses of halocarbons, such as in refrigerating units, should be phased out more slowly. The later phasing out would occur only if other sources did not provide sufficient control over the release of these chemicals into the atmosphere.[10]

In the early 1970s there was growing concern over the integrity of the stratosphere because of the advent of supersonic flight. It was believed that large fleets of supersonic aircraft would discharge their exhaust products into the atmosphere. These exhausts contain nitrogen oxides which act as catalysts to reduce the ozone content of the stratosphere which protects man from excessive solar radiation. Preliminary research carried out by France, the United Kingdom, and the United States indicates that the present number of supersonic aircraft flying into the next decade would only cause a minor reduction in stratospheric ozone. The research reports held that the amount of reduction would be too small to be detected by current observing systems or networks.

However, increased research into the chemistry of the stratosphere led to the realization that chlorine may be a more potent agent for the catalytic destruction of ozone than the nitrogen oxides. By 1974 research indicated that the chlorofluorocarbons released into the atmosphere from propellants in aerosol cans and to a lesser extent in refrigeration and air conditioning units might provide a significant source of the chlorine in the upper atmosphere. Also in 1974 the Royal Commission on Environmental Pollution expressed its concern about this potential hazard to the upper atmosphere. In 1975 a United States report indicated the same danger and suggested regulatory action might be required.[11]

The specific nature of the problem is that the ozone in the upper atmosphere acts as an optical filter screening out much, but not all, of the ultraviolet radiation from the sun which can have harmful effects. The effective reduction of the ozone layer would produce a substantial increase in the amount of damaging ultraviolet light that reaches the surface of the Earth. In turn, this would lead to a larger increase in all forms of skin cancer, including life-threatening malignant melanoma. There is also reason to believe that an increase in ultraviolet radiation would undoubtedly have negative effects on animals and plants although these effects are not yet fully known.

The National Research Council Report concluded that the release of fluorocarbons into the atmosphere at a rate corresponding to the use in 1973 would eventually produce somewhere between a 2 and a 20 percent reduction in stratospheric ozone, with the most likely figure being about 7 percent.[12]

Once released in the atmosphere, present evidence suggests that the fluorocarbons are not broken down in the troposphere as are most other chemicals but gradually are lifted upwards into the stratosphere. Their normally desirable property of stability, for which the fluorocarbons were developed, becomes in the atmosphere an undesirable property. The average lifetimes of the most heavily used commercial fluorocarbons are estimated to be about 29 to 205 years.[13] Since the beginning of measurements in 1970 there has been a measurable increase in the concentration of these fluorocarbons in the troposphere. It is only in the stratosphere that these chemicals are, in fact, changed to produce individual chlorine atoms. The chlorine atoms produced from this process can catalyze and bring the destruction of stratosphere ozone. If the release levels of CFCs continue indefinitely at the 1973 rate of production, theoretical models estimate an ozone-depletion rate rising to an equilibrium of approximately 8 percent after about one hundred years. The reason for this long period to reach an equilibrium level is the very slow rate of vertical transport across the atmosphere and through to the higher reaches of the stratosphere. On the other hand, any reduction in the rate of release of the fluorocarbons would take a similar period before becoming fully effective. This situation means that action would need to be taken long before the ozone reduction reaches any agreed-upon critical levels and indeed possibly before any measurable ozone decrease can be detected by present instruments. Until recently, worldwide production rates of CFCs increased at a rate of some 10 percent per year. And if this trend were to be resumed, then the models predict that correspondingly greater ozone depletions would eventually result.

In understanding the impact of such chemicals upon the atmosphere, one must also realize that a variety of other volatile fluorocarbons have also been detected in the atmosphere. Some of these come from dry-cleaning and metal-cleaning processes, whose annual discharge into the atmosphere is somewhat comparable to that of the CFCs. The effects of such compounds on the world's ecology depend on details of their atmospheric chemistry which is only partly understood at this time. Some scientists believe that the most significant of such compounds, carbon tetrachloride and methyl chloride, are thought to cause more ozone destruction than the CFCs. Most believe that the methyl chloride appears to have a significant natural source, while the origin of the carbon tetrachloride is probably man-made.[14]

In 1975, the world production of CFCs was estimated at 687,000 metric tons, having declined from a maximum amount of 805,000 metric tons in 1974. Most of the CFCs are produced in Western Europe, the United States, and the Soviet Union. In the United States about 20 percent of the CFCs are used in air conditioning and refrigeration and about 50 percent as aerosol propellants. The United States produces approximately 40 percent of the world's key CFC elements (these are commonly called F-11 and F-12). It is estimated that in the United States nonessential aerosol uses account for approximately 70 percent of United States production. United States curtailment of these emissions will reduce the world's fluorocarbon impact on the ozone layer by approximately 30 percent. Thus, the rest of the world contributes 70 percent to the outstanding problem. The banning by the United States of the release of the CFCs would simply prolong the time in which the depletion of the ozone layer would ordinarily occur. But it will not stop it. The problem cannot be solved by merely unilateral United States regulations.

The effect of the CFCs appears to be such that for each 1 percent of ozone reduction there will be an increase of ultraviolet radiation of approximately 2 percent. Thus, a reduction of 8 percent in the ozone concentration would lead to an increase of about 16 percent in the incidence of ultraviolet rays at ground level. While there is some dispute about the required amounts of additional ultraviolet radiation which could cause an increase in the incidence of skin cancer, it appears clear that some increased danger takes place as a result of such higher levels of ultraviolet radiation. While it is difficult to establish a direct quantitative relationship between the decrease in the ozone level and the incidence of skin cancer there appears to be from most of the literature a feeling that such a relationship does exist.

There is also a certain amount of information which indicates that increases of ultraviolet radiation on plants and animals might be causing a certain amount of damage. The effect of ultraviolet radiation on animals appears to include such things as eye cancer, bacterial infection, and other conditions.

There is also a possible impact on climate due to the release of CFCs. The CFCs act in similar ways to carbon dioxides producing the so-called "greenhouse effect." The British believe the impact on climate of increased ultraviolet radiation is relatively small and it is unlikely that the postulated depletion of the ozone layer of about 6 to 8 percent would give rise to such effects as to change the earth's weather in general or the agricultural systems specifically. On the other hand, some scientists hold that the halocarbons anywhere in the atmosphere will absorb infrared radiation emitted from the Earth and prevent it from radiating into space, thereby warming the atmosphere. This is similar to the impact of carbon dioxide.

It is difficult to assess the magnitude of such potential temperature increases since very little is known about the variables that affect climate. One calculation noted by the National Research Council suggested that continued release of CFCs at the 1973 rate might produce a global temperature increase of about 0.3° C. in some fifty years. This would be half the effect predicted for carbon dioxide during the same period. It is believed that were the release of CFCs to continue to increase at the same rate as in the past, the calculated effect on global temperature by the year 2000 would be as large as that from carbon dioxide. These calculations are crude but point to areas of growing concern over the impact of the release of chemicals into the atmosphere. Most climatologists agree a global temperature increase of even 1° C. would have a major effect on climate.

The Committee on Impacts of Stratospheric Change of the National Academy of Sciences recommended the following:

—The regulation of halocarbons should be selective to produce the greatest immediate reduction in release. Aerosols should be banned by 1978 and other uses should be restricted.

—The United States should make every appropriate effort to encourage other countries to adopt similar restrictions.

—Restrictions on CFC use should be reviewed every three to five years as the amount of knowledge about the climate increases, to determine if such restrictions still are appropriate.

—Better knowledge of atmospheric chemistry and better measurement of atmospheric changes should be undertaken and obtained.

—Better information should be obtained about the effects of ultraviolet radiation on humans and particularly about its effects on plants and animals.

—More information should be obtained about preventive medicine procedures needed to protect humans against ultraviolet-induced skin cancers.

There are many uncertainties about the impact of CFCs on the ozone layer and thus we can expect many disputes over its effect for a number of years. Despite this uncertainty, however, there seems to be little question that the theory of its impact is valid. Given this it appears equally clear that the danger can be reduced only by eliminating on an international basis, by all producing countries, unnecessary use of CFCs.

Finally some experts have also pointed to another threat to the stratospheric ozone from various surface nitrogens especially nitrogen fertilizers. So far, data on this phenomenon is not available to enable decision makers to take any corrective action. The main problem is the difficulty in distinguishing between the various sources of nitrogen reaching the stratosphere. Thus very high priority should be given worldwide to research by scientists on this problem. Should clear evidence indicate that nitrogen fertilizers are an important factor in depletion of the ozone layer the impact could be very great. Especially the developing countries would be affected by limits on the use of these chemicals.

A major lesson for the global community from the ozone-layer-depletion issue is the degree to which all countries share in the high risks of change in the world's ecological balance. While aerosol cans are a product of a rich industrialized society, their impact is worldwide. Only the advanced industrialized countries (the producers of CFCs) are able effectively to reverse the impact.

On the other hand, the use of nitrogen fertilizers is universal and they are used extensively in many developing countries. Here the costs and benefits must be measured carefully since not only the world's ecological balance is at stake but also its food producing capacity. We see again in this issue how different sectors, normally seen as independent, are in fact highly interdependent. Because of this interdependence, changes in even one sector can increase the risks for all peoples.[15]

MAJOR CLIMATE CHANGES

Scientists are not agreed on whether the Earth is getting colder or warmer. The Earth has been experiencing some abnormal weather, including in 1976 the Midwest droughts, Western Europe's hot summer, and the 1976-77 very cold winter in the eastern United States. Scientists are agreed, however, that some changes are taking place as a result of man's activities, especially the combustion of fossil fuels. (Sunspots and changes in ocean temperatures are among the other suspected causes of climate changes.)

On the one hand, as a result of the increase in carbon dioxide due to burning of fuels, the consequence is likely to be the creation of a "greenhouse effect." The carbon dioxide permits sunlight to pass to the

Figure III-1. CO_2 air quality concentrations, Mauna Loa, Hawaii, and Antarctica

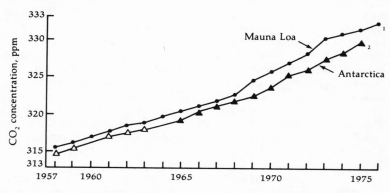

[1] Average annual concentration (based on Scripps 1974 manometric calibration).

[2] Δ = average based on limited data.

Source: C. D. Keeling and R. B. Bacastow, "Impact of Industrial Gases on Climate," *Energy and Climate* (Washington, D.C.: National Academy of Sciences, 1977), p. 77.

Earth but it prevents the long-wavelength heat radiation produced by the Earth from escaping into the upper atmosphere and space. The result could cause a warming of the Earth over time by several degrees Fahrenheit. The end product could be, over a number of decades, the melting of the polar ice caps which would increase the levels of the oceans. From 1915 to 1950 there has been a significant warming of the Northern Hemisphere. Some scientists have held that the concentration of carbon dioxide in the atmosphere could increase several times over the present level if we continue to burn hydrocarbons at the present or predicted rates. So far since the Industrial Revolution it has increased 10 to 15 percent.[16] (See Figure III-I.)

On the other hand, there also appears to be a general cooling trend in the Earth's climate especially in the Northern Hemisphere, which acts against the increase in warmth from carbon dioxide. From the 1950s up to 1970 there was a cooling trend, but it was reversed after 1972.[17] The increase of particulates (from industry, volcanoes, and agriculture) in the air is seen as a major contributing factor to a cooling trend since the particulate matter acts to reduce the amount of sunlight that reaches the Earth by reflecting back the sun's radiation away from the ground.

There is a division among scientists about which factor is the more important. Some believe that particulate matter has screened out enough sunlight to decrease the average temperature of the Northern Hemisphere by almost one degree.[18] In theory a six-degree drop could produce a new ice age. Should the average temperature of the North Polar area fall, the result would cause the upper level western winds to bring cold polar air farther south. The result would be a critical change in the grain-growing regions which would move farther south. The present rich growing areas of Canada, the Soviet Union, and China would become too cold to support the production of major grain crops. The outcome would be a major shift in power and economic capacity on a global scale. It could also produce disaster in world food production. Some hold that the cold wave could advance by 2000 A.D. sufficiently to destroy the capacity of vast areas for crop production.

Yet a warming trend could produce equally disastrous results for global food production. Through the "greenhouse effect" temperatures in the North Pole could increase, and this would reduce the southerly movement of the westerlies. The result would be the loss of spring and summer rains that the westerlies provide. The grain areas would thus become too arid for significant food production. This would hit the United States particularly hard. Another consequence could be the melting of Arctic ice which would create more ocean surface that in turn would absorb more heat than the original ice areas. The result would be to move grain growing regions farther north.

While we are not sure in what direction the Earth is moving, the result either way would reduce the Earth's food production. This would cause worldwide shortages. One problem has been the higher than average food production in recent years which has lulled the governments of the world into believing they could count on good weather as a usual event and thus get along, with just adequate stockpiles without provision for carry-overs in case of several years of sustained bad weather and poor crops. The other impact of cold winters is the need for additional fuel supplies. The winter of 1976-77 proved that we were poorly prepared for a very cold winter. If the cold trend were to continue, the need would be very great for more fuel and increased efficiency, conservation, and insulation. Otherwise, we could be running into serious shortages of fuel and food without adequate emergency supplies. The results could have health, economic, and even security implications of astounding proportions. While the rich areas might still have enough food, there would be little left, if any, for export to poorer areas. The consequence could be widespread famine.

Governmental concern over this topic was sufficient enough for the United States Central Intelligence Agency to conclude in an unclassified report that "climate is now a critical factor. The politics of food will become the central issue of every government."[19]

With the recent wide fluctuations of weather it appears prudent for governments to assess carefully the impact that pollution has upon climate and to take corrective action against such pollution. The cost of such corrections can only be far less than the consequences of major climate change and the massive risks inherent in such shifts for all peoples. One informal United States government paper described the situation thus: "The impacts which future energy needs will have on global atmosphere/environment conditions are not yet uniquely determined. However, it is clear that there are possibilities for catastrophe in several different directions."[20]

CONSERVATION OF NATURAL RESOURCES

Over the past decades with the increase in population and in economic development there have also occurred many examples of misuse of natural resources, including the flora and fauna and especially the quality of the soil structure. Most recently we have seen vast areas experiencing soil degradation including an increase in the rate of desertification. These negative environmental factors can have an important impact on food production. Short-term misuse can destroy for decades the beneficial process of nature. For example, an inch of top-soil takes centuries to form but can be destroyed in years or even months by mismanagement.

Forests worldwide are decreasing as a result of man's activity and through natural processes. The greatest problem is in the tropical areas with their very fragile ecology. Increased population has created additional pressure on forest resources, which in turn has resulted in the destruction of vast natural areas needed to protect the Earth's soil and rare species of plants and animals. One important factor has been the use of forests for firewood by one-third of the world. Most of the rest of mankind depends on forest products in one form or another. Yet forests hardly exist any longer in much of Central America, the Middle East, and North Africa. For example, forests that once covered a third of much of North Africa are now just a tenth of their original size. Deforestation is especially dangerous in the Himalayas and for the Indian subcontinent's major river systems. In Africa, the Ivory Coast's forests were reduced 30 percent between 1956 and 1966.[21]

The prudent and wise management of soils can make the difference between starvation or abundance for a large number of people in any given region. Conservation of resources and careful use of soils increase their productivity markedly. Soil management can return damaged land that is unproductive to high levels of fertility. It can also ensure that already cultivated areas remain productive and even bring higher yields. It can transform areas not now being cultivated into food production.

While it is estimated that inherent soil resources are more than ample in most countries for the present population, they must nevertheless be protected for future generations since vast areas are experiencing overgrazing or deterioration in other ways. Also the burning of the forest areas on the savannah contributes to losses of nitrogen and sulfur and to the encroachment of weeds and grass. Overgrazing reduces production of forage and exposes the soil to washing and blowing. It can cause serious flooding and sedimentation because the bare soil often forms a crust that forces the rain to run off.

Within the United States, recently, we have seen wind cause great dust storms which strip the topsoil and destroy large western farm areas. In one day, 300,000 acres of cropland in one county were damaged by wind. Some fields underwent thirty years of normal soil loss in twenty-four hours.[22] This will result in very poor production in these areas for many years to come.

We see now that the cycles of dependence and interdependence, of population growth combined with overgrazing and deforestation are creating major denudation of the rural areas of many developing countries. The result is the rapid spread of soil erosion. Experts have estimated that millions of acres of cropland, mostly in the poorer countries of Africa, Asia, and the Middle East, are abandoned each year because soil erosion has made agricultural activities uneconomic with the technology at hand. One example of this loss is the destruction of the ancient "Fertile Crescent" in the Tigris-Euphrates Valley, which was rich enough in the pre-Christian period to support a larger population than it does today. Deserts in this and other areas were expanded by overgrazing.

In the industrialized countries the problem is the encroachment of highways, shopping centers, and houses on farmland. Often the most productive soil is also the most attractive for nonfarm purposes. During the last decade about 400,000 hectares were preempted for urban uses, and this land is now forever lost to food production. Not all available land should be farmed. Not all swamps should be drained, nor all rivers dammed. These actions can hurt the overall ecosystem and frustrate the aims of good soil conservation, and must be weighed carefully.

Problems of soil conservation are national or perhaps regional in their impact, but like some other problem areas, the cumulative effect can be global. We are seeing a worldwide trend towards general soil erosion, particularly through wind and water action which often carry soil very long distances.

Another threat to good soil management is the misuse of pesticides and other toxic substances. Fungicides, for example, can injure beneficial soil microorganisms and thereby inhibit transformation of nitrogen compounds. This problem is rare but care should be taken that such chemicals will not have undesirable long-term effects on agriculture and create wider environmental costs. Very often these chemicals are transported away from the site of application and find their way to pollute streams, lakes, and other waterways, harming the fish and animals that use the contaminated water.

The costs to the land are great even in thinly populated but water-poor areas such as North Africa where populations are increasing each year by 3 percent. In fact, the population of arid Northern Africa has multiplied sixfold since the beginning of the century. This has brought degradation of land quality which causes movements of population and livestock, which can exacerbate the pressure on the land in new areas. This overgrazing and deforestation have assisted the spread of the Sahara Desert along its southern fringe from Senegal to Northern Ethiopia. The United Nations Food and Agriculture Organization (FAO) estimates that more than 250,000 acres of farmland in North Africa are lost to the desert each year. The result is starvation for people and animals.

In the last few decades, a great deal has been learned about arid lands management. The United Nations Conference on Desertification held in September, 1977, gave special attention to this aspect of the soil conservation problem. The conference examined ways of developing and utilizing new technology for use in the Sahara and other arid land areas.

In sum, it appears that soil erosion and consequently overgrazing and desertification are increasing, mostly due to accelerated population growth. Technology, which sometimes could help prevent or slow down this process, has not been effectively applied in many areas. The availability of water is another important factor as well as the knowledge of better farming methods. Thus to help preserve our thin shell of soil, significant improvements must be made not only in controlling the growth of population but also in spreading better knowledge of irrigation, farming techniques, and soil conservation. This will require giving these problems a higher international priority, increased local resources, and, most importantly, knowledge and assistance from the richer countries. The key to action in this as in many other areas is an acknowledgment by people and governments of the serious nature of the problem. Unless corrective action is taken soon, the world will lose for centuries vital cropland and the food that this land can produce.

Finally, it would be wrong to leave out of our consideration of the protection of natural resources the examination of endangered plants and animals. Man's encroachment has resulted over the last century in the destruction or the extermination of thousands of species of animals and plants. Man himself threatens the very survival of countless thousands of animal and plant species. The balance between human, plant, and animal life has been upset. Not only have natural habitats been urbanized but wastes from industry have spread toxic chemicals which threaten to break the life cycles of many species.

There are numerous examples of this problem in the United States where 10 percent of the 20,000 species, subspecies, and varieties of plants native to this country are threatened with extinction, and in Central America which has lost nearly two-thirds of its tropical rain forests.[23] Many animal species are endangered by toxic materials, especially the vital plankton which marine biologists fear could be destroyed by pollution and in turn this could destroy not only the ocean food chain but also Earth's life-support system.

The list of endangered wildlife of the International Union for the Conservation of Nature and Natural Resources has been growing rapidly. While it is natural for extinction to take place, the pace of such loss has increased and far exceeds now the number of new species appearing. Therein lies a special danger to our ecosystem.

Man's progress in feeding himself and in protecting human health depends on our knowledge of plant genetics and maintaining crucial genetic material for supporting scientific advances. Plants have provided keys to improving food supply and nutrition and for increasing sources of natural chemicals which can help in conquering diseases. (For example, science suppressed malaria with quinine which comes from a Latin American plant, the cinchona tree.)

Clearly, therefore, man runs a risk to himself in the destruction of plant and animal species. Some experts believe that as the process of "man-made" extinction is accelerated, the chances increase that the complex ecosystem which supports all living things could be dangerously and perhaps irrevocably harmed.

The United States has been in the forefront of a number of international efforts to protect various endangered species. United States law, in some cases, requires such action. The Marine Mammal Protection Act requires the United States government to foster international protection of marine mammals. Thus America has moved to protect the whales through participation in the International Whaling

Commission (IWC) and by pressing for adherence by additional nations to a moratorium on the killing of whales. So far, this latter goal has not been accepted by those countries most engaged in the slaughter of this great mammal. Russia and Japan continue to oppose a halt to high seas killing of whales; but through largely United States efforts, IWC has been able to decrease the quotas on certain endangered whale species.

There is a great need to develop more effective international conventions for marine mammals inadequately protected at present. In particular, action needs to be taken to protect Antarctic seals, North Pacific fur seals, and the magnificent polar bears.

Within the United States, policy has been guided by the requirements of the Endangered Species Act which prompted the United States to support the International Endangered Species Convention. But there is a great need for stronger enforcement by various domestic agencies of the convention's signatory parties.

Also the global community needs to work to preserve native habitats of genetically important plant and animal species. A plan has been developed establishing special "biosphere reserves" supported by funds from the richer countries or international organizations when such "reserves" are located in a developing country. The United States can bilaterally be of some assistance by supporting programs helping endangered species and establishing or strengthening national parks which not only preserve wildlife but can also be an important source of hard currency by attracting tourists. The United States has signed the World Heritage Trust Treaty which seeks to promote the conservation of natural areas and of cultural sites. Yet this convention remains weak and has, so far, done little to preserve areas of importance in the developing countries.

It is essential that early action be taken to draw up an international convention or perhaps a series of regional or limited agreements to systematically preserve and "bank" the genetic resources of the world. In addition, it would be helpful to increase the amount of research devoted to identifying endangered plants and animals so that both national and international corrective action can be taken.[24]

The Crisis of Fresh Water

The United Nations Water Conference at Mar del Plata, Argentina, in March, 1977, helped increase the attention given by the public and governments to a growing crisis shared by both developed and developing countries—the pollution and the increasing scarcity of fresh clean water. Yet this conference only said what most people of the world have already experienced. Drought, rampaging floods, and contaminated water supplies are now common in almost every region of the globe.

Much of the water in the world is unsuitable for direct human use, for domestic purposes, industry, or farming. That water which man can reasonably utilize is seldom consistently available in sufficient amounts from assured sources. Droughts parch the soil, dry up the rivers, and lower water tables. Man-made wastes contaminate rivers, lakes, and groundwater, and pollutants make these water supplies unfit for normal use.

Drinking water is vital to the very survival of every individual but it is only a small part of man's basic requirement. The production of food requires large quantities of water. Up to 120 gallons of water are necessary to produce a loaf of bread, and a pound of meat needs 200 times that amount.

Within the United States per capita daily water use has increased more than 75 percent in the last twenty-five years. Worldwide water use is expected to triple by the early twenty-first century if projected population and per capita consumption trends materialize.[25] For the future, therefore, it will be increasingly difficult to satisfy the growing demand. The most accessible sources of water have already been tapped in many areas. The best irrigated farmland has already been developed and in the future such land will take more effort to use and will increase more slowly than in the past. The shortage of fresh water for irrigation could severely constrain efforts to expand world food supplies. According to United Nations experts, the two uses of water where shortages are contributing most to human misery are in food production and in the supply of drinking water.

What exactly is the profile of global water use? First, 80 percent of the world's people have no access to tap water. Most of these people are in the developing world and obtain water from streams or wells. Often these waters are contaminated with human wastes. The United Nations Children's Fund estimates that about one billion rural people in the developing world and 200 million inhabitants in urban shantytowns such as in Mexico City and Lagos, Nigeria, must use unsafe water sources. Seventy percent of the world's population in developing countries still lack safe drinking water. There are an estimated 250 million cases of water-borne diseases yearly. The human cost is that more than 5 million people die every year from water-borne diseases.[26] Some experts believe that the single most effective measure that could be taken to improve human health in developing countries would be to provide safe sources of drinking water.

Second, agriculture currently accounts for 80 to 90 percent of all the water used by mankind, not counting rain. Most of this water is for irrigation. While irrigated land represents only 15 percent of the world's total farmland, it produces from 30 to 40 percent of the world's food.[27] Most of the world's additional food will probably have to come from new irrigated land if the growing population's food needs are to be met, particularly since the new high-yielding seed varieties require irrigation to obtain maximum production.

Third, the United Nations Food and Agriculture Organization estimates that to feed all those who will be alive in 2000 we will need to double the amount of water now used for irrigation.

Fourth, the need for water by industry, already growing, will expand greatly in the next decades. For example, in the energy sector, refining a ton of oil uses 180 tons of water while making a ton of paper consumes 250 tons of water. The result of this use has been the dumping of industrial waste into rivers and lakes, which destroys water for other industrial and domestic use. While such pollution is common in developed countries, it has now become increasingly common in the urban areas of the poor parts of the globe.

One example illustrating the danger pollution has for water quality is the recent destruction of brook trout and the spotted salamanders in lakes in New York State's Adirondack Mountains because of deadly rain and snow containing corrosive acids that kill these species. A recent Cornell University study showed 90 percent of the lakes above 2,000 feet were devoid of fish life, while in the 1930s only 4 percent were barren.[28] One new "pollution control" measure, the high smokestacks, may have helped to spread this problem since it is the industrial complexes far away from these lakes which cause the pollution. A similar problem exists in Europe where acid rain from Great Britain falls on Scandinavia.

Human and industrial waste also can destroy lakes and waterways in developing countries. African lakes, once rich in natural wildlife, have become cesspools for polluted water including agricultural runoff. Birds leave such areas and the lakes are unsuitable for many other important uses.

Finally, we need to remember that while water is one of the most abundant materials on Earth, well over 99 percent of it is not available for direct human use. There are about 333 million cubic miles of water on the planet—97 percent is in the oceans and a little more than 2 percent is frozen water in the polar regions. Of the remaining fresh water, 0.65 percent, nearly half is located more than a mile underground beyond the reach of conventional technology. An equal amount is located up to one-half mile deep (groundwater) and is already being tapped. Lakes and rivers contain 0.01 percent of the planet's water or about 33,000 cubic miles. Most farmers depend on the water that is stored in clouds and delivered as rain. This amounts to only 0.001 percent of the world's water, and most of it goes into the oceans.

Under pressure of population growth and industrial development water can be a focus of international and domestic conflict. Often a river or lake is shared by two or more countries, with pollution from one destroying the use of the water by others. Also the sharing of bordering waters becomes a high political problem where there is not enough to satisfy the needs of all.

The outlook for the future is filled with risks that sufficient water will not be available, or at least not available in a usable form, to meet the basic needs of a large proportion of the world's growing population. In the next twenty-five years, we must make twice as much fresh water available as the world already uses. Thus, new technologies will need to be developed to supply this water and to see that it is kept or made clean.

Towards a Global Water Development Strategy

There are a number of actions that the global community and individual countries can take which will reduce the risks of a future water crisis. Different efforts will be required in different areas and will relate to the nature of the local situation. In general, however, they include the following:

Water Recycling: A major way of meeting the industrial and domestic needs for clean water is to clean dirty water and recycle it for industrial or other uses. Japan has developed this approach and now that country's industries obtain more than 62 percent of their water by cleaning their own wastes and reusing the water.[29] Over the last fifteen-year period, Japan has been able to quintuple its industrial use of water while having to increase its consumption of unused "fresh" water by a factor of only 2.3.

Desalting Seawater: This technology still must progress before it will prove economic in most parts of the globe. New technology is being developed using ion exchange and special membranes, but the costs—at present levels—are too high.

Use of Water in Icebergs: From time to time, it is proposed to utilize the polar region's icebergs as a relatively cheap source of water for the desert and semidesert areas. Three-quarters of the world's fresh water exists as polar ice. Dr. John Isaacs of the Scripps Institute of Oceanography suggested towing the icebergs from Southern Antarctica to southern California to supply the rapidly rising needs of Los Angeles, San Diego, and neighboring areas.[30] Saudi Arabia has even commissioned a study to check on the practicability of using icebergs in that country where they would be melted for drinking water and for irrigation. The price could be half the cost of desalting seawater. One interesting question raised by this bizarre concept is who owns the icebergs and who should regulate their use? In any case, there are major technological and environmental obstacles at present to this technique.

Building Dams and Reversing the Flow of Rivers: It has been traditional to build dams on rivers to preserve water for human use in one form or another. There is still some room for this in developing countries but there are real limits on how far one can go in developed countries with this practice. The Soviet Union, for example, is examining the possibility of diverting whole rivers that now flow toward the Arctic and directing them more southward to irrigate farmland. Already a 175-mile canal is being constructed to divert a small portion of the waters of two rivers. Yet experts caution that such diversion can upset the Arctic ecosystem.[31]

Use of Fossil Water: Many areas are now exploiting "fossil water," that is, underground water left over from the Ice Ages which is not being replenished by rainfall. It exists largely under deserts and, unlike common groundwater which is replenished naturally, it can and is being used up. Where it has been used it has resulted in the fall in the area's water table and caused many wells to run dry. Once gone it cannot be replaced. In Africa there are vast quantities of such fossil water under the Sahara, and it has been estimated that this water could irrigate a large area for several decades. But the problem is that once used up, the area would be as dry as before.

Irrigation: This technique has been the traditional and relatively successful method of using water for the production of crops in areas lacking sufficient rain. However, irrigation can also cause environmental problems by saturating soil with mineral salts that are dangerous to plants. Rainwater does not have this problem as it is free of minerals. In general, irrigation water comes from rivers or wells in which the water has picked up large amounts of dissolved minerals. The water evaporates from the irrigated soils leaving the minerals behind; they can accumulate to toxic levels. This is a problem shared by the people on the lower Colorado River and the Indus River Valley of Pakistan. To control this problem, there has been an increased use of "trickle irrigation" which distributes water through small plastic pipes that drip water at the base of individual plants. It minimizes wasteful spraying of water and somewhat lessens mineral buildup. Also, technologies are being developed to deal with soil oversaturated with salts. Reduction of water loss through evaporation or seepage is possible by a number of techniques including the use of mulches and plastic sheets.

Rainwater Harvesting, or Catch Basins: This technique has been used since ancient times in arid lands. By reshaping the land surface into broad bowls, the little rain that does fall can be concentrated into one small area where fruit trees or other crops can grow.

Other Technologies: There are a variety of other ways to increase usable waters, including even irrigation with saline water for new plant varieties that tolerate brackish water. Tunisia has begun growing date palms with such water.[32] Satellite technology has been able, through photography, to develop information that may guide hydrologists to previously unknown sources of groundwater.

In the last analysis, however, we will need not only to develop new sources of water but to conserve the old or existing sources. Our success in pollution control of both air and water will in large measure determine whether we will have in the future clean, safe, and fresh water for our needs. The risk exists that this will not be the case, yet we have now at least the knowledge of the dangers and some of the necessary tools to preserve this vital resource.

TOXIC SUBSTANCES

Already serious environmental and health damage has been caused by rising levels of toxic substances being introduced into the globe's ecological system, and the risk to all living things is growing. This has given rise to concern about the long-term effects of chemicals in wide use. Toxic compounds such as DDT, PCBs, arsenic, and especially the heavy metals are now in the food chain. These dangerous chemicals affect all environmental media including our oceans, fresh water, and air. When man eats fish contaminated with high concentrates of heavy metals or drinks water with high metallic levels, the result has been sickness, genetic damage, and death. Another very dangerous group of substances are the carcinogens which include asbestos and vinyl chloride. While most publicity is focused on short-term events like the poisonous chemical cloud released over Seveso, Italy, in July, 1976, the main threat is the long-term impact of these chemicals on human health. New Jersey, for example, has long had one of the largest chemical industries in the world, as well as this nation's highest cancer-mortality rate. The high cancer rate and the dumping of chemical wastes into New Jersey's environment are almost certainly related.[33]

Heavy Metals

Mercury poisoning has killed hundreds of persons and the extent of sickness or birth defects it has caused cannot yet be fully measured. Even such a wide-ranging species as swordfish has levels of mercury above that permitted by American regulatory bodies.[34] It was mercury that poisoned the people of Minamata in Japan after they ate fish from their bay. Another toxic chemical also found in fish is cadmium, which is used by a number of industries. This chemical is especially dangerous because it persists in the human body for very long periods. Again it was in Japan, in the Jinze River Basin, that the world found an example of the impact on humans and nature of soils contaminated with cadmium from upstream mines and smelters.

While we have known for a long time that lead was poisonous, it has only been in recent decades that it has spread from being a specific and local problem into a worldwide danger. Lead is found in very high concentrations in people exposed to auto exhausts. In urban areas the lead content of the air is often twenty times that found in rural areas. In addition to the large amount of lead absorbed by humans from automobile exhaust fumes, lead reaches man through older plumbing and lead-based paint.

Pesticides and Herbicides

We have already mentioned that pesticides and herbicides can cause serious environmental dangers. They are used widely in the production of many crops in tropical and temperate areas, and are used extensively in urban areas.

Pesticides are often highly persistent in soils (persistence can be somewhat less in wet tropical regions). Occasionally, pesticides remain in the soil after the harvest of the crop to which they were originally applied, and may injure a more sensitive crop planted later.

In some areas toxic levels of copper and zinc have built up in plants in some sandy soils after extended application of certain fungicides containing these elements. Also, phytotoxic levels of arsenate are present in some old orchard sites following long-term use of arsenical insecticides. So far, fortunately, permanent harmful effects of pesticides on soil productivity are relatively rare.

In dealing with toxic chemicals governments will have to regulate the use of all of these pesticides to be certain they will not have an undesirable long-term impact on food production and on the ecology in general. Greater care is needed to ensure that pesticides do not find themselves swept away from the original site of use, to damage other areas, especially streams, lakes, and drinking water supplies. (Kepone, a pesticide, contaminated the James River in Virginia, causing the river to be closed to fishing. The workers manufacturing the product were poisoned as well.) With these dangers known the United Nations Food and Agricultural Organization needs to develop and more widely distribute better information on the proper use of pesticides, to disseminate more complete information concerning possible short- and long-term dangers, and to promote research on safer substitutes for toxic chemicals.

In the examination of the benefits of using pesticides, governments must consider the present and future potential risks of such use. Within the United States the government made recommendations to restrict greatly the use of DDT and certain other "hard pesticides," based on its evaluation of their hazards to human health, availability of effective alternatives, movement in the natural environment, concentration in food chains, and other environmental considerations.[35] It should be noted that while DDT may be banned or restricted, residues will continue to be found in the ecological chain for many years.

The discovery of excessive concentrations of DDT in coho salmon caused the United States government to launch its 1960s study of the use of pesticides and their effect upon food safety and human health. Also, it was found that much of American red meat, many dairy products, some eggs, fowl and fish—all parts of basic food groups deemed necessary for a balanced diet—contained very small pesticide residues from the ecological chain. It was clear to the government that DDT and similar chemicals were very dangerous to human and animal health. Action was taken particularly to examine and review the established tolerance levels of specific pesticides in food and drinking water.

The United States, however, continued to export DDT on the assumption that the risk/benefit balance had to be determined by each country on its own. It did ask the Agency for International Development (AID) to review with developing countries its programs involving the use of pesticides in light of the damages experienced in the United States. So far, however, few countries in the developing world have acted to restrict DDT in a way comparable to the action taken in the United States. By increasing agricultural productivity and by killing malaria-carrying mosquitoes, DDT has certainly saved many lives in developing countries, and for this reason, it has been very difficult for some of these countries to ban its use.

Regulating Toxic Substances

The scope of the problem of regulating and controlling pesticides can be seen from the fact that over 600 active pesticidal chemicals are in use in the United States and they are formulated in more than 60,000 ways.[36] Among the first steps to control such substances nationally and internationally are the registration of all brands of pesticides and the worldwide dissemination of such information along with warnings of possible hazards.

In weighing the use of specific pesticides, the relative trade-offs between the needs for public health protection and the need for producing an adequate food supply must be considered. This was one of the reasons DDT and other pesticides were not completely banned in 1969. On a national and international scale experts have recommended that we:

—accelerate programs to evaluate better the benefits of specific pesticides and alternative methods of pest control;
—develop less hazardous pest control techniques that are highly specific and leave a minimum of persistent chemicals in the environment;
—improve our understanding of the relationship between man and his food chain and of tolerance levels, and especially to improve our techniques for predicting the effects of chemicals on man;
—control the disposal of surplus or unusable pesticides; and
—use, where feasible, integrated pest management techniques that rely more on natural controls and less on chemicals.

Within the United States the Toxic Substances Control Act of 1976 (TSCA) was enacted to provide a general framework to deal with long-term as well as acute effects of chemicals on human health. Its aims include: (1) to regulate chemicals now in use that may seriously threaten human health or environmental quality and (2) to prevent new compounds from coming on the market until their safety has been evaluated. An inventory of all produced chemicals will be created to help determine which require further testing. The hope is that the provisions of the TSCA can be "internationalized" by other countries adopting similar procedures and cooperating in their implementation.

A principal problem of dealing with toxic substances is that there still is not enough information about tolerance levels, persistence, chemical interactions, and detection. For example, we still are not sure that our instruments are sophisticated enough to determine the presence of some toxic elements at very low but possibly dangerous levels. We are not sure of the tolerance levels for certain chemicals in many animals, fish, and especially man. Many chemicals are being introduced into use every day, and for most of them we do not know what their ultimate impact will be on the environment.

A first step in dealing with the toxic substances problem on a regional or global scale is the creation of more effective methods of worldwide information exchange and technical assistance. Better monitoring and control of effluents from industrial plants manufacturing, formulating, or using toxic substances may be vital to prevent serious harm. Chemical firms that manufacture and formulate toxic materials should carry the burden of proving their safety and efficacy before each chemical can be marketed.

One action already taken by the United Nations Environmental Program (UNEP) has been agreement to establish an International Registry of Potentially Toxic Chemicals (IRPTC) which will emphasize the gathering of information on selected chemicals. This registry will contain information about hazard assessment, health criteria, etc. Also data about regulation of chemical substances and their justification will be contained in the proposed registry. The information will be open to all United Nations members. Yet this is just a start. Much will depend on how governments use the registry and their enforcement of laws or regulations dealing with toxic substances.

Within the Organization for Economic Cooperation and Development (OECD) chemicals group there is a program to harmonize testing. If successful, common testing protocols will be established and utilized by the main industrial countries. In 1978 the Swedish government, at the urging of the United States, hosted a meeting in Stockholm of key environmental ministers of producing countries. They discussed cooperation on selection of priority chemicals for testing and regulatory action, development of common testing protocols, creation of standards for quality assurance, development of common methods of risk assessment and the possible creation of new international mechanisms for the control of toxic substances. Because of the nature of the problem, multilateral cooperation in this field makes most sense.

Finally, progress in dealing with this risk will only be possible with ecological research on a very large scale. Some idea of the complexity of the problem can be seen when it is realized that there are more than 70,000 chemicals in use in the United States alone and thousands come to the market every year. Further, there has been an increase in the number of chemicals manufactured and in their volume over the last thirty years, and this trend is accelerating. One step is to develop better standards and methods of evaluating chemicals and their risks.

It is also necessary to learn more about the basic metabolic processes of man and animals. In the future, mankind will have to be more careful in the introduction of chemicals, since such substances build up for years without apparent danger, but ultimately have disastrous and even irreversible consequences for us all.

ECONOMIC AND RESOURCE CONSIDERATIONS

Pollution control standards are an important part of international economic and trade issues. If one country can manufacture certain goods without utilizing any pollution controls, it can undercut and underprice another country or firm which must use often expensive pollution abatement methods. This creates unfair competition, and undermines the development of strong pollution control regulations and the use of abatement technology in many countries. Most industries will argue with their governments that strict regulations will result in the loss of vital export markets. This point of view weakens a cooperative approach to pollution control and the advancement of realistic pollution control standards in different countries.

The United States has recognized this problem and supported in the OECD the adoption of the "polluter must pay" principle which, in effect, holds that each firm should bear the full cost of controlling the pollution it causes and that this cost should be reflected in the price of the goods in the international market. The United States as a "high standard country" has played a leading role in seeking that roughly equal pollution standards and control technology be adopted by all the industrialized countries. Under this theory, no country would gain an undue advantage over another country because it has lax pollution standards.

To achieve this aim, it is important that the highest standards be utilized rather than the lowest. One dangerous element in an environmental negotiation is the tendency to adopt as the "international standard" the standards of the country with the lowest or weakest criteria for pollution control laws. This is called adopting the "lowest common denominator." Often this approach is urged or used by industry in "high standard countries" as a way to lower those strict standards so that they can pollute more and make a greater profit. One way around this in the international arena is to push for the adoption of a minimum average standard among industrialized countries with a period of time allowed for improving standards.

Another element in the global economic environmental picture is the so-called "pollution haven," a country which has little or no pollution control laws or regulations. A government often encourages "dirty" industry to invest in its country to gain a trade advantage over other countries which have stronger regulations. Korea, for example, was such a country and was a haven for especially "dirty" Japanese industry which could no longer build new plants in its home country without investing in expensive new pollution control technology. Some developing countries have sought to become pollution havens in order to attract industry and increase employment. The problem is that, over time, these "dirty" industries often cause serious harm to the local environment. The price is high and is paid by the people with the least ability to protect themselves against it or to obtain adequate health care for the problems that develop.

Some former pollution havens have seen that there is a real cost in permitting "dirty" industry to pollute the air and water and have taken action against such industries. For example, Brazil often was considered a pollution haven until the public became so outraged at some of the worst offenders that they forced the introduction of environmental protection laws.[37] Yet pollution control standards are still very loose or nonexistent in many developing countries. Most of these countries if given a choice between employment and "dirty" industry versus no employment and no industry would still prefer the "dirty" industry.

One way to deal with this environmental and economic problem is to place special countervailing duties on goods imported from countries that do not require pollution control efforts. These duties would be equivalent to the pollution control costs of the importing country or those approved through international agreements. A more direct solution would be for the developed countries to assist the poor countries in obtaining the funds for investment in pollution control technology. A voluntary code of ethics among multinational firms might also be desirable. The code could be adopted on an industry-by-industry basis and provide for minimum, but adequate, levels of pollution control in all countries where the specific industry or firm was located.

The costs to a country of polluting the air and water are another economic factor of pollution control. These costs are often not taken into consideration when the decision is made to allow an industry to establish itself in a country. Presumably water is seen as a "free good" rather than a priceless, limited commodity; likewise, clean air. Over time, as pollution destroys clean water and air, a community learns their real value, as they must pay more and more to obtain them. Also, the sickness caused by pollution is a real cost, through the loss of work productivity and increased medical expenses. All these "costs" should be internalized in an industry and added to the cost of goods that are produced if the "true cost" to society is to be fully reflected.

Rarely is it possible to identify or assess the true full cost of pollution, thus it is much better to prevent it rather than just ensure that "the polluter pays." It will be important for the concerned international organizations such as UNEP and the OECD to undertake extensive studies on how best to deal with the environmental and economic disruptions due to industrial pollution. At the planning stage all relevant and important environmental impacts should be taken into consideration so that developing countries do not have to repeat all the environmental mistakes which the industrialized countries have made and are still trying to rectify.

An important element of environmental protection is an examination among the industrialized countries of their growth patterns. These countries need to avoid disruptive growth which can bring a number of undesirable environmental hazards and dangers. To avoid dangerous growth and its pollution by-product, it is important that within the industrialized countries cooperation takes place to harmonize environmental standards and methods of regulation. It is unlikely that identical standards could be obtained in every developed country, but it is possible to ensure that no country gains a superior competitive edge by allowing unfettered pollution by industries.

The industrialized countries can reduce industrial pollution by cooperation in resource extraction, conservation, environmental protection, and in the avoidance of certain types of trade distortions. There can and should be systematic exchanges of information on which patterns of growth might be desirable or undesirable, and on ways of dealing with growth problems.[38]

As noted earlier, the most serious long-term difficulties in the global social and economic structure arise from the gap which is growing between the rich and the poor countries. The search on the part of the poorest countries for rapid industrialization can seriously exacerbate the global ecological imbalance and increase enormously the pollution and health costs of such growth. Yet such growth and development must take place for the good of all parts of the world, and a way must be found for these countries to avoid the horrendous environmental costs which have been paid through rapid industrialization by the richer countries. The difficulty is to find ways of extending the time left before reaching the ultimate limitations which exist on our globe's material growth. We must also accelerate the shift of the richer countries towards consumption patterns which are least environmentally harmful—towards services, leisure activities, and high-technology, knowledge-intensive production and away from goods and services with high resource, energy, and environmental costs.

Further, it is necessary to develop new international economic relationships which can reconcile slower material growth in the industrialized countries with a faster material growth in the less developed regions. This means that the developing countries may be increasingly the producers of goods which are needed by all, rich and poor. On the other hand, the developed countries may produce many goods and services needed by the developing world to undertake new growth patterns within the context of rational planning and pollution controls. Certain industries will more and more under these kinds of patterns locate in the developing world, while other industries in the developed countries will be producing goods and services with the least harm to the environment.

Another environmental trend worth mentioning is the movement of population from the countryside into the cities which is taking place in many of the developing countries around the world. There are many forces at work contributing to this pattern including the flow of investment and the availability of new technology and of social services within urban areas. Also the relative wage levels are a strong determinant of migration to urban areas. Thus, one of the most important factors of the quality of life in these countries is whether or not the rural countryside can be a productive, healthful, and rewarding place for its people to live. Often this is not the case and the burden to the ecology of increasing populations concentrated in urban areas with inadequate food, housing, and sanitation can be disastrous for a country desiring a balanced growth pattern and a minimization of poverty. Migration also exacerbates the problem of the rural poor as there are fewer and fewer skilled people to serve the needs of the rural population over time.

Another element of the environmental equation is the increased scarcity of natural resources. Increased growth, population, and development has put horrendous burdens on both living or renewable and mineral resources on the globe. For example, in recent decades the United States has been producing almost half of the world's industrial output while occupying less than 7 percent of the Earth's surface and with only 6 percent of its population. Thus, our high grade minerals are being depleted relatively quickly and we are turning more and more to higher grade and lower cost resources abroad. Also, the high environmental standards which we are adopting in the United States through controls on mining and smelting and other phases of production have all brought limitations upon certain polluting activities here in the United States. This produces more demand for minerals and resources abroad which adds to the burdens of other countries and increases this world's interdependence.

In the area of living resources United States' demand for imported goods from other countries has steadily increased. For example, imported supplies of forest products now account for about 12 percent of domestic consumption and this proportion of imported goods will probably grow in time. The United States' need for wood products will contribute to a certain degree to the deforestation of many land areas in developing countries.

It is likely that demand in the mineral area will increase the pressure for mining, with all its environmental consequences, mostly in developing countries abroad. For example, projections foresee an increased United States import dependence on iron jumping from 30 percent in 1970 to 67 percent by the year 2000; for copper from almost 0 percent to 56 percent; for zinc from 59 percent to 84 percent; for lead from 31 percent to 67 percent, etc. Already many other minerals such as bauxite (aluminum ore), nickel, manganese, chromium, and tin are largely imported from abroad.[39] With tremendous population growth and rising global development, and the world increasing its per capita use of depletable minerals, some experts have predicted worldwide exhaustion of crucial minerals within a number of decades.

Yet one must be careful in examining such projections since the discovery of new minerals takes place each year and new technology makes the extraction of lower and lower grade resources more economically feasible. For example, exploration has been more than able to keep ahead of consumption for most of the minerals in the recent decades. With few exceptions, known reserves of lower grade ores greatly exceed those of present commercial grade. There is also an increased opportunity to use available substitutes. For example, in the future aluminum extraction could take place from very widely available clays instead of from bauxite. The oceans, as we have noted, also can be a source of minerals which in many cases equal known land resources.

There seems to be a consensus among the experts that there are sufficient supplies at manageable costs if we develop a cooperative posture with the developing countries where many of the new mineral reserves are to be found. With such cooperation we can speed up geological surveying and thereby assure the exploitation of promising new sources but with careful environmental safeguards. The world as a whole will benefit, hopefully within the context of balanced growth. A concern for long-term needs and for the ecology of each country and even for the world as a whole will help ensure a less dangerous growth pattern.[40]

TOWARDS A GLOBAL ENVIRONMENTAL STRATEGY: ROLE OF GLOBAL ENVIRONMENTAL INSTITUTIONS—PUBLIC AND PRIVATE

One important event of global significance was the United Nations Conference on the Human Environment held in Stockholm in June of 1972. This first major environmental worldwide governmental meeting brought together representatives of some 113 countries. It was not a conference to sign binding treaties or agreements but focused primarily on the development of a large number of general resolutions. Most, but not all, were aimed at protecting our ecosystem and an important one called for the establishment of a new global environmental organization.

From the conference results it was clear that most of the world's nations were still in the dark about not only what to do to preserve the environment but also about the true nature of man's impact on our global ecosystem. The first needs, therefore, were to call for better scientific information to tell us what is happening as a result of man's activities, to identify the major trends, and finally to establish the order of priorities in cleaning up.

Perhaps the most important achievement of the United Nations Conference on the Environment was its establishment of the United Nations Environmental Program (UNEP), already mentioned, and its call for a global program titled "Earthwatch" to monitor, to share information about, and to evaluate the quality of our global environment. Subsequently, the monitoring part of this effort became the Global Environmental Monitoring System (GEMS). Originally, the GEMS program had seven goals. These were to develop or undertake:

—an expanded human health warning system;
—an upgraded international disaster warning system;
—an assessment of global atmospheric pollution and its impact on climate;
—an assessment of the extent and distribution of contaminants in the world's biological systems;
—an assessment of the state of ocean pollution and its impact on marine ecosystems;
—an assessment of the response of terrestrial ecosystems to environmental pressures; and
—an assessment of critical problems arising from agricultural and land-use practices.

This program is aimed at a dual implementation strategy, one using proven methods and existing facilities and the second focusing on developing new methods and facilities. This effort is a truly pioneer approach to a very difficult problem area. In effect what is proposed is a kind of global health report with a strong "state of the art" scientific base. We must, however, be realistic and know that the actual establishment of such a capability will be difficult, especially the development of a capability for prediction and forecasting trends. Baseline data first must be collected over a number of years before hard and accurate data are available in forms useful for decision makers. Clearly, such a continuous assessment of the status and direction of the Earth's environmental quality is a prerequisite to effective environmental management.

The hope now is to utilize to the extent possible already existing or planned national and international monitoring activities. These include the Integrated Global Oceans Station System (IGOSS), the World Weather Watch run by the World Meteorological Organization (WMO) and the Global Atmospheric Research Program. Also regional programs and national systems that exist in such countries as the Soviet Union and the United States will be an important part of this effort.

Perhaps the most important element of the Earthwatch program is the periodic evaluation and review of global environmental conditions. This includes examination of major ecological trends. Yet the program does not provide for a real environmental management function since UNEP has not been given any responsibility for actual programs to halt pollution or decision-making authority with respect to carrying out clean-up activities.

The evaluation function has not even started and unfortunately may never get off the ground since there are both technological and political reasons for this function being avoided by United Nations member countries. Will the organizations controlled by and dependent on their member governments point their fingers at a specific country as the cause of acid rain in another country? Who will accuse a nation of spilling into the ocean toxic waste which destroys living resources and eventually enters the human food chain? There is little proclivity towards this kind of hard but necessary "blowing the whistle" against international polluters. Unfortunately, there is no international enforcement machinery against the polluters of mankind's fragile environment.

In addition to such global institutions as UNEP, WHO, and FAO there also exist a number of regional governmental organizations that have environmental programs. Most of these organizations concentrate on cooperation among industrialized countries. Clearly, the greatest contribution to the world's pollution from industry comes from this group of technologically advanced nations, which also have the capability of doing something effective about this type of pollution.

Those regional organizations with fewer members and a common experience and ideology often can act more effectively than global institutions which require agreement of a hundred or more countries before any action is taken. Smaller and highly competent organizations can often achieve more significant results in shorter periods than larger, more diffused institutions. One innovative organization in this field is NATO's Committee on the Challenges of Modern Society (CCMS). It operates not through large international bureaucracies but rather through the use of individual country-led "pilot projects." These projects or studies are coordinated, conducted and funded by pilot countries with the assistance and collaboration of other interested countries. This approach focuses not on abstract or academic papers but rather on concrete exchange of information and technology between participating countries. Member countries are represented by the substantive agencies concerned with the relevant subject and not primarily by diplomatic or "international" staff personnel unfamiliar or not directly related to the line office with domestic responsibility for the subject at hand. This approach fosters direct technical exchanges and it has also catalyzed national actions on problems and new efforts by other international organizations. Its main accomplishment has been to transfer relevant technology among participating countries and thereby advance environmental improvement.

Among the areas covered by NATO/CCMS in the past are air pollution, oil pollution of the oceans, transboundary freshwater pollution management, road transportation safety, toxic substances, waste-water treatment technology, and urban transportation. In each case the projects were for specified periods of time with concrete goals and included an important provision for later review and follow-up action by NATO member countries to ensure proper implementation. Also non-NATO member countries participated in individual projects on an ad hoc basis.[41]

Another important "regional" organization working on environmental matters has been the Organization for Economic Cooperation and Development which has an Environment Committee which focuses especially on pollution problems and their economic impact or relationship. They have worked on issues of common concern to the "market economies" or industrialized countries. They have examined the impact on trade and economic growth of environmental policies and agreed to exchange information on toxic substances. They originally put forward the concept of the "polluter must pay" which essentially attempted to obtain international agreement that the cost of pollution clean-up should be integrated into the cost of goods produced and traded internationally.

There has been some criticism that rather empty general resolutions are passed by the OECD Environment Committee without specifically ameliorating the real problem or changing actual polluting practices by various countries. But much good work has been done by this organization and it needs strengthening in carrying out the function of examining the interrelationship between economic policy and the environment.

Finally, another organization concerned with environmental matters is the United Nations Economic Commission for Europe (ECE) which has representatives from both Eastern and Western Europe in addition to the United States. It has been seen as a multilateral bridge with Eastern Europe in the environmental field. Among its program areas have been the long-range transport of air pollutants and the development of low-waste technology. It has had some problems in creating concrete and relevant programs given the ideological diversity existing in its membership and the unpredictable hot and cold blowing of the winds of East-West relations. Further, there has been a certain amount of criticism of some of the ECE's activities since a number of its committees are dominated by industry representatives with little representation of consumer or environmental interest groups.

The work of all these organizations put together has not halted the continued spread of pollution or increases in the danger to our ecosystem. The risks are so great to all of mankind and the supporting instruments of protection so weak that it would take a madman to believe we could avoid disaster by proceeding in the future as we have in the past. Already we know not too little but too much to believe those who tell us that all will be well. The Earth's absorptive capacity is not unlimited. What we do not know is where those limits lie.

Some have argued that only with environmental information of unquestioned credibility will national governments then be moved to action; only then will prompt ameliorative efforts be undertaken and be effective. For those who believe in the idea that to know right is to do right, then the solution of our global environmental problem lies simply in obtaining good information. (Perhaps this author can be forgiven for noting that within the United States, knowing that smoking tobacco causes cancer has not resulted in the banning of its use or even its production.) To this end we need to develop and test new global functions for alerting the world—governments and peoples—to the probability of risks to their health and well-being. It is a necessary step if not a determining one. We must first know the dangers of mercury in the flesh of fish, or DDT in the oceans and rivers, or PCBs in our water to decide whether we should undertake efforts to rid our ecosystem of these chemicals. We need to establish, therefore, massive, serious, professional, and unimpeachable international authorities to whom we can look for guidance and disinterested advice and information. This will be costly. Such a function can only be performed by the best scientists in the world. It should not be influenced by the usual petty concerns of national, ideological or regional personnel balances normally found in international organizations including UNEP. The best experts, no matter their nationality, should be utilized to ensure that a wide variety of the keenest minds available are applied to this problem area.

Some hope that perhaps UNEP could become this great intellectual force in environmental matters by utilizing and taking advantage of the best experts in the international community.[42] This hope has not yet borne fruit and UNEP continues to experience serious growth pangs and management weaknesses. It has concentrated its efforts at building up management and programming capabilities for individual developing countries. While this is a worthwhile activity, it has taken money, resources, and personnel away from the major task of assessing the overall state of the vital life support systems of the entire globe. A true global environment monitoring system will not be established unless a greater priority is given to this activity by UNEP.

The time has also come to search for new ways for the scientists of the world to communicate with not only governments but also the public directly about the risks they face from pollution and the impact of new technology. To this end information about the destruction of the quality of our environment should be provided through radio, TV, newspapers, through universities, learned societies, etc. For this function to be adequately and effectively performed a certain degree of freedom of expression, which certainly does not exist in many countries, is required. Thus, the reduction of our environmental risks somewhat depends on the increase in the free flow of information unhindered by governmental or other censorship.

The protection of the global environment requires going beyond a description of the problem and its risks. Scientists can outline changes that are taking place in the Earth's ecological system and note the implications for human health, but someone must also be able to prescribe—much like a doctor—what courses of action are necessary to bring the body back to a healthy state. Specific professional judgments must be made about necessary actions to reduce our risks.

One alternative approach to efforts so weakly started by the United Nations might be to establish one or more new institutional mechanisms (perhaps funded by governments) to carry out this kind of function using information made available by international organizations, national institutions, universities, and private research establishments. In effect, the functions of both "whistle blowing" and making recommendations for risk reduction could come from one or more highly independent, highly competent groups. They would provide annual "state of the world environment" assessments which could be the basis of cooperative action. One problem with this suggestion is that the carrying out of such a function is expensive and must be done constantly for essentially centuries.

The establishment of one or more quasi official but independent international environmental entities which would make assessments of trends in pollution and recommendations for corrective action would not mean that individual private or governmental environmental research would no longer be needed. On the contrary, such efforts would be even more important. Only when there is a multiplicity of efforts underway in each area can there be some assurance that results or assessments are in fact accurate and reflect the considered judgment of the scientific community. Thus, it is not an either/or choice between the normal freedom of scientific inquiry and large-scale directed comprehensive research looking for new dangers. Simply we need badly a more intensive, focused effort given the very high risks we are running.

Pollution Control Technology Sharing

One area of cooperation is through the sharing of pollution control knowledge and technology. International competition in new methods of reducing pollution can produce pressure toward the introduction of new technology and of new standards for emissions and air quality. An example of this is the gains foreign automobile producers have made in the reduction of engine emissions. Foreign companies have developed lower emission engines such as the stratified charged type (Japanese) and the diesel (German) which can meet the tough proposed United States standards without the use of the costly and inefficient catalytic converter now favored by domestic companies. Also research is being done in other engine designs by foreign countries from which we should learn. But unless we are willing to encourage this kind of foreign competition this new knowledge contributed by foreign researchers will be of no use. There are a number of bilateral and multilateral cooperative mechanisms by which governments can encourage and promote cooperation on pollution reduction technology especially in such organizations as NATO/CCMS, the OECD and UNEP.

The United States has also signed cooperation agreements with developed and developing countries to help each other deal with pollution problems more efficiently. The United States, for example, has signed an agreement with Iran to fight air pollution. Iran, which has serious problems in this area in its cities, already has enacted laws to improve air quality. Even the cold war has not stopped the United States and the Soviet Union from signing a major environmental cooperation agreement which is coordinated by the EPA Administrator and his Soviet counterpart. As a result of this agreement, regular and frequent high level and technical exchange visits take place in each country to discuss common problems and joint solutions for pollution control.

Another important focus for reducing pollution is commercial research, development, production, and distribution of technology to reduce and monitor pollutants. For the United States the export of pollution control know-how and hardware is big business, with foreign spending estimated to grow to $11 billion in 1978 for pollution control technology.[43] The Japanese also are building new pollution abatement equipment on the order of $3.2 billion annually. The Japanese government is spending for environmental administration, research and assistance some $1.6 billion.[44]

The Developing Countries

There is a major need for appropriate pollution control techniques and equipment which can be utilized by the developing countries. Many of these countries have the worst pollution of the world. There is an increased awareness in many of these countries of the need to improve air and water quality. Already very serious health hazards exist in such diverse cities as São Paulo, Nairobi, Ankara, and Tel Aviv. One reason for increased concern has been the spread of information about the impact of pollution through modern communications. These problems are now well known even in the poorest countries through publicity in the mass media. These countries are faced with the dilemma of not being able to afford the very expensive pollution control equipment which is in use in the developed countries, and yet wanting to minimize pollution, especially when it affects the health of their citizens. These countries need specific assistance either to import cheaper equipment, adapting it for local conditions, or to design and build indigenous technology from the ground up. There will thus be a need for the developing countries themselves, perhaps assisted by UNEP or some other international mechanism, to exchange relevant experiences on how poorer countries can control pollution. There may be an increased need to provide, either through governmental or private means, some assistance to bring together pollution control technology companies on the one hand and developing countries on the other so that low cost and effective technology is available and used efficiently. The 1979 United Nations Conference on Science and Technology for Development is a forum in which the nations of the world can examine ways of helping the developing world obtain and apply the best techniques for protecting their environment.

A Strategy Towards Global Environmental Protection

As much as an individual community or a single nation needs the capability to do ecological analysis of all major aspects of human activity and to assess their relative costs and benefits to that community, so must the global community ensure its own capacity to understand all elements and activities which could affect the global environment, especially those activities which cause transboundary pollution. As we have in the United States an Environmental Impact Statement (EIS) required under the National Environmental Policy Act of 1969 so we need a global environmental impact statement for major ecologically dangerous actions which could upset the basic elements of our ecosystem.

Such a global impact statement must be based upon the best available scientific knowledge and should not be subject to political or economic pressure from individual governments or from any international organization. Yet it must be acknowledged that there exists a tremendous gap between scientific knowledge and public policy making, and between the policy maker and the scientific experts. For example, while the United Nations has established the Earthwatch program to monitor environmental pollution, there is no mechanism to translate the data gained from such scientific monitoring programs into specific governmental action to ameliorate global pollution problems. Current economic and national forces are strongly opposed to any kind of international authority which can have a direct impact upon industrial or other activities in a given state. In order to move from this situation of stalemate, with its inevitable disastrous consequences for the human environment, towards a context where there are in place effective mechanisms to deal with threats to the global ecology, the following basic changes in our international institutions should be considered:

First, we need a specific global body designed with overall policy and decision-making power to deal with environmental problems which threaten the entire world community. The body could be the United Nations General Assembly, perhaps with some special role given to the Security Council to ensure the participation and weight of the larger nations, or an entirely new mechanism. It might also be a strengthened and restructured UNEP. The consequent decisions on transboundary pollution issues of these political bodies would be binding on all agreeing governments. The actual implementation could, however, be up to individual countries. Thus the "international body" could agree that Freon should not be released into the atmosphere, but each government could decide on how best to prevent this from happening.

Second, we will need to establish some kind of dispute settlement or judicial function which can act directly in cases where transboundary pollution affects other nations and their people. Access to this dispute settlement tribunal should be given to private bodies and not just national governments alone. This would require a radical revision of many of the current sacred cows of international law. However, the simple fact is that changing technology and its ecological, health, and economic impact require just such a revision if we are to enter into the next decades with a good chance of reversing the present deteriorating ecological situation.

Third, there is a vital requirement for effective global environmental public interest groups. They can keep watch both on the ecological and pollution trends and on the international organizations, much in the same way they perform this function in the industrialized democracies. This means that such international pressure groups must be permitted to have contact with similar groups on the national level—even in countries we cannot call traditional democracies. A start in this direction has been made by some existing groups, especially the so-called Nongovernmental Organizations (NGOs). One such organization is Barbara Ward's International Institute for Environment and Development. But the present impact of these groups is not very great on either national government decision making or on international intergovernmental bodies. Far more effectual, unfortunately, is the continued lobbying of industry and private interest groups seeking to preserve their economic position and their profits.

Fourth, there should be established some kind of operational and funding mechanism to act directly to improve environmental conditions which have a global or major transboundary character, especially when they impact on the marine environment or affect seriously the upper atmosphere. This operational mechanism should have the capability to assist directly nations and regions, especially in the Third World, with specific transboundary pollution problems. It should be able to provide technical assistance to deal with pollution abatement problems, assist in establishing governmental pollution control programs, and provide training for both technical and management personnel. This operational arm, which could be part of the existing United Nations Environmental Program, should also have responsibility for carrying out, directly or under contract, research and development programs which advance our knowledge of pollution abatement technology and which are especially focused on those sources of pollution with an international character.

Further, the establishment of a new and innovative funding mechanism to provide necessary economic incentives for countries and regions to implement sound environmental policies and behavior is greatly needed if all facets of the problem are to be adequately addressed. Basically, such funding must come, to a large degree, from national government sources, but a new "Environmental Development Bank" or fund, perhaps tied into the World Bank, should have direct access to private lending institutions and be able to float bonds on its own authority. It in turn would be able to make relatively long-term loans to governments and even directly to businesses either to clean up an environmentally dangerous global or transboundary problem or to help get established new efforts towards the development and manufacturing of pollution abatement control technology aimed at the pollution problems of the poorer, developing world.

For this purpose loans to specific countries or industries could be tied to a "tax" on pollution levels which have an international impact. The tax could be collected by the national government but paid into a fund from which the country could draw for the loans to the industry for cleaning up. This would both provide an incentive for industries to clean up and also provide assurance that repayments would be made from the polluters themselves. Another source of funds for such an Environmental Development Bank could be fines levied by an international judicial body on polluters—national and private—which affect the global, or international, environment. As with the tax, these monies from fines could be utilized as loans by the very same industries found guilty of pollution. Such loans would be paid back to the bank eventually over a number of years thus permitting further clean-up programs. This concept would require a much greater willingness to give up some elements of sovereignty by countries and probably would not be accepted until such time as the globe has experienced severe ecological disasters to prove the need for such a mechanism.[45]

International law was not established with the problems of protecting the global environment in mind. It does not, for example, give standing to an individual in one country against another individual in another country who is polluting the former's air. Over the years it has been very difficult to obtain the assistance of international law in effectively stopping transboundary pollution. Yet some progress has been made.

The most famous international case is the "Trail Smelter Decision" between the United States and Canada, in which some experts believe it was held that a country is responsible for the harm its polluted air does to another country. The case was not a clear victory since both countries accepted arbitration and Canada acknowledged its responsibility before damages were arbitrated. So far the strongest cases appear to be those of over-the-border air and water pollution control problems of immediate neighbors.[46]

There is a greater need for a more innovative approach to international law to deal with environmental problems. For example new conventions might be agreed upon to deal with the water management of large water basins or air shed areas. The conventions would have to be broad enough to ensure to each participant concrete advantages in addition to any possible liabilities which might be undertaken for accepting responsibility for pollution and its clean-up. New regimes can be established which can begin standard-setting and enforcement. Without such conventions or other international agreements, the present international legal regime for pollution remains weak since it requires specific individual acts by governments to agree to new rules and powers given to international bodies to determine damage and appropriate clean-up activities. Development of a new global or regional environmental regime will take some time since few governments will accept liability for damage before they know the specifics in costs and benefits.

Given the global environmental dangers likely over the next decades, a comprehensive framework that can operate at a global level, yet also is related to regional and national institutions, appears necessary. Such an overall framework could include the following elements or requirements:

A global human health warning system which can be sensitive to any long lasting or persistent deviations in human health and especially alert to widespread indications of sickness due to environmental factors. It should be able to assess an increase in death or sickness rates in a given region and analyze the possible causes. Its findings should be made by an independent body of experts not responsible to governments and its conclusions and recommendations should be public.

A Global Atmospheric Assessment Authority should develop a quantitative global index of atmospheric pollutants which can give governmental decision makers and the public a monthly and yearly report on how well or badly the world is doing in cleaning up its atmosphere. Already the United Nations Earthwatch is scheduled to undertake some elements of this function. Also the World Meteorlogical Organization should participate in this effort. This program should also examine the impact of pollution on climate. This is important since all waters in the biosphere come from condensation of water vapor circulated in the atmosphere as rain or other forms. The evaporation-precipitation exchange cycle links with the larger land, atmospheric and marine environment which carries quantities of materials placed into the cycle by human activities. For this reason the Atmospheric Pollution Report should also break down atmospheric pollution into its component parts and indicate clearly and without bias the source of the pollutants by industry and region. Further it is vital that eventually some kind of predictive capacity is established so that short- and long-term trends can be recognized and therefore evaluated by the relevant decision-making bodies.

A global assessment of contaminants in the ecological system, especially in food chains, should be established. The global community must develop better methods for assessing toxic substances in the human environment, especially those that can affect human health. Even national capabilities for evaluating this kind of problem are largely inadequate. Therefore a stronger national base must be built and these national efforts must be supported and linked to an international mechanism. But the start of such a global toxic substances control and analysis function cannot await the development everywhere of similar national institutions. Already scientists are seriously worried about the introduction of more and more new persistent toxic substances into the environment without any kind of control or understanding about their long-term impact on human and animal health. It would be useful through international agreements and appropriate bodies to determine the best methods for identifying toxic substances, to compare experiences on how best to limit or to control toxic substances from getting into the environment, and finally to control toxic substances that travel in international trade.

A new expanded global disaster warning system would identify potential disaster phenomena such as earthquakes, tropical cyclones, volcanic eruptions, and tsunamis. Also certain man-made disasters such as hazardous marine pollution spills should be included in the system. The need is to develop information, forecasts, and analysis of such phenomena in a form which can be utilized and acted upon by the competent bodies. World and regional centers will need to be established which can deal with each type of disaster or possibly a number of types. These centers should be in close contact with the appropriate national centers which must be responsible for national alert activities. There is already an internationally designated Tsunami Warning Center in Honolulu. National centers can be expanded into international centers through the addition of international funding for expanded capabilities. Beyond the establishment of centers there is a need to create a capacity to mobilize international resources to deal with major disasters during and immediately after they have occurred. International response teams should be established which can provide technical assistance when a disaster occurs. This technical assistance would provide such functions as impact assessment, clean-up methods, and long-term recovery planning.

Here again emerging and existing technology can be of great help. Satellites can provide information on hazardous marine spills and provide data on tropical cyclones. They can also be utilized for rapid communication of information about potential and actual disasters and for facilitating international assistance. International centers with computer banks can provide information about the availability of necessary resources, such as food, emergency equipment, and medicine which could be supplied to disaster areas. The data banks could also contain the names and location of experts who could be called upon to assist in case of certain types of disaster. New technology can be used to create a system for the collection of disaster related environmental facts, especially from automated remote sources and also to transmit such information to appropriate international and national centers. Such centers and their data banks could contain collected information about atmospheric, seismic, marine, and hydrologic observations. New and more sensitive sensors can and should be developed for key phenomena to improve the information available.

Some of the international centers can also act as educational institutions where experts, especially from the developing world, can gain additional expertise and skills. Such training activities could form the basis for national centers—the teaching of teachers.

The establishment of a world *Oceans' Protection Authority and Marine Environment Center* would assess the state of the marine ecology and in particular the ocean pollution situaton. The impact of ocean and land based pollution on marine ecosystems would be studied and annual reports could be made to the United Nations General Assembly, the International Maritime Consultative Organization (IMCO) and to other interested bodies and the public. As with atmospheric pollution these reports would contain scientific data with specific numerical levels for pollutants and an evaluation of their impact on the oceans' life cycle with indications of short- and long-term trends. The Oceans' Protection Authority as outlined elsewhere would be the global enforcement and policy arm for dealing with marine environmental problems.

The center's first priority will be to develop baseline and long-term trend data. Also the center would help coordinate national research programs and their resulting information. Much of the actual research could and must still be done under national governmental or private sponsorship.

The most difficult and yet the most important research and assessment would be monitoring the impact of pollutants on the marine ecosystem. Studies would have to be done examining pollution resilience, transport, degradation, and deposition.

The center would have to perform a host of other complex scientific functions including publication and dissemination of standard reference materials, quality assurance, and intercalibration methodology. It would also need to have some kind of financial capability so that it could have its own technical and research ability as well as the necessary resources for contracting with countries and private groups to carry out specific projects. In particular, it should be responsible for the expansion of the capacity of developing countries to participate in marine research including the outfitting of research vessels and providing technical assistance and equipment for poorer nations with the understanding that research results would be incorporated into the global marine pollution monitoring system.

The key to future marine pollution monitoring would be the establishment of regional stations and specialized research centers, mainly through the expansion of already existing institutions. These stations or facilities, all linked through computers with each other and the global center, would sample air, water, organisms, and sediments on a regular basis for such pollutants as petroleum residues, chlorinated hydrocarbons, heavy metals (including mercury, lead cadmium, and arsenic), and radioactive nuclides.

A population census of some species selected for each aquatic environment would be carried out to provide comprehensive data on the distribution and on the effects of pollutants in the marine environment. All of this data would also be related to physical measurement of other conditions such as air and sea surface temperature, atmospheric pressure, wind direction and speed, and surface salinity. The main purpose would be to look for trends in the condition of the ocean and overlying atmosphere. Close integration between marine and atmospheric pollution monitoring programs would be needed so that the interconnection between the two environments can be fully studied. There is a growing body of data which indicates that much of the most dangerous marine pollution comes from the atmosphere.

Both the Atmosphere and the Marine Authorities could conduct periodic reviews and assessments of findings focusing on the preparation of annual reports to the United Nations and member countries on the state of the environment including recommendation on action necessary to improve technology for monitoring and prediction. The larger and critical task of making the needed recommendations for ameliorative action to stop or prevent pollution must be the task both of scientists engaged in environmental studies and of other experts knowledgeable about abatement technology, waste control, and political and economic factors. The drawing up of recommendations might be given to a body of independent experts, not responsible to governments, who can make hard and honest recommendations. These recommendations for ameliorative action should be made public. These reports should provide an opportunity for a wide ranging debate on what needs to be done not only by experts or in the United Nations General Assemblies, but also in universities, public agencies, the media, and private interest groups in all countries.

Political Follow-up

In the last analysis each of these mechanisms or institutions can be effective only if it can relate to decision-making bodies with real powers and access to the necessary resources for carrying out approved recommendations. There is thus a need to examine in a new way the evolution and reform of these institutions as we develop the necessary capability to understand scientifically what is happening to our environment. Scientists must speak the language of political leaders and political leaders must pay attention to the knowledge and judgment of scientists or we will fail in any global environmental strategy.

CHAPTER IV

The Oceans

Introduction

There are few areas offering better illustration of the interdependent character of global challenges and their attendant risks than the oceans. Growing population, the need for more food resources, and the demand for additional energy and minerals all impact on the oceans—the Earth's main source of oxygen and rainfall. We also see the effect of new technology on the oceans, which makes possible the intrusion of man into places which were unreachable even a decade or more ago. This combination of increased world need and the availability of new technology have brought the oceans to a point of unforeseen vulnerability to man's encroachment. New deep-sea oil drilling technology, the construction of massive oil tankers, and new "factory" fishing fleets are all examples of how recent technology has made the oceans an area of increased human activity of a kind never seen before.

The changing patterns of global political and economic conditions also have had a significant impact. With the addition of new states there has been an increase in the demand to exploit to the fullest the resources in the oceans. Many of these states have given priority to economic development rather than to the preservation of marine ecology or long-term needs. The older industrialized nations also have contributed significantly to this vulnerability of the oceans through their exploitation of ocean resources. They have drilled indiscriminately for oil, they have built larger and larger fishing fleets which have depleted fish stocks, and they have expanded their transportation fleets which have poured millions of gallons of oil into the oceans with unknown long-term ecological effects.

There appears to be a growing conflict between the concept of total freedom of the uses of the oceans and the need to ensure that the marine environment is not impaired. In another age, the oceans were so vast and their uses so few that conflicts were rare. Today such a concept of total freedom cannot deal with the reality of new technology and many competing uses. In addition to visible pollution, there is congestion from shipping and the drilling for offshore oil in many parts of the world. Depletion of living resources is now more imminent. All of these factors call for new measures of management and conservation.

Application of the concept of rational management of scarce resources is hardly acknowledged among the nations that utilize the oceans today. Their main impetus appears to be short-term advantage which in the long term will prove disastrous for all. Already the catch of a large number of commercial species of fish exceeds the estimated sustainable yield. Thus, in place of a growth in diet of protein from the oceans, we could have a decline. In turn this will affect adversely fulfillment of the protein requirements of a rapidly growing population.

Probably the most serious consequence of the current political and economic situation has been the extension of national jurisdiction over increased areas of ocean space once considered the high seas. The unilateral extension of the traditional territorial sea to 200 miles by some states illustrates the growing pressure by nations and their citizens upon the oceans. Many coastal states wish to restrict scientific research off their coasts at a time when our basic information on the oceans is wholly inadequate.

While there has been a manifold increase in man's use and abuse of the oceans, there has not been an equivalent increase in the creation of new institutions or methods to manage these new intrusions of man into marine space. While man has been busy at work exploiting the ocean and its resources, he has not devoted the same attention towards the task of ensuring that his actions will not result in long-term harm to the environment that provides him with vital life-giving oxygen and other requirements of a healthy existence. The few institutions that do exist to protect the oceans are weak and often dominated by those interests whose only aim is short-term profit or the protection of various national industries.

PROTECTING THE MARINE ENVIRONMENT

It is not the oil clots, not the toilet flush or the empty containers which the rich man can see that ought to occupy all our attention, but the invisible and indestructible pollutants that move about, unseen and unchangeable, performing out of our control the duty they were intended for: to serve as one of man's weapons against the equilibrium evolved and required by nature. —Thor Heyerdahl, "Man Against Nature," Council of Europe, January 1972

The oceans are vital to the survival of all living things on earth. They contain 317,000,000 cubic miles and 97.2 percent of the world's total water. Yet they have also become the common ultimate waste sink of man and his civilization. Human activities have now started to endanger the natural ability of the oceans to regenerate and remain healthy and thus carry out their necessary ecological and natural functions. Already many streams, rivers, lakes, and subsurface waters have become irreversibly polluted. Pollutants from these freshwater sources find their way into the oceans and thereby endanger bit by bit this great ecological life-giving storehouse. There are a number of factors— increased industrial activity and increased population among others— which have affected the growth in marine pollution over the last few decades and will continue to do so into the foreseeable future.

Sources of Pollution

Overall the greatest impact of pollution is probably from waste dumped directly into the sea from rivers and land-based outfalls although pollution from the air is increasingly suspect as a major source. Some of these outfalls are from domestic sources, largely organic sewage, but increasingly they contain industrial chemicals and other synthetic and toxic elements. About 80 to 90 percent of all pollutants in the ocean originate from land, coming to the ocean through rivers, the atmosphere, or carried in pipes.

A great deal of this marine pollution is due to direct dumping of waste into the oceans. Some comes indirectly through polluted rain or particulate fallout from the atmosphere. Other "direct" sources include oil spills from ships—largely due to "cleaning" of ballast and oil-holding tanks at sea, and a small amount from ship accidents. Estimates are that about one-third of all oil pollution in the world's oceans is caused by marine transportation activities, with oil tankers providing the largest single contributor of such pollution.[1]

Looking at land-based pollution we must first recognize that a great deal of the volume of materials entering the oceans from land is sediments resulting from the natural erosion of the shore. Little can be done about this natural process. But there are many and dangerous man-made pollutants, such as sewage sludge and raw chemical wastes, which are dumped in the oceans. Local and national governments can prevent or at least mitigate this dumping.

Land-based pollution takes many forms. One form comes from an excess of nutrients introduced to the ocean through the use of certain chemicals, such as phosphorus and nitrogen. They are used in chemical fertilizer on land and in the disposal of domestic sewage. The nutrients cause the eutrophication of estuaries and adjacent coastal areas, thus removing oxygen and killing living resources. With the increased need for more food for a rapidly growing population we can expect this type of chemical pollution to expand over the years, in both developed and developing countries.

Another kind of ocean contamination comes from highly toxic substances. These go into the oceans in a wide variety of forms. The most recognized and discussed include DDT and other toxic substances used in pesticides, generally called chlorinated hydrocarbons. Here an international consensus to decrease the use of such substances would move in the right direction even if it is not a total solution to the overall problem.

These chemicals now being introduced into the marine environment in large amounts were previously present in only very small quantities or not at all. For example, the cited chlorinated hydrocarbons are now being dumped into the ocean in ever larger amounts. These could alter the composition of the oceans significantly.[2] In some cases, the amounts being dumped by industry as waste are doubling the normal or natural concentration of these minerals or chemicals. The introduction of totally new chemicals has added a number of unknowns about the quality of the oceans. We are not at all sure what the long-run impact will be since we have no previous experience with these highly toxic chemicals or compounds in the marine environment.

The heavy or toxic metals constitute another source of ocean pollution. These metals include lead and mercury. For example, mercury dumped into the oceans is transformed by seaborne bacteria into methyl mercury, a very toxic compound which could reach hazardous levels of concentration on entering the food chain.[3] Much of this kind of pollution enters the oceans through the atmosphere, for example, from lead in automobile exhausts finally dropping into the sea far from its place of origin. Considerable changes in industrial practices and newer pollution control technology will be required if we are to reduce on a global basis this kind of pollution.

Yet another major element of marine pollution is domestic water including human sewage and the direct use of various products such as detergents, which find their way through municipal disposal systems. In many developed as well as developing countries there is an almost total lack of any sewage disposal plants, with raw sewage simply being dumped into the oceans from outfalls. Some more developed countries treat their sewage in varying degrees. Few utilize a completely "tertiary" level disposal system which returns almost clean water to rivers, lakes, and the oceans.

As noted, one major pollutant—oil—now covers much of the oceans. The oil pollution we see in the oceans is an inevitable consequence of our oil-based industrialized society. By one estimate, in 1967, the washing of cargo tanks at sea alone could have dumped some 2.8 million tons into the oceans. By 1970, the potential amount grew to about 6 million tons. Other estimates are lower, with the National Academy of Sciences using 1.5 million tons of oil going into the marine environment from tankers alone in 1973. It should be noted that the lower estimates are based on extrapolations from records kept for individual ships, assuming that the ships would be following the "best" practices, which may not in fact be true. The higher estimates may, therefore, be closer to reality.[4] By the early 1970s we were dumping about 2.1 million tons of petroleum as a minimum figure into the oceans from all transportation activities. The pumping of bilges by non-tankers contributed about 500,000 tons. Another expert stated that losses during loadings and unloadings and from collisions added an estimated 1 million tons.[5]

Other sources of oil in the ocean include accidents on the high seas or near shore and losses during the exploration and production of oil drilling. Also, pipeline breaks add more oil. One key source of oil in the oceans, however, is from used lubricating oil. An estimated level of 2 million tons is annually unaccounted for in the United States, much of it eventually ending up in our coastal waters.[6] On a global basis, urban and river runoff contributed about 1.9 million tons of oil to the oceans annually with coastal municipalities providing an additional 300,000 tons.[7]

The total estimated oil influx into the marine environment is something between 5 and 10 million tons with 6 million the "best estimate."[8] Again, given these wide ranges and the possible dangers, we probably need to assess better than we have in the past exactly how much is going into the oceans. It may be that more, not less, is going in despite such new techniques as load-on-top, used for tankers, or oil and water separators, used on cargo and other ships.

Overall Impact of Pollution

Some strong evidence indicates that oil has already seriously affected ocean life. Oil absorbs insecticides and the oil and insecticides are in turn absorbed by plankton, shellfish, oysters, and clams.[9] We do know that oil occurs in the stomach of surface-feeding fish and in the fat of fish and shellfish.[10] Probably it also negatively affects whales. We know that oil and other toxic waste can upset plants and plant life cycles and thereby also be detrimental to fish.[11] The short-term impact of oil includes mortality to seabirds, damage to bethic and intertidal organisms, and changes to plant life, algae, and salt marshes.[12]

One researcher, Max Blumer of Woods Hole, has especially cited the impact of low-level effects of oil pollution. While we are rather ignorant about long-term and low-level effects of oil spills, there is some fear that they may be more serious and long lasting than short-term effects. Blumer notes that "many biological processes which are important for the survival of marine organisms and which occupy key positions in their life processes are mediated by an extremely low concentration of chemical messengers in seawater."[13] There is a belief that pollution interferes with these processes by blocking the taste receptors and by "mimicking" natural stimuli, leading to false responses. Both high boiling and saturated oil fractions and aromatic hydrocarbons can have this effect. Thus low-level oil concentration may have a disastrous effect on the survival of some marine species. Blumer in this connection notes: "Research in this critical area is urgently needed. The experience with DDT has shown that low level effects are unpredictable *and may suddenly become an ecological threat of unanticipated magnitude.*"[14] (Emphasis added.) Here again we have another example of those elements of our modern technological age which contribute to the creation of a high risk world.

Further, one of the most dangerous aspects of oil pollution is its method of decomposition. In the process of the crude oil being broken down by marine microorganisms, intermediate products are formed in each stage or new substances created requiring other species of bacteria to further break down the crude oil. Unfortunately, the most readily attacked fractions of crude oil—the normal paraffins—are the least toxic of all. But the highly toxic aromatic hydrocarbons, particularly the carcinogenic polynuclear aromatics, are not very rapidly attacked.[15] We know that certain crude oil fractions are rich in multiring aromatic compounds which are capable of inducing cancer.[16] Finally, our knowledge of the effects of petroleum in the oceans is incomplete. There is no consensus on the quantity of hydrocarbons that the oceans can assimilate without threat to the marine ecosystem.[17]

Specific Impacts on Marine Life

We do know that oil and other wastes affect a number of marine species which at some stage in their life cycle utilize the shores along the seas and oceans. Oil has hurt this important habitat of nesting birds, seashell life, and plants. Further damage may result from invisible, absorbed insecticides, particularly chlorinated hydrocarbons.[18] We have found, for example, that estuarine fish-eating birds are building up very high body burdens of DDT and its degradation products. As a result, they are suffering extensive failures in their reproductive process.[19] Further, a wide range of marine life, including plankton, crustaceans, mollusks, fish, and birds are adversely affected by the chronic toxicity of chlorinated hydrocarbons. In sum, among the observed results after exposure to these toxic chemicals are: decreased growth rates, increased mortality, failure in the development of young, reproductive failure, eggshell thinning, etc.[20]

This evidence of the impact of chlorinated hydrocarbons is strengthened by the following background conditions. First, the oceans are the final depository for the persistent chlorinated hydrocarbons. (About 25 percent of the DDT compounds produced to date have probably ended in the sea.) Second, there has already been a demonstrable negative impact on the ocean environment. Third, man is increasing his total production of these complex chemicals, many of which are hard to degrade or highly toxic with half-lives in years or decades. Many of these chemicals will find their way into the sea. Fourth, the large bulk of already used chlorinated hydrocarbons (about 75 percent of the total) will eventually find its way into the ocean. Thus we are likely to see over time an increase in these chemicals even if they are no longer used widely. With half-lives of decades or longer, these compounds will leave mankind with "no opportunity to redress the consequences."[21] It is this last significant fact which is characteristic of many of our global environmental and technological problems.

Another characteristic of the impact of chlorinated hydrocarbons, also with larger implications for other areas, is that the more scientists examine the problem the more unexpected effects are identified. One conclusion was that "in view of the findings of the past decade, our prediction of the potential hazards of chlorinated hydrocarbons in the marine environment may be vastly underestimated."[22] Again we see a case where we are playing a kind of Russian roulette with nature with unknown odds and with still largely unknown but possibly disastrous results. This is only one case but there are many many others—some undoubtedly completely unknown to us now.

Despite this evidence, the majority of nations of the world have done very little to stop the impact of either oil or chlorinated hydrocarbons on the marine ecology. The cited National Academy of Science panel recommended in 1971 the following action:

A massive national effort should be made immediately to effect a drastic reduction of the escape of persistent toxicants into the environment, with the ultimate aim of achieving virtual cessation in the shortest possible time.

Programs should be designed both to determine the rates of entry of each pollutant into the marine environment and to make baseline determinations of the distribution of the pollutants among the components of that environment. These should be followed by a program of monitoring long-term trends in order to record progress and to document possible disaster.

The laws relating to the registration of chemical substances and the release of production figures by government should be examined and perhaps revised in light of evidence of environmental deterioration caused by some of these substances.[23]

While these are largely national recommendations aimed at the United States government, it is clear that the problem is global and will not be solved by any single nation. Unfortunately, even all of these rather mild recommendations have not been fully implemented by the United States. The Toxic Substance Control Act of 1977 in the United States has at least established the basis for specific action. Yet, without strong American action, as the largest producer of these dangerous chemicals, there will be little hope of significant global progress.

Above all, it is the long-term, cumulative impact of many different toxic pollutants (and their interaction on each other) which may be the most dangerous and quite likely the most irreversible result. We do not yet know how much pollution the sea can accept and still recover from.

Limited Capacity of the Oceans

Many scientists believe that we are fast approaching the limit of the capacity of the ocean to absorb, degrade, and digest the wastes being dumped into it. For example, the waste being dumped by New York and other East Coast cities, in combination with tanker discharges, has formed a constant sludge of oil and plastics 1 million square miles out into the Atlantic, down to the Caribbean and beyond.

Thor Heyerdahl, the great ocean explorer, has reported vividly on the ubiquitous solidified oil and waste floating in mid-ocean. He has posed the question whether humanity can survive in the conditions of the present technological civilization, citing the pollution of the high seas as a prime example of this kind of challenge. He has stated that:

As one who knows the oceans from close contact and deliberate observations, I would like to stress three points which I feel have a direct bearing on the question of whether our own civilization can survive unless it is modified and improved to suit reality.
1. The ocean is not endless.
2. There is no such thing as territorial waters for more than days at a time. The ocean floor can be mapped, but the water above it is in permanent rotation and, like the atmosphere, must be a common heritage.
3. Pollution caused by man has already reached the furthest sections of the world ocean.[24]

In the same speech Heyerdahl cited the key problem of marine pollution, that the oceans, unlike rivers or lakes, cannot dispose of water in some outlet but rather the "ocean only evaporates clean water, retaining all pollutants in an ever increasing concentration."

Past and Present Marine Pollution Control Efforts

The international community through its environmental and maritime institutions has largely concentrated on the 20 percent or less of pollution that comes from the dumping and discharge of oil and other wastes at sea by ships. Very few of the existing international agreements to limit pollution or the marine environment really get to the vast major problems of shore-generated wastes.

The Inter-Government Maritime Consultative Organization (IMCO) in 1969 amended an earlier 1954 convention to deal with the deliberate discharge from ships of oil and oily wastes.[25] Yet these new provisions were not effective in stopping much of the oil pollution problem. For example, it was proposed but not adopted that a new technology be used for separating oil from water on board ship to ensure a relatively clean discharge. Also there was and is a need for better arrangements and facilities for the disposal of oily bilge and ballast water from ships in ports. Further, the building of ships with separated cargo and ballast tanks can ensure over the long run that there will be no dumping of oil from ships in the future.

One relatively minor cause of oil pollution in the ocean is due to ship accidents. The 1967 stranding of the *Torrey Canyon* brought great publicity to this problem and there were some follow-up actions taken by IMCO to improve both ship safety and to deal with the resulting pollution.[26]

In 1970, NATO's Committee on Challenges of Modern Society held a major conference on oil pollution in Brussels and agreed to support a ban on international oil spills from ships by 1975 if possible, but not later than the end of the decade.[27] In 1972 the IMCO Assembly agreed to a resolution (A.237 [VIII]) that the 1973 Conference was to adopt a new Convention that "should have as its main objective the achievement by 1975 if possible, but certainly by the end of the decade, of the complete elimination of the willful and intentional pollution of the sea by oil and noxious substances other than oil, and the minimization of accidental spills." Thus IMCO incorporated the NATO/CCMS objectives. This led to agreement on the 1973 Prevention of Pollution from Ships Convention. This convention sets new standards for ship construction and discharge requirements for all polluting substances and was designed as a substitute for the Amended 1954 International Convention for the Prevention of Pollution of the Sea by Oil.

The 1973 Convention itself, yet to be in force globally, includes measures to control more pollutants than ever before and places more stress on prevention rather than cleanup. The treaty has the following features:

1. regulates ship discharges of oil, various liquid substances, harmful package goods;

2. controls for the first time tankers carrying refined products;

3. requires segregated ballast for all tankers over 70,000 cwt contracted for after December 31, 1975 (but does not require double bottoms);

4. prohibits oil discharges within fifty miles of land (as did the 1969 amendments);

5. mandates all tankers to operate with the load-on-top system if capable;

6. reduces maximum permissible discharge for new tankers from 1/15,000 to 1/30,000 of cargo capacity (there is no *total* discharge prohibition);

7. regulates the carriage of 353 noxious liquid substances with requirements ranging from reception facilities to dilution prior to discharge;

8. controls harmful package goods in terms of packaging, labeling, stowage, and quantity limitations;

9. prohibits discharge of sewage within four miles of land unless the ship has an approved treatment plant in operation, and from four to twelve miles unless sewage is macerated and disinfected; and

10. prohibits disposal of all plastic garbage and sets specific minimum distance from land for disposing of other kinds of garbage.

One problem in obtaining adequate environmental provisions and enforcement through IMCO is that this organization has been criticized as being dominated in practice by maritime and oil interests. Often shipping industry representatives serve on IMCO delegations, while the environmentalists are largely left out in the cold. The weak enforcement of the 1954 Convention and slow process of entering into force of the 1969 and 1973 Conventions indicates that some of this criticism is justified. Further, since IMCO is mainly focusing on ships, its approach to other forms of pollution has been too narrow. Also it has not worked enough on the prevention of pollution, while mostly dealing with clean-up and limiting their own (the maritime interests') liability.

There are international and regional conventions to deal partially with dumping of certain wastes from vessels at sea. The IMCO Ocean Dumping Convention of 1972 is the most comprehensive of the international agreements in this area.[28] There also exists an agreement among the Mediterranean countries to work together to deal with the serious pollution problems in that sea. Unfortunately the agreement does not contain specific articles on prohibiting toxic and other discharges. While all such efforts are necessary, and despite these conventions, the oceans continue to receive additional pollution from land and from ships flying flags of countries, not a party to the applicable provisions of these conventions, which permit large amounts of oil and other substances (including atomic waste materials) to be dumped into the sea. Further, marine accidents such as the *Amoco Cádiz* incident in 1978 continue to add more oil and other waste to the overall pollution total.

A Strategy Towards Global Cooperation to Deal with Marine Pollution

The main fact we must remember is that the oceans' deterioration, caused by man, can be reversed through the application of technically feasible precautions. But to preserve the marine environment the global community will have to undertake extraordinary efforts in providing resources, political will, and organizational skill. Some marine pollution problems can only be solved on a global basis while others will require cooperation on a regional or local level.

A major difficulty is that our current international organizations reflect the reigning nationalism of the day rather than the reality of our common problems and their concomitant risks. The irony is that unless we can organize ourselves for these complex global tasks we are more likely than not to lose any benefit that national "sovereignty" can provide. No single nation can save itself in a world where the oceans are poisoned. Yet most nations remain incapable of organizing any, even local, efforts to reverse their continued pollution of their coasts and adjacent waters. Therefore the prognosis for the continued health of the world's oceans is dark indeed. We have a situation with very high risk for mankind, with little probability of being solved in the foreseeable future, while continued deterioration brings us closer and closer to the possibility of an ocean catastrophe. The solution will be an undertaking of unbelievable complexity.

One major difficulty is that many of the developing countries, which contribute especially to land-based pollution, believe that the pollution problem is for the developed countries alone to solve. They hold that pollution results from technological developments and therefore the problem should be exclusively solved by the more affluent countries. Further, they argue that strict pollution control measures are too expensive for poorer countries. This attitude creates misunderstanding and retards progress towards a realistic program of action which must require considerable effort by all nations—poor and rich.

Having said all of this is not thereby to counsel inaction or despair but rather to proceed with specific actions to reduce our risks from ocean pollution. Like many areas of great complexity there is no single solution which will put an end to the pollution of the ocean. The international community will need to take a comprehensive and systematic approach, aiming first at decreasing the most dangerous forms of pollution so as to ensure the long-term ecological balance of the entire ocean area. No approach can be effective without the establishment by the international community of some kind of mechanism or regime, including the widespread participation of coastal countries, to eventually enforce effective sanctions against any party which breaks treaty provisions and continues to pollute.

The first step should be the calling of an international conference to examine systematically marine pollution and to make recommendations for action to governments and to suggest the provisions of a comprehensive convention to regulate *all* forms of marine pollution, including enunciation of basic principles governing the discharge of pollutants into the ocean from any source. A major part of such a convention would be the establishment of standardization procedures for the disposal of waste into the seas—going beyond the existing ocean-dumping convention to include land-based sources. The conference could also make recommendations for institutional reform to improve the way the global community "manages" the oceans.

A second and related step would be to deal with the large gap in our scientific knowledge about the oceans in general and in particular in our knowledge of the impact of long-term pollutants. Given this, the global community should immediately institute a large-scale and coordinated marine scientific research program, including basic monitoring and impact assessments probably within the United Nations system. A major expansion of resources devoted to marine pollution research appears to be of the highest priority.

A third step may be establishing an international detection and enforcement system against all forms of marine pollution. Only when we recognize that the oceans are indeed a vital global "commons" will we accept cooperative procedures for pollution verification, consultation about necessary action, and an effective detection, investigation, and enforcement system supported by coastal and maritime states as well as the whole international community. In this connection a new international agreement might include a provision in which any major new technological development which could be used in the marine environment should have an "international environmental impact statement" before its initial application to the marine area.

However, immediate implementation of such a program is probably impossible. Given the cost and the negative attitudes of many developed and developing countries, this proposed convention will probably have to provide for the gradual increase in standards of discharge of pollutants over a reasonable period of time. It should, however, have stringent standards dealing with the disposal of persistent, highly toxic wastes. These actions should be taken within the context of an international organization focusing on environmental issues rather than by organizations dominated by industrial or special interests. Whatever approach is taken, all polluters will need to be exposed to effective enforcement and be assured of effective penalties. Eventually the international community must look upon the oceans as a single system and develop an organizational framework which reflects that fact. Until that time we probably will have to make do with partial efforts towards marine pollution control.

One important element which must be taken into consideration is the danger that certain marine pollution controls might transfer pollution to other environmental media or sites. Thus there is a need to relate marine pollution controls to a comprehensive national and global environmental strategy which will prevent present marine pollution from being transferred to other areas. For example, prohibiting the dumping of sewage sludge into the oceans might increase river dumping or incineration of sludge which could increase atmospheric pollution. These trade-offs will need to be carefully examined before new pollution control regulations are adopted.

In the future the global community needs to ensure in the exploitation of living and nonliving marine resources that appropriate environmental standards are established as integral elements of any relevant international convention. The Law of the Sea (LOS) negotiations in the United Nations include provisions in the draft text to safeguard the marine environment against pollution resulting from the exploitation of deep marine seabed minerals. Other provisions relate to enforcement of international marine pollution standards regarding vessels. Also provisions are necessary to provide for minimum environmental safeguards in drilling for oil.

Economic and Legal Implications

Economists would hold that we now are entering into a situation where the oceans have moved from a "free" resource or a "common property resource" into a condition in which ocean resources are "economically scarce."[29] But this economic perspective, however interesting, is still too narrow to take into account problems of long-term environmental damage (not easily assessed in economic terms) or equity. Further, technological change is hard to take into account when establishing a system based on present economic factors. There is a growing tendency for polluters to use a "common property resource" such as the oceans as a means of waste disposal since it is free of economic cost to the polluter and is only costly for the other beneficial user of the resource. Where there is a common resource which is being damaged, clearly the community in question has a right to prevent the destruction of its shared resource. This is a basis for mutual collective environmental control and enforcement.

In this context, the Law of the Sea negotiators have created a compromise between the interests of some coastal states in strict enforcement of environmental standards by the coastal state itself and the navigational or maritime nations which desire only flag state or perhaps port state enforcements of pollution offenses.[30] The navigational interests were generally stronger in the LOS negotiations since environmental interests do not have a strong domestic constituency and are thereby disadvantaged in influencing government policy and individual national LOS delegations. One additional consideration in the LOS context is the need for uniform environmental standards with respect to the design and operation of ships. Different standards for each coastal zone would be inefficient. Yet there is also a danger that international standards (not specifically set in the LOS Convention but left to other organizations or treaties) will be too low, reflecting the lowest common denominator rather than the most effective and required high standards.

Probably the LOS treaty, if it is finally agreed to, will share responsibility for pollution from ships between flag, port, and coastal states, having them enforce penalties for violations of international environmental discharge regulations and other environmental rules. Jurisdiction within the proposed 200-mile Economic Zone will be given to port and coastal states, especially if flag states fail to carry out their responsibilities. On the question of land-based pollution the LOS draft treaty does not contain any provisions which will seriously deal with the problem.[31]

In summary, whatever the outcome of the LOS Conference it will be necessary for the international community to initiate major new activities and specific new treaties, derived from the very general principles set forth in the Law of the Sea Convention. Among the tasks or issues which will require immediate consideration and action are:

—The establishment of very detailed uniform and enforceable standards of discharge for all forms of waste from ships and from other sources;
—The establishment of specific means of enforcement and penalties against those who pollute, especially on the high seas;
—The establishment of specific regulations for protection of the marine environment and for the exploitation of living and nonliving marine resources beyond national jurisdiction; and
—A comprehensive approach to land-based pollution including the international recognition that this type of pollution is an act against the common good of mankind.

THE OCEANS AND GLOBAL HUNGER

There has been much written about the future potential of the oceans as a source of food for a growing and hungry population. While there have been and will be set limits on the finite land available for cultivation and inherent limitations on increasing productivity in already cultivated land, there probably is still room for growth in the effective utilization of the oceans as a source of human nutrition and also for animal feedstuff.

One of the greatest nutritional needs of mankind is for protein. Protein shortage in early childhood can affect brain development adversely. The result of such protein deficiency has been to reduce seriously the learning capacity and, thereby, the productivity of large numbers of poor persons, especially in Latin America, Africa, and Asia. This early brain damage is unfortunately irreversible. Thus a global program to increase the protein content of the food for the world's poorest is a major international priority. The oceans are especially suited as a source of additional protein from fish and other marine creatures.

Figure IV-1.   Fish catches.

MILLION METRIC TONS

REGION	1960	1965	1970	1975	Growth Rate 1965-75 % PA
World	40.00	53.20	70.00	69.70	2.74
Africa	2.31	3.17	4.44	4.52	3.61
America, North	4.09	4.45	5.09	4.81	0.78
America, South	4.43	9.19	14.76	5.97	-4.22
Asia	17.90	20.26	26.24	31.69	4.58
Europe	8.09	10.89	12.00	12.62	1.49
Oceania	0.13	0.15	0.20	0.24	4.81
USSR	3.05	5.10	7.25	9.88	6.84

	1965	1975		1965	1975
China .... a	5.72	6.88	Norway	2.31	2.55
Denmark	0.84	1.77	Peru	7.63	3.45
India	1.33	2.33	Spain	1.36	1.53b
Japan	6.93	10.51	USSR	5.10	9.88
Korea, Republic of	0.64	2.13	United States ...	2.70	2.80b

a) Includes Taiwan Province;
b) FAO estimate.

Source: *World Statistics in Brief,* United Nations, N.Y., 1977, p. 179.

Traditional Fishing

Fishing has been a traditional source of food for centuries. Yet today we are experiencing the depletion of many traditional fish food stocks. This has resulted from not only the expansion of the world's population—greatly increasing total demand—but also from new technology which has improved our capacity to capture fish on the high seas and off the coast. The total worldwide catch today is about 70 million tons. This has increased the exploitation of the most easily caught and the most desirable of species. The resulting depletion has led to a waste of effort and low profitability. (See Figure IV-1 for global fish catches.)

Underutilized Stocks

On the other hand, there are a number of underutilized species of fish in the world's oceans which could, with a certain degree of effort, be used by man directly or indirectly for food. An important characteristic of such underutilized species is that such living marine fisheries represent a renewable resource which would be a complete waste if not utilized.[32] Estimates of the potential of such underutilized species range from yields equal to the total present world fisheries catch and upwards.[33] For example, one estimate of the ratio of total world fish landings to the annual available primary production of fish stocks is about 1:3,000.[34] While this suggests that we are poorly exploiting the biological productivity of the oceans, these estimates remain unproved and more research, especially about the interrelationship of species, is needed.

For utilization of species not now fished to occur, major changes in eating habits and food distribution would have to take place. We need first of all to learn much more about individual, potentially available, fish species to provide guidance for early effective management and to ensure economical fishing over the long run. National governmental and international assistance may be required to encourage interest in new fishing areas and to ensure a global management perspective which would include looking at the entire ocean ecology as a single system. Unless this is done, we may see the same depletion of these still underutilized species as we see now of scarce stocks.

The reasons for this relatively imbalanced and poor exploitation of the oceans are many. Some of these reasons include environmental factors, inaccessibility of species in central ocean gyres, and length, structure, and transfer of efficiency of the food chain, as well as overall difficulty in exploitation.

Limits on Ocean Fishing for Immediate Future

Despite these potential areas of expansion, so far fishery products provide only a small percentage of the world's total food production. Total consumption in 1970 was 43 million metric tons of fish or about 2.6 percent of the world's total tonnage of food.[35] Fish only provided about 2.3 percent of the world's protein supply. The total tonnage of fish caught in 1970 was greater than the above figure since about 38 percent was used in the manufacture of fish oils and meals. One reason for this relatively small share fish have in the world's food supply is that only fifteen countries make a major effort to fish: these countries account for about three-fourths of the world's fishery catch.[36]

The makeup of the world's total catch is composed of about three-fourths marine fish species, about one-eighth freshwater fish, while the remainder includes anadromous fish (mostly salmon), mollusks (including oysters), and crustaceans (crabs). Some 50 percent of the world's fish catch comes from the Pacific Ocean, and about one-third from the Atlantic. Yet some areas remain underutilized, such as the Indian Ocean.

Global seafood catches and aquaculture increased around 7 percent per year from 1948 to 1968, but have leveled off or declined in recent years. Most of the loss has been the result of reduced catches of anchovetta. This decrease or slower rate of increases indicates we are reaching maximum sustainable yield for much of the world's traditional fishery resource. However, there are major unknown factors about the basic productive capacity of the seas. As noted, little is known about the economic or technological feasibility of harvesting unexploited species where the greatest potential probably rests.

One key factor in future ocean food production relates to overall global and worldwide demand. This demand is projected to increase from 11.8 kilograms per capita per year in 1970 to about 14 kilograms in 1985.[37] While it is very difficult to project future production given the recent wide fluctuation of catches, some experts believe we can have a total fish harvest in 1985 of more than 199 million metric tons compared with some 70 million tons in 1977. Other, more moderate, estimates now project a 1985 catch of some 80 million metric tons. The great difference between the two estimates is due to various assumptions about the probable sustainability of a significant rise in fishery catches.

Despite its importance as a rich protein food for some countries with relatively high per capita consumption, fish are not now projected to contribute significantly to total world protein requirements in the next few decades. But, even at the low end of the scale there is room for significant additions to the world's food resources if fishing and harvesting can be expanded for non-conventional species.

The great unknown in this area remains the natural production limits of the ocean. We still do not know the ability of the oceans and the various species to sustain increases in catches—especially beyond the 100 ton figure. A final remaining unknown is the future potential of aquaculture.

New Fishing Exploitation and Potential

One approach which could greatly affect the total exploitation of ocean living resources would be to utilize species lower down in the food chain—the so-called "primary production." Through a shift of fishing interest and utilization to more abundant groups of organisms which are closer to the primary ocean production, a significant increase in the total availability of ocean-based food could take place. Other methods exist to increase the food potential of the oceans. One is the transplantation of one useful species into an area where it does not occur naturally in order to increase its production. (Some have suggested shifting some salmon to the Antarctic to feed off of the krill.) However, experience to date has been very mixed and not wholly successful.

Among the most promising areas of future exploitation of the ocean's living organisms would be, for example, the utilization of krill, the mass cultivation of mussels, and the possibility of a fishery for plankton.[38] With respect to krill, the resource is already being utilized by a number of ccuntries including the Soviet Union. The Soviets convert this plankton into fish meal which is used as a food supplement for poultry and swine. The Soviets harvested about 200,000 tons of krill in 1974, but the annual total catch is now about 20,000 tons. Japan has a limited catch and is developing palatable krill products. Also, the United Kingdom, Germany, Norway, and Taiwan are examining the potential of krill fishery.

While it has proved very difficult to estimate the total amount of plankton in the sea, with respect to krill even the smallest estimates indicate immense quantities. These estimates range from 40 to 100 million tons of stocks which might be available, with 50 million tons considered a reasonable annual harvest projection. This would almost equal the total catch of the world fisheries in the late 1960s. Krill's food value is similar to that of other crustaceans, with high protein and fat content, one pound being equal to 460 calories. However, there are a number of problems including easy spoilage. Krill must be processed into meal on the spot within a few hours of capture. In such form, it could be used either as a human food supplement or more normally as a feedstuff. It could be used directly as human food, but its very small size presents a major handicap (an average size animal weighs only one gram). In addition, there are other plankton fishery such as the red crab which could be utilized.

There are added difficulties in developing an economical plankton fishery. Technology for catching and processing is still in the primitive stage. There is little normal "human" direct demand for plankton. The poorer areas that need great improvements in diet do not normally eat fish, let alone processed plankton. Further, some experts believe that protein deficiency is not the major nutritional problem for the large populations of Africa and Asia—but rather obtaining necessary energy (calories) levels.[39] Even so, in a world of serious population growth, low per capita income, and severe nutritional and food problems, the use, development, and harvesting of the large quantities of available plankton from the oceans should be a high priority for all concerned countries and the world community.

New Processing Technology

While the question of the exact extent of protein deficiency on a global scale is still being debated, nevertheless, in certain areas it remains a serious problem. One estimate is that at least 500 million people throughout the world are short of necessary levels of protein.[40] Animal protein, including fish protein, can solve some of this problem when used as a concentrate in human meals and it can also provide some of the essential amino acids which are lacking in many plant proteins. Fish meal, however, is used largely for farm animals and, in particular, it is used in the American poultry industry. Until recently, most of this fish meal was in the form of anchovies caught off the coast of Peru. More than half the fish landed in the United States goes to feed farm animals in addition to the enormous imports as fish meal. Fish meal is not only high protein, but it also has a good amino acid balance and is rich in vitamins which give it high nutritional value. Further, for many uses fish meal is the cheapest source of high-grade animal protein. Consequently, there has been a phenomenal rise in the utilization of fish meal worldwide until the recent decreases in catches of anchovies. In 1968, a high harvest year, about 4.8 million tons of fish meal were produced as against only 627,000 tons in 1938. Despite criticisms that indirect usage of fish meal is inefficient, it has contributed to total human nutrition, and otherwise might never be utilized at all for direct human consumption. The task remains, however, to utilize, as much as possible, such products directly.

In this context, a much greater worldwide effort is required to produce a high quality fish protein concentrate (FPC) which will be acceptable to many different palates. Already progress has been made and such a concentrate can be produced, but it is still relatively costly for markets where it is most needed—the poorest countries of the world.[41] Also there is a need for the proper marketing of such a concentrate so that it can be a regular part of the meals of most people in the developing world. But there are many difficulties. Some are economic, as noted, but the social or psychological barrier is a major one requiring comprehensive study and effective planning. Success in achieving widespread acceptance will require a systems approach since the issue is not just supplying fish protein concentrate or some other new nutritional element but dealing with population growth, income levels, sociological patterns, distribution systems, and other nutritional needs.

The development of fish protein concentrate as a human food source is only one very partial answer to the complex global food and nutritional problem. It may not even work, and other food sources may prove to be more efficient. Yet, unless we carry out large development and research efforts employing presently underutilized food products, we may never solve the difficult challenges we face in feeding the world's growing population. A relatively cheap food protein concentrate which can be stored without spoilage and integrated into a variety of normally used foods could be a major contribution to global nutritional problems.

Despite this fact, there is little commercial production of FPC.

Consequently, there is little experience of large-scale usage over time.[42] There is evidence that the small-scale use of FPC, mostly as an additive in other normal food, has already had significant success in increasing the health of its users, especially children. A positive element is that previously "undesirable" species of fish can be used in making FPC, species which are now not caught at all or which are highly underfished. Further, the third of the world's fish catch which is presently used to make fish meal could be used to make fish protein concentrate.[43] The utilization of unused species of fish for human food could contribute, by some estimates, tens of billions of pounds on a sustained yield basis.[44]

On the other hand, krill and other plankton may prove ultimately an even larger source of FPC than larger fish, and the Soviets have already utilized it for meal. Here technology may yet provide an answer in reducing costs and producing an acceptable product. A sense of priority and governmental action will, however, be required before real progress is made.[45]

Potential of Aquaculture

At present aquaculture (the breeding, feeding, and harvesting of fish or shellfish in controlled habitats) contributes only a very small percentage to the total world food supply. Aquaculture now ranges from such specialty items as trout and oysters, mostly raised in the industrialized countries, to relatively low cost fish protein produced in extensive pond systems mostly in Asia and Africa.

With the inherent limitations of worldwide fishery and with some species already reaching their natural production limits and most others likely to reach this level by the end of the century, new methods and projects in aquaculture could contribute to additional significant increases in the world's fish supply. In the long run, perhaps the greatest hope for a wise utilization of ocean space for food would be setting aside vast areas of the sea as marine equivalents of land farms, in which man will apply the same basic approaches as he uses on land. He will then gradually abandon "hunting" for fish as he has abandoned "hunting" for animals as a major source of protein rich food. Given the great need of mankind for food the time is long past when we should be learning the techniques of sea farming.

Yet we remain relatively ignorant about farming the sea. We do not understand nearly as much as we should about the sea creatures which could potentially be used in aquaculture. Their life patterns are complex and their environment covers so much area that it is very difficult to know what is needed to domesticate most of the useful species let alone even effectively catch them.

As mentioned, there has been for years some aquaculture particular-ly of freshwater species including trout, catfish, and carp. In salt water we have had hatcheries for cod, lobster, salmon, and shad. But saltwater fish production has not usually been true farming since there has not been control over the full life cycle of the creature. Therefore, many past efforts to increase total ocean stocks have not been very successful, except in the hatchery production of coho salmon. The basic aim of sea farming must continue to be the control of fish throughout its entire life until it is ready to be harvested. Very few species have been successfully cultivated throughout their entire cycle.

Most aquaculture probably will take place within the coastal areas on the continental shelves in shallower water of less than 200 feet. Even so this opens vast areas for potential farming. The only danger is the increasing pollution of the seas, mostly still concentrated in these coastal areas. The productivity of these "farms of the seas" can be much greater in per acre protein production than most land farms. Fish farms can produce for example up to some 1,500 pounds of fish per acre annually.[46] Thus, with additional research and improved methods, shallow water farming can bring large fish crops.

Despite some progress, "farming" the sea still has great problems. A far greater investment including research by governments, industry, and international organizations will be required before this method can add significantly to global food production. Some research is being done by governments but it is very small. One project, partly financed by the United States government and private industry, is raising the giant California kelp (a form of seaweed) together with other plants and marine animals. The basic concept is to produce land animal stock feed, energy, and food through the use of deep-water nutrients and solar energy on the water's surface.[47] Here we see the combination of technology (the process of uniting deep-sea nutrients and surface sunlight) with the natural environment so as to produce greatly added amounts of plants, food, etc. These efforts are only at the experimental level. Any commercial production of this system's output is probably decades away. Also most farming has been restricted to expensive species and therefore of little help in feeding the world's poor.

While we cannot expect too much in this area if we are seeking substantial quantities in the near future, there is some hope over the longer term. For this very reason a major and early global effort should be started to respond to the world's growing need for food from all sources. A realistic goal would be to expand sea farming significantly so that it can make a major contribution to the world's protein supply by the end of the century. As with many other suggestions to improve the quality of life of the globe it will require considerable action on a number of levels: reduction in ocean pollution, increased scientific research, and not least, cooperation among countries and diverse international organizations.

Management Problems—A Future Perspective

The possibility of combining new technology in catching ocean living resources, new scientific information about the habits and quantities of various species, and the growing demand for food from more and more people have created the need to manage global fisheries resources that are within and beyond the increasingly accepted 200-mile coastal economic zone. Unless this is done, we will be faced with the same situation we see with the depletion of highly desirable table grade fisheries or with the ruthless exploitation of whales by the Japanese and a few other nations. Even these immense quantities, now untouched, of living resources will be scarce and threatened with extinction in the same way modern whaling has brought to near annihilation the biggest sea creature—the blue whale. It is vitally important also that we fully understand the entire marine ecological system, so that we do not upset its balance through overfishing for certain species which may be vital links in the food chain for other important species.

For these reasons we must look upon the living renewable resources of the open oceans more and more as a single whole and develop an international resource management system. At present no such system exists. There are a few highly limited (and largely unsuccessful) efforts like the International Whaling Commission or the old Inter-America Tropical Tuna Commission. The proposed Law of the Sea treaty will only create a very general framework which permits the establishment of such organizations for fisheries which cannot be managed within a single 200-mile coastal economic zone, but it has nothing in its provisions in the way of specifically mandating the rationale and wise management of open oceans or wide-ranging fisheries.[48]

What is required is a global authority with real powers and resources. One approach could be through an Oceans Protection Authority. It could conduct studies of fisheries, their life cycles, feeding habits, and would set limits on catches. A fair allocation system among different nations also would have to be established when total catches reached the Maximum Sustainable Yield (MSY) levels. There are arguments against using a pure MYS approach as a conservation basis, but the important point is that management principles should be developed on the basis of equitable sharing, long-term conservation, maximum yield, and also in the context of maintaining the overall integrity of the total ocean's ecology.[49]

MINERALS AND ENERGY FROM THE OCEANS

The sea can also provide important mineral resources for a growing world economy. In addition to the relatively small amount of oil which exists under the deep seabeds (much of it inaccessible, even with the most modern drilling technology, unlike the vast and tappable reserves of the continental shelves) there are minerals on the surface of the deep seabed rich in deposits of manganese, nickel, cobalt, and copper. We have known of the existence of these minerals for almost a century but we did not know how to extract them. Now modern technology is rapidly advancing the time when their extensive exploration and exploitation will become a reality. With new technology it will soon be possible to exploit these deep seabed ores, and add a significant new source of raw materials to supply industry and to improve the world's economy.[50]

While manganese nodules were discovered first by the scientific research expedition of H.M.S. *Challenger* in 1873, they were not considered rich enough for commercial exploitation and the technology did not exist for their recovery in large quantities. Since then, there have been widely divergent estimates of the value of seabed minerals and when they would be commercially viable. Some contemporary experts even foresee large and profitable production levels as early as the 1980s.[51] But with new technology the basic conditions now exist for beginning their exploitation.

Some "nodules"—only one form of ocean-based minerals—consist of up to 50 percent manganese content and, therefore, despite containing other important minerals, are called "manganese nodules." These nodules are formed by gradual accretion of minerals chemically precipitated around some minute nucleus. They range in size between those larger than basketballs to just grains of sand. The main minerals contained in the richest type nodules include the following properties: 1 to 1.5 percent nickel, 25 to 30 percent manganese, 0.5 to 1 percent copper, 0.25 percent cobalt, and 0.05 percent molybdenum. There are about thirty other minerals present, but at the moment, nickel, copper, and cobalt are the most commercially interesting components.[52] They generally are located about 15,000 to 20,000 feet below the ocean's surface and are usually far from land. We believe the largest concentration is located in the Pacific Ocean, with some deposits scattered in the Atlantic and Indian oceans.

The current economics of seabed mining are such that a mine site must have high-grade abundant nodules and produce about three million tons (dry weight) of nodules per year. It is believed that there are more than 400 mine sites providing the necessary mineral concentrations. If all of these sites were ultimately exploited, the seabeds would provide a substantial portion of total global consumption for copper, cobalt, nickel, and manganese. Short term, it is unlikely that seabed mining will make up a very large percentage of world mineral production except for cobalt. Over the longer run, most nickel and manganese will probably come from seabed sources.[53]

By most estimates, the total potential of seabed minerals is considerable. For example, one appraisal calculates some 14 billion tons of nickel existing in seabed nodules—or some 150,000 years' use at the 1960 rate of consumption. This compares to only about 100 years' supply of land-based ore.[54] The potential reserve situation is similar for other minerals (not always contained in "nodules") including aluminum, manganese, copper, cobalt, and molybdenum.[55]

In addition, extensive minerals also exist in the water itself and in the deeper reaches of the ocean bed. Unfortunately, most of these minerals (with the exceptions noted below) are too dispersed to be economically exploitable with even the most advanced existing technology. However, progress has been made in the exploration and exploitation of "manganese nodules." It is likely that we will be able to recover these economically in the late 1980s if the prices for the key constituent minerals, especially nickel and copper, are at sufficiently high levels compared with other competing raw materials. We should not expect that commercial development of these minerals will be of great significance to total worldwide demand until the 1990s or even later.

It must be noted that it remains difficult to estimate exactly when deep seabed exploitation will reach a "take off" stage of sustaining and substantial productivity, since advances in technology are continuing and new breakthroughs are always possible. In addition, new discoveries about the location, concentration, and content of seabed nodules could have a significant bearing on the viability of the industry in competition with land-based mining operations. For example, a nodule of 1.5 percent nickel is far more attractive than one of only 0.5 percent and the difference could mean the existence or nonexistence of a successful seabed mining industry. As we have indicated, evidence does suggest that there are a large number of ocean sites with nodules of a "high grade" ore content which could sustain economic activities for a long period of time.

Another potential source of minerals from the sea is found in mineral rich mud deposits lying in the ocean depths, especially those found in mid-ocean ridges that are formed by volcanic eruptions, with the original material becoming very fine particles and eventually forming accumulated sediment. The material consists of oxides and sulfides of manganese, copper, iron, lead, silver, gold, tin, cadmium, nickel, and cobalt. These metals from the ridges may help in the formation of nearby manganese nodules. At today's prices, the muds contain billions of dollars' worth of recoverable metals.

These deposits of vented material from subsea volcanic eruptions have been known to scientists almost as long as they have known about manganese nodules. Explorations are currently being carried out by a number of countries to determine the extent of these mineral deposits, which might be very widespread and in a number of different ocean areas. As with nodules, extraction is difficult. Some of the muds appear to be rich enough in mineral content to be economic for mining even at great depths. The amount of metals contained in these muds could be more extensive than those found in seabed nodules. Together with nodules, the processing of these minerals will require extensive use of energy, demonstrating again the interdependent nature of the world's technology, economy, and ecology.

Environmental Impact

As with much of industrial and land-based mining activities, the mining of metal-rich muds and seabed nodules can take place only at some environmental cost. The most impact is likely to be at the original site of mining. With the muds the problem is the spreading of the waste material, less the metal particles, until it is returned to the ocean's floor. The distribution of waste sediments over the surface could greatly reduce the level of sunlight reaching the ocean layers. This could adversely affect the production of aqua life (especially plankton) and endanger the ocean's food resources. This lack of sunlight could reduce the phytoplankton population of large ocean areas. The waste sediment would probably remain in the water column before finally resettling on the ocean floor for very long periods. Thus strong environmental standards and regulations would be required if these negative impacts are to be minimized. One way of mitigating the consequences of this kind of mining would be to require that mining waste be returned to depths well below the ocean's euphotic (sunlight) layer.

There are a number of other negative environmental impacts on marine life which mining would probably produce. And, as with all new activities, there may be effects totally unknown today. Thus, caution is required to assure that no serious harm to ocean life takes place. The basic problem, however, is that no authority yet exists to control such pollution (outside the territorial sea or 200-mile economic zone), and an international authority over mining still awaits further acceptance in a Law of the Sea treaty.

Establishing a Legal Regime for Seabed Minerals

The combined advances in technology and the growing demand for key minerals have brought about a need to clarify the legal status of the ocean bed. They have made obsolete traditional concepts of international law and undermined the authority of existing global institutions.

The issue facing our world community now is how to exploit these mineral riches in the ocean. The United Nations has declared the deep seabeds to be "the common heritage of mankind." But this phrase, like many others in international debate, creates almost more problems than it solves since each country gives it a different interpretation. The Law of the Sea Conference is addressing the question of how the world community will manage the clash of diverse national and regional interests involved in deciding how seabed minerals are to be exploited. In particular, there is a great disparity of views between those countries with the technology for seabed mineral exploitation (e.g., the United States, Japan, Canada, the Soviet Union, and some European countries) and other nations (especially the developing ones) which are not likely to have such technology for several decades. As Secretary of State Henry Kissinger, in 1975, said: "Ultimately, unless basic rules regulate exploitation, rivalry will lead to tests of power. A race to carve out exclusive domains of exploration on the deep seabed even without claims of sovereignty will menace freedom of navigation and invite a competition like that of the colonial powers in Africa and Asia in the last century. This is not the kind of world we want to see. Law has an opportunity to civilize us in the early stages of a new competitive activity."[56]

This statement of the basic conflicts of interest and their larger implications indicates the difficulties in establishing a widely acceptable legal regime for the seabeds. The combination of the rapaciousness of all groups of nations, a traditional international law made obsolete by modern technology, and the general widening gap between the developed and developing world create a negotiating context which could be harmful to the long-term global community interest.[57] Yet, we cannot somehow put these issues off. Technology marches ever onward and does not always await the existence of favorable political conditions or adequate decision-making institutions.

The major task of the present Law of the Sea negotiations is to provide a legal and widely acceptable framework to give reality to the United Nations supposition that the seabeds are "the common heritage of mankind."[58] One significant and indeed precedent-making proposal in the United Nations Law of the Sea negotiations was the concept that revenue sharing should take place from seabed mining operations, the revenue going to a common fund for use largely by the developing countries. This is a promising start towards a kind of international tax system to sustain global public interest and welfare needs. The eventual revenues from exploitation of these resources may total, over time, billions of dollars. Further, there is a proposal before the Law of the Sea Conference for the establishment of an International Seabed Authority which can both license others to exploit and also directly manage itself the exploration and exploitation of seabed minerals. This concept makes great sense since it would maximize the potential of the oceans for the world's ever-growing population, which is increasingly in search of additional raw materials to sustain and improve its quality of life.

Extensive exploitation of nodules and other forms of seabed minerals will have a major impact on world mineral markets by increasing the supply of these scarce metals. Traditional land-based ore producers will need to reevaluate their future productivity and income in light of this new potential. Conceivably, land mining and processing technology will also progress apace, and land-based producers will try to ensure a continued significant, even dominant, role for themselves. One possible political approach would be, for example, that some land-based mining countries (such as Canada, Chile, and Zaire) might attempt to block exploitation of seabed minerals. They might prevent or limit such mining through control of any international authority which might be given power over seabed mining by the proposed Law of the Sea Convention. In the end, this kind of limitation on production will probably not succeed given the demand of mankind for additional raw materials. Consumer countries would have a very great interest in ensuring their long-term access to seabed minerals.

The best policy would be to encourage the fullest exploitation as is economically feasible, by as many parties as possible. This would increase competition both for seabed miners and for their land-based counterparts.[59] There are important trade-offs to be considered also in the setting of levels of revenue sharing since too high levels will discourage mining and thereby restrict the total availability of minerals for the economy. On the other hand, revenue sharing can tax the so-called "scarcity rent" without loss to economic efficiency.[60] But there are other good reasons to encourage as great a number of miners as possible. Given the number of mine sites noted earlier, and with only about five to seven potential mining firms initially seriously interested in mining "first-generation" type areas (1985-95), there are ample resources for a large number of miners. In particular, the richer developing countries should be encouraged to invest in this area, especially the oil rich countries with few if any other resources and with large surpluses in their balance of payments.

It would, however, be a serious mistake for the developing countries to look upon this area as an exclusive preserve for them alone to exploit. Not only would this lead to a breakdown in cooperation between the North and the South, leading to growing conflict with all its implications, but it would delay the effective benefits of these areas to those who need them most, since the technology and financing for exploiting these areas are now in the hands of industrialized countries. There is also no doubt that the capability and skills of the richer countries must be fully engaged in the process in order to ensure that these resources are exploited without serious damage to the world's environment. Planning and wise management in the context of a long-term exploitation policy with care for the needs of future generations could establish a framework in which the world community can make the maximum use of its "commons" areas.

Energy from the Oceans

The oceans can be an important source of energy, both of the conventional and more unconventional type. First, they can provide conventional hydrocarbons through offshore drilling for oil and natural gas. Many rich fields are being explored under the bed of the continental shelves. There are equally large gas and oil deposits off the coast of some Pacific islands. It has further been proposed that there could be some oil under the deep seabed of the oceans. The latter possibility will take some time for exploitation. Commercially available technology has not advanced sufficiently to make possible extensive drilling and recovery at the great depths of these central ocean areas. Some estimate the total hydrocarbon deposits in the oceans may equal those known on land. (It should be noted that most of these deposits are relatively close to shore.) In this energy-intensive world, the potential exploitation of these resources adds yet another pressure on our ocean spaces.

While the question of global energy needs will be more extensively dealt with in another chapter, we should note here the improvement in ocean drilling technology over the last few decades. By 1960 almost all commercial quantities of offshore petroleum had been produced from wells in waters 340 feet deep or less. Only a few exploratory wells had gone beyond 1,300 feet.[61] Since that time, new technology has made it possible to drill and extract oil in depths of several thousand feet. Now, technology is moving towards undersea drilling that can be operated by remote control. Further, the technology of large oil rigs on platforms above the surface of the oceans, thousands of feet above the seabed, has also advanced. With the depletion of land-based resources, we can expect that a greater and greater proportion of the world's oil wealth will come from marine areas. Already many marine oil fields are economically competitive with oil found on land. With continued advances in technology, such as the building of platforms to service multiple wells, offshore production expenses can become even more competitive with onshore costs.

It was the knowledge of these oil deposits and the development of new technology which created new pressures on coastal states to extend their control over the adjacent continental shelves and thereby decrease the area which was part of the "common heritage of mankind." The tendency of nations to extend their territorial jurisdiction as technology advances the opportunity for profits has become a common characteristic of this most recent period of man's history. Now, more and more countries are intruding into spaces which previously were thought to be open for all to use without the right of exclusive claims.

Another source of energy from the oceans exists in the inherent motions of the seas themselves—either through tidal action, current movements due to temperature gradients, or wave action. Also in the future, when we learn to use hydrogen for energy, the seas will provide an almost inexhaustible supply of that material. In addition, the oceans can and already do supply cooling water for nuclear power plants located along the coast. In the face of these forces, the present legal ocean regime is largely insufficient. Unavoidably, change must and will take place in the oceans and in the international law which covers this vast area.

MANAGEMENT OF THE OCEANS—A GLOBAL TASK IN A HIGH-RISK WORLD

The Law of the Sea negotiations are establishing an ocean regime which essentially is a compromise between, on the one hand, the desire of coastal and maritime states to protect or extend their powers and jurisdiction and, on the other, the needs of the entire international community for global, responsible management of ocean resources and environment. The treaty probably will neither satisfy the extreme nationalistic ambitions of some states nor the idealistic hopes of some groups or individuals who seek a universal ocean's regime over all marine space in the name of common humanity. It will be an imperfect instrument reflecting the serious imperfections of our current global political and economic system. This balance between limited global management approach to the oceans and national extensions of control is seen in the following LOS negotiating issues or elements:

—Establishing an International Seabeds Authority with specific management responsibility for the mining of seabed minerals in the area beyond national jurisdiction. Included in this Authority is control over pollution only from mining.

—There would also be established the basic framework for control of marine-based pollution through provisions designating responsibilities and duties of coastal and maritime states over pollution. Specific follow-on conferences would be required to give concrete realization to the general principles of the treaty.

—There would be some provision for international management of highly migratory and anadromous fish. (Coastal species within the new 200-mile Economic Zone would come under the management and control of the coastal states.)

—There would be revenue sharing from seabed mineral mining which would go to the international community especially for the poorer countries. This would be in partial fulfillment of the concept that the seabed should be the common heritage of mankind.

—Finally, there would be a dispute-settlement mechanism for conflicts over ocean uses which should lead to peaceful resolution of different viewpoints about the meaning of the treaty.

In addition to these positive elements enhancing an international approach to oceans space management there are other elements of the forthcoming LOS Convention which strengthen national control over some marine space. These include:

—Extension of the limit of a territorial sea to 12 miles;

—Establishment of a 200-mile Economic Zone with coastal state control over living and nonliving resources in that zone (this will deny to the global community about one-third of ocean space now open to all); and

—Granting of largely coastal-state control over scientific research within the Economic Zone (this normally is a high seas freedom which may be lost by the global community).

The final product of the LOS negotiation will be far from perfect. It will provide only a very small and very limited step in the direction of common management of a common resource. The negotiations reflect both the realities and the problems of current political forces and the result of technological change. They do not reflect as much the pressing long-term needs of preserving the integrity and balance of the marine environment. They do provide some important beginnings. They establish for the first time an international authority over a nonliving resource; also for the first time the international community will receive independent revenue from seabed mining. These revenues are a kind of international tax to provide "for the general welfare."

Beyond the LOS Negotiations

Beyond these small steps should they finally materialize in one form or another, more difficult tasks are ahead. What has been done up to now is not sufficient to deal with the increasing risks to mankind from the abuse of the oceans. Other efforts must be made towards a more comprehensive and far-reaching regime for managing the many and often conflicting uses of the seas.

The first priority must be in protecting the oceans and their living resources. Some suggestions on how to proceed have been made with respect to dealing with specific sources of pollution. But it is clear that some kind of Oceans' Protection Authority may need to be established, whose primary aim is to prevent harm to the marine environment and not to exploit it. The first task would be to establish, through the United Nations Environmental Program's Earthwatch activities, a monitoring and baseline data program for marine pollutants throughout the world. Further, such an organization would fund and carry out research to discover not only what pollutants are in the oceans but also what impact they would have. The Oceans' Protection Authority would have their own oceanographic and scientific service of the highest professional quality to do this work. It also would be the focus for gathering and evaluating marine research throughout the world. It could be funded, in part, with revenue from seabed mining or, eventually, from an international fee on catches from fishing on the open ocean. It might also manage all living resources outside the 200-mile zone initially— perhaps expanding its services over time to within the 200-mile zone as countries realize that fish and marine pollution do not recognize such boundaries.

The perspective of such an Oceans' Authority would be long-term management. Its concerns would be to ensure that future generations would inherit an ocean abundant in living resources and free of dangerous pollutants.

Another function of the Authority could be to manage international ocean "parks" (or Marine Preservation Areas). These would be specially designated areas of the oceans, which because of their special characteristics—unique ecological systems, living creatures, or physical elements—require special protection. To carry out the role of protection, preservation, and research, an International Marine Protection Service might be established responsible only to the Authority.

Other functions of such a Marine Protection Service could include:

—Enforce international fishing regulations on the high seas to maintain sound long-term agreed-upon conservation goals.
—Protect completely marine mammals such as whales and dolphins.
—Enforce international regulations on the dumping of waste into the ocean including a ban on the discharge of all toxic wastes, especially heavy metals.

—Help establish and maintain and enforce marine navigation systems including those from satellites in space.
—Assist ships in distress on the high seas.
—Establish and maintain monitoring satellites looking for sources of marine pollution.
—Enforce seabed mining regulations.
—Control dumping of radioactive waste into the oceans.
—Maintain marine automatic monitoring stations examining the quality of the oceans at specific locations as part of a Global Environmental Monitoring System (GEMS).

However, before this "ideal" organizational approach is agreed upon more limited immediate and practical action will probably have to be taken by the industrialized countries to limit their dumping of wastes into the oceans. Thus a first priority would be cooperative action by OECD member countries on land-based pollution. New and more strict discharge standards need to be developed for both ships and land activities. A beginning by the rich countries to control their pollution is vital. It must be done on a cooperative basis since this would prevent more competitive "polluters" from taking economic advantage of nations or industries maintaining a high quality environment.

Looking at the positive side of managing the oceans, there is need for greater cooperation among nations in developing conservation measures to deal with the exploitation of living and nonliving resources. International efforts should be made towards a major cooperative international project to utilize aquaculture as a key approach to supplying food from the marine environment in ways that are more efficient over the long-run than traditional fishing methods.

The management of fish stocks through the utilization of a modified conservation theory of "maximum sustainable yield" for certain fish stocks would increase the efficiency of the global fishing industry and at the same time maintain the desirable ecological balance in the oceans' food chain.

Finally, a major new cooperative effort is required to increase mankind's knowledge of the oceans. This knowledge is vital for developing any effective program of environmental protection and conservation. An important step would be the establishment of an International Oceanographic and Marine University and Research Institute which would particularly be aimed at education of students from the developing countries and at training the international civil servants required to manage the oceans' riches for all mankind.

The principles of such an international approach to managing the oceans must be based on open and non-discriminatory access by all countries to the resources of the oceans. It would be unwise and ultimately self-defeating for any group of countries to deny access to any other group based on political, ideological, or geographic grounds. Further, both coastal and landlocked countries should share in the benefits of the oceans. Given the present distribution of technology and resources the industrialized countries need to take a position of enlightened leadership in this area. They can help provide the necessary funding and the technology which can start to accomplish the extremely complex task of protecting the marine environment and conserving its resources for future generations.

CHAPTER V

Global Energy Needs and Problems

Introduction

The energy crisis is a clear example of the kind of high risks the global community will continue to experience in the coming decades. The dependence of most industrialized nations on abundant energy (especially petroleum) from a few countries has created new vulnerabilities in an uncertain and dangerous age. The choices nations and the international community make in their energy policies influence our quality of life, our personal security, the world's climate and food supply, and our overall economic well-being. These "energy choices" will, for example, determine whether consumer countries will be open to economic or political blackmail, whether we will be subject to highly polluted air, or whether we experience irreparable ecological damage through strip mining or other environmentally harmful activities. Further, the availability of cheap or expensive energy could determine whether many people in the poorer countries have any hope of improving their marginal existence.

Much has been said about interdependence, but in the energy sector it has come home to the industrialized countries with a vengeance. In one short year the industrialized countries learned vividly about how dependent their economies were on a few developing countries' oil production. (This has its opposite counterpart in the dependence of the developing world on the food exports of the industrialized countries.) Within a few short years, the increased dependence of the West on imported energy has transformed the very foundations of the global political system. It has created new risks for all countries in the resulting rapid shift of power and money. It illustrates the weakness of the various international institutions which are supposed to protect the post-World War II global system from serious disruptions. The foundations of a more stable, more equitable, and safer global energy or overall economic system are still not in sight. Each group of countries, even those that have benefited from being rich in energy resources, has discovered new vulnerabilities from the disruption of the old order.

THE WORLD'S USE OF ENERGY

Much of the recent historical period can be called the Age of Petroleum. Before that it was coal that provided the main source of commercial energy. Today oil and gas together are responsible for two-thirds of the world's commercial energy. Some fifty years ago coal made up 80 percent of global commercial energy use, with oil and gas consisting of 16 percent. In 1950 coal provided 60 percent and was only passed by oil in 1960.[1] About 96 percent of the world's commercial energy now comes from the burning of fossil fuels. Hydropower, nuclear, and other forms of energy make up the remaining amount. About 40 percent of this "commercial" energy is used by industry, 25 percent by transportation, and 25 percent in the residential and commercial sector.[2]

Another key factor in the energy sector is the recent rapid growth in consumption. World energy fuel use tripled in twenty-five years. Oil and gas use quintupled while electricity use nearly reached a sevenfold increase.[3] Yet for a very large proportion of humanity, especially in the poorest countries, use of commercial or modern forms of energy is still only a remote dream. This group obtains most of its energy needs via noncommercial sources such as wood and cow dung. Such noncommercial consumption is estimated to be about 10 percent of the world's total energy consumption. While small in percentage terms this form of energy is important for a very large number of people. Further, in many countries in the developing world energy use is doubling in ten years versus twenty years for North America.

The high price of energy and especially oil as a result of the global energy crisis has had its greatest impact on the non-oil exporting developing countries. The high cost of imported energy has slowed or even completely halted progress towards development and a higher quality of life for many of the world's poorest. The payments for oil have in some countries had to compete with the cost of importation of food or other goods to meet basic human needs.

Another serious consequence of the energy crisis in the developing world is that the combination of increased population along with overall higher energy demand has resulted in depletion of indigenous noncommercial energy sources such as firewood. This has caused serious environmental harm and also affected the well-being and productivity of the rural sector of many developing countries.

These developing countries increasingly were growing in their dependence on petroleum during the period of relatively cheaper prices. Their dependence on this fuel source is likely to continue even under conditions of higher prices, in the absence of competitive and available alternatives. Thus, for the immediate future the poorer countries will probably have to maintain expensive oil imports.[4]

On the other side of the economic spectrum, the United States while having only about 6 percent of the world's population consumed about 36 percent of the world's energy during the 1970s. In the 1950s, it was 48 percent of the world's total. On a per capita basis it was 76 times the level for India. Over time this proportion should decrease so that by 1985 America may account for only a quarter of the total since consumption abroad is growing faster than in North America.[5]

The patterns of energy use among the industrialized countries differ in both sources of energy, in efforts at conservation, and with respect to per capita consumption. The United States imports about 46 percent of its oil but less than 20 percent of its energy. On the other hand Japan must import some 90 percent of its total energy requirements.

Looking at electricity consumption, in 1969 the average world per capita consumption level was 1,200 kilowatt-hours (kwh), but for the United States the level was 7,175 kwh while for India it was only 94.4 kwh. On the other hand, Norway consumed 15,730 kwh per person but Japan only 2,675 kwh. Norway's cheap hydroelectricity sources, 99 percent of total, make possible its high consumption. Population growth will also influence future per capita energy and electricity consumption levels. The impact for many of these developing countries will mean that while total use will expand rapidly, per capita growth will be considerably slower, taking hundreds of years to catch up even with the slower growth rates of the United States.

There are also important differences among the industrialized countries in other patterns of energy use. Europe and Japan are far more efficient in the transportation sector than is the United States. The United States for example uses almost twice the energy per capita for transportation as does Great Britain. Within countries there are imbalances in energy use. For example, within the United States, the 20 million wealthiest households use twice the energy consumed by the 20 million poorest households. The richest use four times the electricity of the poorest.[6]

Future world energy demand or consumption is very hard to predict given the great changes we have seen in energy prices over the last decades. In the early 1970s the world consumed about 190 quadrillion BTUs (190 "quads") annually. The world consumed only 50 quads in 1938 and reached 100 quads in 1953. This represents a horrendous growth rate which is continuing.[7] According to some (the optimists) world energy demand could reach 800 quads in the year 2000.[8] On the other hand, some foresee a slowing down of the growth of energy demand over the next few decades.

Looking at the future, electricity will probably continue to grow faster than most other forms of energy. Within this sector it has been predicted that a growing proportion of new electrical generating capacity is expected to be nuclear. However, in the face of increased criticism of this technology because of its weapons proliferation, nuclear waste disposal, safety, and environmental problems, the pace of new installations of this type of power may slow. In 1968 nuclear power accounted for only 1.4 percent of all electric generating world capacity. By the year 2000 some have predicted it will amount to 40 percent.[9] Yet this figure must be seen very much in relationship to the many uncertainties of the future makeup of the world's energy framework. A more recent projection is that by 1985 nuclear power will meet no more than 6 percent of the world's total primary energy demand.[10] Another brake on nuclear energy development may be the scarcity of uranium. In particular, it may very well be possible to produce electricity more economically over the next two decades via cheaper hydro power or even via solar energy. This could be especially significant for the developing countries.

Environmental Aspects of Energy Use

Energy scarcity can lead to a decrease in the overall quality of life including degradation of the natural environment. We have already mentioned the increasing phenomenon of the deforestation of large areas in the developing world caused by man's search for energy. This deforestation, in turn, leads to soil erosion which destroys productive croplands. There also is pressure on water resources as more and more countries attempt to maximize the use of limited hydroelectric power. The decrease of food producing lands, the movement of people from rural areas to large cities, and the destruction of large sometimes unique natural areas are all concomitant problems of our energy shortages.

As some countries attempt to turn to other domestic energy sources such as low-grade high sulfur content coal, the outcome is often massive air pollution of urban areas where the coal is burned. This results in a higher incidence of respiratory diseases, increased sickness, and lower work productivity.

The scarcity or high price of energy particularly damages the quality of life in the poorest countries, since energy imports sap funds which could otherwise be employed to import food, fertilizer, medical supplies, and construction equipment. This impact hurts the improvement of many different sectors important to the overall environment. The siphoning off of developmental resources which could otherwise improve or protect the quality of life and environment is one of the major tragedies of the fourfold increase in oil prices. Part of the reason for this situation is that these countries have (like the industrialized world) become highly dependent on cheap imported oil without providing for any reasonable domestic alternative.

Global Security Implications of the Energy Situation

Another result of the sharp increase in oil prices has been a move towards the increased use of nuclear energy. With the high price of oil, nuclear energy became more attractive both for industrialized and developing countries. Further, the nuclear option appeals to some poor countries because it can be bought "off-the-shelf" from a number of countries and provides a kind of prestige for the country seeking to have the most advanced technology.

As we have seen, nuclear power is not today a major source of energy, but over time it might provide one-seventh of the total energy requirements of the non-Communist world.[11] As noted elsewhere the growth of this form of energy technology has serious security implications for all areas and countries. The main problem will be how to ensure that those developing countries that choose the nuclear option will do so only for energy reasons and not to utilize the technology for military applications. The history of this problem does not provide much hope for optimism.

Ensuring the peaceful use of this energy source will require nuclear technology exporting countries to guarantee that their products, both fuel and technology, are not diverted into military programs. Adherence to the Non-Proliferation Treaty (NPT) may need to be a minimum prerequisite for the export of any nuclear energy items if the dangerous spread of weapons is to be stopped. In addition, the exporting countries, together with the importing nations, will have to work to strengthen the international framework of cooperation in nuclear matters. This should be done chiefly through the International Atomic Energy Agency (IAEA), using its system of international safeguards and inspection of all peaceful nuclear facilities to guard against diversion to military uses.

Over the long run, we must examine all of the inherent problems and very high risks of nuclear energy and decide whether it would not be better for industrialized countries to accelerate their research and development of other energy technologies which would be safer for future global security and more appropriate and efficient for use by the developing countries.

Another key change resulting from the energy crisis of 1973 was the shift away from numbers of people as a factor of power between nations and towards countries with the ability to control a vital natural resource needed by all nations. This control and the high prices obtained for the needed resources further shifted power via the newly rich Organization of Petroleum Exporting Countries (OPEC) to control financial markets. With money these nations could also buy a measure of modernity in other sectors such as education, technology, and military equipment and capability. For example, one oil rich country, Iran, is seeking to expand its nuclear power capability as well as modernizing its armed forces so as to be equal in power to many of the older industrialized countries. This shifts power balances and could create new risks for the international system. We see here how an independent event, the rapid rise in the cost of energy, can bring to the international system new dangers and challenges.

Developing Countries and the Global Energy Situation

The non-OPEC developing countries with 41 percent of the world's population consume 9 percent of the world's commercial energy. Before 1973 their energy growth was rapid: up 250 percent between 1970 and 1974. However, their per capita energy consumption in 1974 was only 6 percent of the United States' level including commercial and noncommercial fuels. For many of these countries per capita consumption levels are sufficient only for subsistence. (For consumption projections for LDCs, see Figure V-1.[12])

Some 2.5 billion people in the poorer countries rely on noncommercial energy supplies which mostly consist of wood, dung, straw, and human and animal power. Most of this energy goes into food production, processing, and preparation. Much of it is relatively inefficient. The fuels are already in a situation of shortage which can only become more critical over time with increased population pressures. In particular the increased use of firewood has depleted forest regions near populated areas and transformed humid tropical forests into deserts and wasteland. Thus there is a vital need to improve both the management of forests and to find more efficient ways to utilize traditional energy sources to conserve these scarce materials. Yet it is

Figure V-1.   Total annual energy consumption projections for all non-OPEC LDCs (current trends case).

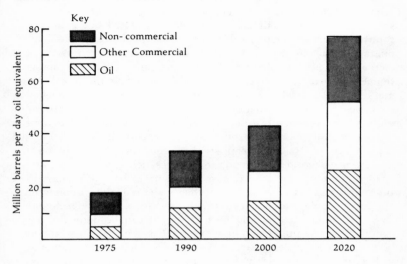

Source: (Document #BNL 50784)

likely that there will be a need to find substitutes for these traditional fuels over time. One of the great challenges of both the governments of many poorer countries and also the assistance programs of the richer countries should be to develop alternative energy sources and train people to use more efficiently existing sources to prolong their availability until better energy technologies are provided. For example, many developing countries have much remaining potential to expand hydro power to supply electricity to urban and rural areas.

Looking at the commercial sector, the developing countries' demand for oil will exceed the current United States oil consumption rate some time between 2000 and 2020 at about 18 million barrels per day. Oil will probably account for 55 percent of total energy demands in the developing countries in 2000.[13] However coal and natural gas will experience a threefold increase. We need therefore to see just how the developing countries will deal with the global energy market.

The poorer countries, without domestic energy sources, are highly dependent on the supplies of oil from a few oil-rich nations. In many cases the rising cost of energy has made many of these countries not only economically dependent on their supplier nations, creating a creditor-debtor relationship, but this has resulted also in a political dependence which has changed the global political situation in a relatively short period of time. It has shifted the focus of political and economic influence from the very poor countries with large populations such as India and Pakistan to the underpopulated but energy rich countries such as Saudi Arabia and Libya. This change has had its military impact since these countries can afford, and are now buying, increasingly modern arms which will significantly change the international balance of power over time. Thus the change in the global energy market, while clearly providing greater leverage for the developing countries in their negotiations with the industrialized countries for economic improvements for poorer countries, may also work to further impoverish the poorest of the poor. The end result is the increased dependence of these poverty-stricken countries not only on the industrialized world but also on the resource-rich developing countries.

One important factor of this resource shift is that the industrialized countries can, over the long term, if they wish to pay the economic price, buy relative independence in energy through investment in technology. The cost undoubtedly could be high but it can be done through a combination of emphasis on indigenous oil and coal reserves, acceleration of work on nuclear reactors, and the development of other energy technologies such as solar and, over the long term, fusion. But this is far more difficult for the poorer countries. They cannot, on their own, develop sophisticated and costly technologies to replace expensive imported oil. For some the alternatives are simply to denude forests, use low-grade coal with all its negative pollution impact, or to simply lower their development expectations. Many of these countries are further caught in a spiral of high population growth which only adds to the overall demand for energy and the products which require energy to produce. Where population growth is the fastest there seem to be few domestic energy alternatives. For example, less than 3 percent of the world's known coal reserves are in Africa and Latin America.[14] This situation, without extrinsic relief, creates a cycle of indebtedness, growing poverty, and helplessness. The results are increasing instability of governments, lower productivity, famine, and perhaps ultimately chaos.

The Oil Exporting Countries

The natural assumption has been that the global energy crisis greatly benefited the oil exporting countries of the world. On the surface this is certainly true. Yet the disruptions that this massive energy change created also brought about new vulnerabilities for these newly rich developing countries. The final balance sheet of advantages and disadvantages has yet to be written. For example, the concomitant international financial and monetary disruptions of the energy crisis created a situation where it was very difficult for the newly rich countries to invest without increased risk. Inflation, exacerbated by higher oil prices, undercuts the profits derived from such investments and, indeed, decreases the real worth of the funds obtained for exported petroleum. Also increased inflation, partly caused by higher energy costs, makes the imports needed by oil producing countries even more expensive.

There is another problem of the choice between keeping oil in the ground or selling it now. The oil rich countries are caught in the dilemma of either selling their oil now and investing the profits for long-term income or hoping that oil prices will increase sufficiently over the long run to make oil in the ground more valuable than any alternative investment. They must weigh in such stakes the future potential of new energy technologies or the new availability of fossil fuel to consuming countries from other sources. For example, coal could substitute for oil and is plentiful in many countries, especially in the United States. By the 1990s or beyond, when various types of solar power will probably be available and economical, what will be the true value of oil in the ground? These are all questions—without adequate answers—which create new problems for the oil rich nations.

Finally, there is one fundamental element which generates new risks for the oil producing countries. With expanded investments in the industrialized world, with larger financial reserves being held in currencies of the Western countries, and with increased reliance on Western technology and imported food, there also is created increased dependence on oil customers which did not exist in earlier periods. Most oil producing countries are very poor in other resources. They are particularly lacking in education for their people which makes them increasingly dependent on outside technical help to run their more modern economic structure.

In addition, these countries have increased their vulnerability in other ways. By being rich they have become a target for aggression by their less rich neighbors. They are more vulnerable to attack within by hostile minorities or an increasingly modernized military class newly outfitted with expensive and technologically advanced weapons. They also are subject to counterattack by the more industrialized countries should they push their advantage too much and try to bring down the economies of the industrialized world.

The Energy Problem and the Industrialized Countries

For the industrialized countries the new risks since the 1973 crisis are perhaps more apparent and immediate, given the very great dependence of every citizen on energy. These countries had taken for granted the continued availability of dependable supplies of cheap oil. Yet international events were fast weakening the foundation of this system. The first signs of increased risk were the founding of the Organization of Petroleum Exporting Countries and the initial price increases in 1971. This was shortly followed by the Middle East War of October, 1973, which resulted in the oil embargo by Arab oil exporting countries and the price increases in December, 1973, and January, 1974. By this time, the industrialized countries were highly dependent on cheap oil and especially on the supplies of the Arab countries.

The problems and the risks for the industrialized world were economic, political, and strategic. The economic risks were the possible dangerous impact on the global financial system which could result from serious balance of payments deficits of many key industrialized countries, especially the United Kingdom and Italy. Further, massive current-account surpluses of the oil exporting countries would also create serious capital outflows from all industrialized nations in huge amounts with the prospect that these surplus earnings would grow over time with increased consumption and higher prices. The possibility also existed that the reinvestment of these funds could disrupt the orderly functioning of capital markets, especially if such funds were used for political purposes. Finally there was and is still some fear that the oil exporting countries would use their investments in the capital markets of the industrialized countries in ways disruptive of the economic system of the latter countries.

The largest risk, however, is possible arbitrary cuts in oil supply and/or unreasonable or unpredictable increases in prices. So long dependent on imported petroleum, the industrialized countries have now become hostages to their own reckless dependence on ever increasing amounts of foreign oil. Indeed, despite the energy crisis and the oil embargo, many industrialized countries are more dependent on foreign oil than before. This is especially the case for the United States which, until recently, had been the world's largest producer of oil. Further, the United States has become even more vulnerable since its imports of Arab oil are increasing. Every day, for example, the United States imports 1.5 million barrels of Saudi Arabian crude oil, and by 1980 that figure is expected to reach 2.5 million.

There is, however, a very great difference in overall vulnerability to an oil embargo or increased prices among the industrialized countries. The United States is perhaps the strongest of all the key countries with its economic power, domestic energy resources, and technology. Certain other countries, such as Canada and Norway and the United Kingdom, are in a relatively favorable position because of domestic energy sources. Others are highly vulnerable and are likely to continue to be so, such as Italy and Japan, both of which import almost all their energy. Although Italy, in particular, is heavily dependent on Arab oil, almost all the other West European countries are similarly dependent.

Thus the political implications of the energy situation are massive.[15] The political leverage which exists in the OPEC countries is of major importance to the global balance of power. So long as most industrialized countries continue to be dependent on imported oil, especially Arab oil, they are and will be subject to political blackmail by these states on a wide range of issues. We see this already in the position of these countries vis-à-vis the Israeli-Arab conflict. Early European public support for Israel has been obviated by the European governments as they set new policies of appeasement of the Arab side at the expense of Israel. The reason is clear: in 1972 imports from the Middle East and North Africa were equal to almost 80 percent of petroleum consumption in Western Europe. By the same token, United States imports from the same area equaled only 5 percent of consumption.[16] The risks are very great for these countries. But because the risks are greater for them is no reason for American complacency, given mutual security ties through NATO and bilateral agreements and through interdependent economies. The resulting possibilities for political and economic instability in these "high vulnerability" countries cannot help but affect American security and stability. (For oil import figures, see Figure V-2.)

Finally, there is a strategic military aspect to the energy crisis for the industrialized countries, beyond the nonproliferation questions outlined elsewhere. Given such great vulnerability, can the countries of Western Europe and Japan be depended upon within an alliance if a few Arab countries can almost bring their economies to a halt within weeks by cutting them off from their principal supply of energy? Are not risks of conflict increased by such vulnerability? Is there not a danger that some countries might, under threat of boycott, consider military action as a way of solving the problem?

Together these elements have increased the degree of risk facing the industrialized world. The next question must be to what extent can this risk be minimized or even eliminated? Can countries individually or acting together in cooperation work to reduce their risks? Already some efforts have been made. These will be examined along with possible choices for the United States and the international community in assuring energy availability, economic stability, and risk reduction for all groups of countries. The leader of such an effort will probably be the United States. Its actions may well determine in large measure the degree and nature of the risks for all countries.

Figure V-2. Net oil imports in 1976 and projections for 1985 and 1990

Million barrels per day

	1976	1985	1990
Austria	0.2	0.3	0.3
Belgium	0.5	0.6	0.8
Canada	0.2	0.7	0.6
Denmark	0.3	0.2	0.2
Germany	2.6	3.0	3.1
Greece	0.2	0.3	0.4
Ireland	0.1	0.2	0.4
Italy	1.8	2.5	2.6
Japan	5.3	7.6	8.0
Luxembourg	—	—	—
Netherlands	0.5	1.0	1.0
New Zealand	0.1	0.1	0.1
Norway	(0.1)	(0.5)	(0.4)
Spain	0.9	1.0	1.0
Sweden	0.6	0.6	0.6
Switzerland	0.3	0.3	0.3
Turkey	0.2	0.6	0.8
United Kingdom	1.6	(0.5)	(0.1)
United States	7.0	11.4	13.9
TOTAL	22.3	29.4	33.6

— Less than 0.05 million barrels per day
( ) Figures are net oil export

Source: Submissions by IEA Member countries reported in *The OECD Observer*, No. 93, July 1978, p. 27.

AMERICA'S ROLE IN GLOBAL ENERGY

In today's modern world it is almost impossible to understand global energy problems apart from an analysis of the United States' role in the world's energy picture. The United States occupies a dominant position with respect to the globe's total consumption and exploitation of energy resources as well as research and development in energy technologies. The United States currently uses approximately 34 percent of the world's total energy. The average American citizen uses approximately nine times the amount of energy as a consumer elsewhere in the world. Further, until very recently, the United States was the largest producer of petroleum in the world. It still ranks as the second largest producer after the Soviet Union.

In 1973 the United States consumed approximately 75.6 quads of energy.[17] Breaking down the total 1973 United States demand we see that approximately 35.2 quads came from oil, 23.6 quads originated from gas, and 15.0 quads were obtained from coal. Only 2.9 quads came from hydro power while nuclear power provided just 0.9 quads. The United States itself produced only about 63.5 quads while it imported a total of 14.1. Actual net imports amounted to 12.1 quads since the United States exported about 2.0. Almost all of the United States imports consisted of oil or its by-products. Thus domestic consumption was 75.6 quads with 77.6 quads for total consumption plus exports.[18]

The United States further influences the total energy picture worldwide through its dominance in energy research and development. The United States maintains a preeminent position in fossil fuel research as well as in new energy technologies such as nuclear technology. It also is in the forefront in the technology of fusion reactors and is fast approaching being the most important researching country in the areas of unconventional energy know-how, such as solar systems.

As the world's preeminent industrial center and foremost military power, the United States provides, in large part, global leadership in the development of international energy cooperation and thus the shaping of international policies. No other single country has the wherewithal, the political unity, and the economic strength to carry out an essentially global energy policy. Further, as the world's most important importer of oil, it can greatly affect total supply and demand for this key energy resource. As the foremost country in reactor technology, in the associated technologies such as uranium separation, chemical reprocessing, and waste disposal, the United States leads in the medium-term alternatives to fossil fuels. Further, the United States has an almost inexhaustible supply of coal which can supply much of its energy needs, if required, for many generations. No other country in the world has a combination of these resources. On the other hand, it also has a great and indeed almost inexhaustible demand for additional energy. This examination of the United States energy picture illustrates how interdependent the world economy is and particularly how great an influence the United States has over the global economy. The choices the United States makes with respect to its own energy situation will greatly influence, for example, the amount of oil pollution that is found in our oceans, the extent and impact of nuclear proliferation on the world's security, and the rate of economic development of many countries.

During the 1950s and 1960s energy was relatively inexpensive and indeed its price was falling. Increasingly the industrial countries depended for their prosperity on the availability of cheap energy in the form of oil. There were few incentives for careful conservation of this depleting resource. Even in the late 1960s the United States was facing a situation of growing energy scarcity with respect to its own petroleum supplies. In 1968 the United States, for the first time, produced less oil than it consumed. Also in this early period little thought was given to the question of protecting the environment or the impact of pollution.

The combination of depleting domestic reserves, a growing economy, increasing dependence on foreign oil, and the need to develop high standards for clean air and water were important elements in the present energy crisis that we see today. Against this domestic background significant political and economic changes were also taking place in the international system which ultimately set forces at work to produce the energy crisis of 1973.

The present global and domestic energy crisis is a good example of the lack of consistent planning and perception of future trends on the part of our societal institutions. While some individual experts wrote about the problem a number of years ago, few governmental institutions, the mass media, or the society as a whole paid much attention, given the then abundance and low price of energy. Only with the oil embargo and the precipitous rise of oil prices in the fall of 1973 did the critical institutions of our society, particularly the government, perceive the nature of our problem and start to analyze new approaches and policies for a world of energy scarcity and high cost.

At that time, however, it was too late to change, over the short term, from a largely oil economy to the utilization of other forms of energy. It could still be well over a decade before significant United States energy demand is shifted from petroleum, especially imported oil, to other energy sources. Even the planned production of new domestic oil reserves such as in Alaska and offshore, while giving some relief, will not change our overall dependence on foreign oil. The United States will continue to risk a major energy shortage should Arab imports be cut abruptly.

Issues Before the United States

There is no doubt that the United States is now at a critical turning point in its decisions with respect to energy policy. These decisions will influence the style of life, environmental quality, and the availability of energy in the coming decades. But these decisions cannot be taken apart from the recognition of the interdependence between energy, the ecology, the world economy and the larger global political context.

In assessing any viable energy strategy we need to acknowledge that the age of cheap and abundant energy is largely at an end. Domestic United States production of petroleum and natural gas is inadequate to meet current needs, let alone those of its growing economy. Almost all forecasts indicate the United States is now and probably will be increasingly dependent upon imported oil. This will be the case unless very severe, indeed almost unparalleled, changes are made in the present course of United States energy policies and particularly actual practices. Over the last several years, despite clear warnings of the dangers of dependence upon foreign oil, United States imports have risen sharply. This has not only increased American dependence upon foreign oil, but has also added to the negative side of its balance of payments. Only the temporary availability of Alaska oil will provide a brief respite.

As an increasing proportion of energy needs are met by imports, this exposes the United States to significant national security dangers. Undoubtedly, this situation uncorrected will bring about increasing oil prices as the United States imports more and more along with other industrialized nations of the globe. There may also be a significant impact on long-term economic stability, flexibility with respect to foreign policy, and vulnerability to international blackmail. In this modern technological age industrial growth and activity—in short the basic health of the U.S. economy—remains highly dependent upon abundant energy supplies.

If this high dependence on foreign oil is an undesirable state, then the choices open to the United States are fairly clear. The only way to lessen this growing dependence is through a major program of energy conservation, development of alternative domestic traditional energy resources, and an increased expenditure by both the private and public sector on new alternative energy technologies.

The American economy, despite critics to the contrary, can generate the necessary capital required for major outlays of not only new production of energy, but also long-term research and development. This is particularly the case if we are to see the continued level of oil prices in the range of twelve to fifteen dollars per barrel. At these prices the domestic private sector could probably generate a considerable amount of revenues and profits for new energy investments. There is a danger, however, that the oil companies might siphon these profits off into other areas. The corollary or necessary prerequisite for continued high prices of oil must be the plowing back of the profits into energy research and development which ultimately will produce comparatively lower cost energy in the future. Indeed, a massive crash program of research and development in alternative energy technologies is very likely to result in future lower cost for energy compared to present high oil prices. But we cannot expect this particular result to take place within a short period of time given the very long lead-times necessary in developing new major energy systems with their concomitant sophisticated and often high-priced technology.

In addition to developing alternative energy resources for the long term, the only effective short-term method of obtaining energy security is the imposition of strong conservation measures. Such measures can reduce the demand for energy and can ultimately also stabilize prices and, in some circumstances, reduce them. There are a number of differing approaches which can result in the conservation of energy. One is to raise the price. This alone, in some cases, depending on elasticities, can reduce total demand. Another alternative is direct governmental regulatory measures. For example, the government can institute minimum insulation requirements in new housing. It also can mandate a minimum mileage per gallon for new automobiles.

In this complex world energy supply and demand affects other areas. It has an obvious impact on the domestic economy. It also has important effects on our environment. Separately, environmental protection measures, developed solely to increase the quality of life of all Americans, can have their own impact on energy production and conservation. However, environmental measures sometimes work in different directions. Some will increase the utilization of energy while others could decrease it. For example, the requirements for the elimination of particulate matter, of sulphur gases, etc., can increase the cost of electricity. On the other hand, good land planning, low polluting/high efficiency automobile engines, and proper siting of power plants will all reduce total energy costs.

The key choice for America (and for the rest of the world) is: should the United States continue to depend on foreign sources to meet an increasing portion of its energy requirements or should the United States adopt a policy of basic self-reliance? While there are a number of advocates of total energy independence, this is probably an unrealistic goal and one which could be ultimately self-defeating if value is given to preserving United States oil reserves for future generations and for valuable petrochemical uses.

Unfortunately, in developing its policies, the United States faces a number of unhappy trade-offs. It will be necessary to make some compromises with a number of differing goals which it must try to balance and reconcile. The following difficult goals would need to be integrated into an overall energy and environmental policy: 1) the establishment of adequate and secure supplies of petroleum and other energy sources; 2) maintenance of a reasonable and predictable price for petroleum; 3) maintenance of national security and international stability; 4) maintenance of viable and beneficial foreign relations; 5) efficient resource utilization; 6) the protection of environmental quality; 7) encouragement of free and effective competition; 8) encouragement of maximum investment in new domestic energy sources; 9) maximization of revenue to the Federal government; and 10) equitable allocation of energy among the competing uses so as to provide equity of price and availability to those sectors most needing the energy. Of the main medium-term objectives, an overarching one of domestic policy is the maintenance of an adequate supply of energy at a reasonable price.[19] These goals have not been listed in any specific order of importance. Indeed it would be impossible to do so since the relative magnitude of individual problems, their risk, or unique relationships could easily change overall priorities. This listing does illustrate how complex the factors are which must be taken into account in formulating and executing a reasonable and balanced energy policy.

A necessary part of the debate over energy policy involves fundamental political, social, and economic questions. For example, some make a case that the government should not intervene in the energy market. Within this overall non-interventionist viewpoint there is also an argument for continued reliance on imports. This viewpoint is often associated with those who would rely heavily on pure market forces. Many who share this view seek deregulation of the present energy industry. They argue that by the 1980s the world will still have a sizeable oil surplus which would make unnecessary a new and costly energy program. They assume that the high price of oil alone will restrict demand and give incentives for conservation. Some would also argue that dependence on foreign imports will enable us to preserve more of our own energy resources for future use.

The other side holds that these assumptions often are not backed by an objective assessment of the facts of the global energy market and, if proved wrong in either assumptions or analysis of future trends, would result in leaving the United States open to unpredictable, uncontrollable, and capricious forces with a possibly catastrophic impact on the American economy and overall security. We assumed in the 1960s a free market and a future of assured cheap imported energy. We were wrong. Thus it is argued that we learned by that lesson and should reduce our risks, including governmental intervention, to the extent reasonable and possible.

Those who support development of a domestic energy program, with minimal reliance on imports, give the following as their basic reasons:

—Heavy dependence on foreign oil supplies for an advanced technological society such as ours jeopardizes our national security and limits our foreign policy capabilities. It would make us more vulnerable to political/security leverage by other states, especially the Arabs.

—The United States balance of payments could be adversely affected by large oil imports.

—The United States economy would remain vulnerable to unforeseen and sudden price increases which could be disruptive of our economy.

—The very high cost of imported oil and even higher future prices at increased quantities will be greater than the long-run cost of developing our own domestic resources.

—Direct investment in new energy resources and research will provide a strong stimulus to the domestic economy and place us in the advance of new energy technologies.

—Continued dependence on oil will delay the introduction of new and cleaner renewable energy sources such as solar, as well as the development of technology for the better utilization of domestic fossil fuels, particularly coal gasification.

THE WORLD ENERGY MARKET
AND THE UNITED STATES

As we have seen the United States has more options in the energy field than almost any other country. Yet its vulnerability to external disruption in the supply of energy will continue for a number of years. The entire industrialized world will continue to pay increasingly higher and higher prices for imported oil. The prices will be set by OPEC, based on governmental action and not necessarily by market forces. The industrialized countries further are facing higher than normal levels of unemployment and are experiencing weakness in economic recovery partly due to growing oil deficits. The outflow of oil money has slowed down their economies, yet little of significance has been done by most countries, especially the United States, to lessen their vulnerability to the power of the OPEC states.

In 1973 the United States imported only 36 percent of its oil. From 1973 to 1975 the world economy was in a recession helped by increased oil prices and the earlier boycott. With increased economic activity in 1976 and 1977 the United States imported more than 40 percent of the oil that it consumed. In 1977 the United States reached a record import level of about 8.7 million barrels a day (b/d), most of it from OPEC. This has since declined as Alaskan North Slope oil has come into full production.

Further, the nature of the American dependence has also shifted since 1973. Canada in 1973 was the largest supplier of imported oil to the United States. It has cut back on its exports to this country, while OPEC shipments were up about 28 percent in 1977 from 1973 levels. Arab OPEC countries have increased their imports to us by about 85 percent. The Arab countries involved in the oil embargo supplied in 1977 around 18 percent of American oil consumption, as against 11 percent in 1973. Thus the United States dependence on foreign oil not only has increased but most of the increase has come from countries that are most likely to use their oil as political or strategic weapons.

The increased interdependence of the world's economy and its energy sources has been more widely recognized, given the experience of the past several years. Not only can the oil producers affect the growth of the world's economy by increasing prices but they can also destroy their own market. They have found that they are affected by the inflation of prices of the goods they import which can easily reduce the real economic benefit of increased oil prices. This awareness may have contributed to the fifteen-month freeze on oil prices starting in October, 1975, and lasting through 1976 and the freeze in late 1977 to 1978.[20]

With increased world economic activity in 1977 OPEC moved to increase its prices and it produced some 31 million barrels a day: some 2 million b/d below the peak production of 33 million barrels daily. It experienced new demands for oil, largely from the United States which did little towards conservation of energy demand. This demand helped create a new sellers' market worldwide. America's partners in the International Energy Agency were particularly critical of lack of action by the United States to stem oil demand, especially since the United States took the initiative to establish that organization as the consumers' forum to deal with the oil producers' cartel.

By late 1977 and early 1978 the combination of new oil from the North Sea and Alaska combined with a serious slowing of economic growth on the part of the industrialized world created a temporary surplus of oil which in turn resulted in cutbacks in production (28–29 million b/d) on the part of the OPEC countries. In part this resulted in an industrial recession accompanied, however, by continued inflation in the price of industrialized goods and an accelerated search for alternative energy sources and new conservation measures.

In the end, if effective energy conservation and new alternative energy sources are not developed, the United States will need to consider the possible advantages of a system of a special import tariff and/or a crude oil allotment program which would force the oil companies and others to import a declining amount of oil over time, and orient American purchases towards those countries which provide for price rebates and promise long-term guaranteed supply without political strings. Such a system might finally break the oil companies' present market role in which, with every increase in oil price, they make greater profits. This system provides no encouragement to keep prices down but indeed works against low prices. Breaking this perverse system will require increased governmental intervention into the global oil market, which is already dominated by Arab governments. The oil companies now have enormous incentives to collaborate with the producers to keep up prices and protect their investments. It is not impossible to construct a new system with incentives towards price reduction.

However, this cannot be done overnight. It would take, perhaps, new legislation and additional governmental funding to support such an interventionist policy. If adopted, it would need to be carried out in cooperation with other International Energy Agency (IEA) partners. It does not have to be done in any aggressive way against the oil producers, but rather as an action of self-defense and self-interest which could benefit the entire global system since it will ensure the strength and stability of its most productive and strongest political sectors.

In addition, action by the United States probably needs to include the revitalization of effective leadership within the International Energy Agency and with other consuming countries. Once massive conservation measures by the United States have started, other countries may regain their willingness to contribute to a global conservation program beyond the measures already taken. Increased American action in the development of alternative supplies will further demonstrate this country's determination not to be dependent on foreign imported oil. This will also assist other consumer countries. A key need is to turn around American oil production levels which fell in 1977 to a low of 8.2 million barrels a day from 9.2 million barrels a day in 1973. In 1978, the United States produced about 8.8 million barrels a day, the increase coming from Alaska.

We can expect American and world oil production to increase once Alaskan and North Sea oil fully reaches the market. It should continue to grow until about 1985-90. But many estimates foresee a decline in production levels by the turn of the century or earlier. Some hold that a new world scarcity could start as early as the 1980s. With increased development levels in the poorer countries, increased population and economic growth in the industrialized world, we could see an extraordinary increase in energy demand with prices pushed to exorbitant levels.[21] The only way to avoid this possibility as we have seen would be a worldwide program of conservation and stepped-up efforts to make available alternative energy sources.

While it is foolish for the United States to leave itself open to potential economic and political blackmail, the even more vulnerable European allies and Japan continue to be so dependent on Arab oil that they are in danger of separating themselves from American policy in the Middle East and in other areas. If economic recovery continues, these countries and the United States will largely depend on Saudi Arabian oil, since that is the only country that could increase crude oil production rapidly enough to meet the additional demand. Thus unless rapid action is taken to develop new alternative energy supplies most of the industrial world will be highly dependent on a single Arab country for its economic and even its national security well-being. There are many energy alternatives to oil, including coal and nuclear power. However, only one alternative provides safe, clean, and abundant energy over the long term. This is the energy that comes from the sun.

THE PROMISE OF SOLAR ENERGY

There is one energy technology that, on a global basis, holds the greatest promise for many countries: that is solar power. Its environmental costs are very low—it does not contribute to the global "heat sink," it is renewable, and plentiful. This makes it the one source of energy which, for the medium and longer term, can be said to be the preferred alternative energy source. For this reason a special analysis of this energy source from a global perspective is needed.

In evaluating solar energy, we should remember that all of our conventional energy sources—petroleum, coal, natural gas, water or tidal, and wind power—are just other forms of energy from the sun. For example, the sun's rays are the driving force of atmospheric circulation. The sun, through the photosynthesis process, forms all of our coal, oil, and even wood.

It will probably be nearly two decades before solar energy makes a significant impact on the world's need for energy. In general, geographic, technological, and economic factors now limit the wide-spread introduction of solar energy. However, should new and foreseeable technological breakthroughs take place, this situation could change in the near future.

The sun is a continuing, non-depletable and pollution-free source of energy. Over the long term, it represents one of the world's greatest hopes for an inexhaustible energy supply. Most of the current applications of this technology have focused on the use of sunlight for heating water, supplying heat for industrial processes, and for space heating in homes.

For the Third World, however, solar energy provides the greatest opportunities for effective utilization of sunlight. In the future, solar power could mean significant savings in these countries of expensive imported fuels. Solar stoves could replace the need for firewood, which is increasingly in short supply in developing countries. With respect to global energy needs, however, the total demand of the developing countries is far less than that of the industrialized countries.

The major problem impeding rapid introduction of solar energy is the high initial cost of the technology. The nature of solar energy (especially its intermittent characteristic) requires costly systems for energy collection and storage. However a number of factors have been at work with respect to improvements in technology and the cost and availability of conventional fuels to radically change the prospects for solar energy. Solar energy can be used in a number of ways such as solar pumps for water irrigation, as space and water heating, and for conversion to electricity.

Solar energy can be utilized to generate electric power either through the conversion of sunlight to heat or use of solar or photovoltaic cells. Largely as a result of the space programs of the United States and the Soviet Union we have pushed forward the technology for the development of the so-called silicon solar cells. These cells convert solar radiation directly into electricity. Generally, solar cells of all types have an efficiency of about 10–15 percent, with the silicon cells towards the upper levels. This efficiency ratio compares, for example, with a thermal generating plant's efficiency of about 30 percent, and nuclear power achieving rates up to 40 percent. Additional technological advances are required if the cost of solar electricity is to compete with conventional sources. Research is also being directed to developing special batteries for the storing of electricity and thereby overcoming the problem of the intermittent nature of solar radiation. A major breakthrough in solar cell efficiency could alter the prospects of this form of energy and thereby radically change the global energy picture over the longer run.

Economies of scale and new improvements in technology have brought down the cost of many forms of solar energy. For example, photovoltaic cell power (PVCs) until recently had cost about $11–12 per

watt peak (Wp) installed, compared with $200 in 1959.* The price for
PVCs in the United States has reached about $6 per Wp. A rough range
of recent estimates for PVC electricity has been between $1.00 to $3.00
per kwh. One application in a developing country (Tanzania) was
estimated at $1.43 per kwh.[22] The United States Department of Energy
looks to 1985 or earlier for prices in the range of 50¢ per watt peak or
about 12¢ per kwh. Others believe we can already obtain this level with
the use of cadmium sulfide cells developed by the French and others.
While there is some dispute about actual figures, clearly costs are
coming down rapidly. This price level is competitive for example with
electricity costs for many areas in Africa and elsewhere. At the same
time the cost of wind power (a form of solar energy) to generate
electricity or perform mechanical work has been reduced. At one time to
be economic this technology required an average wind speed of 18 miles
per hour while today it is only about 12 miles and probably will be
reduced further. Electricity from windmill generators at this speed
would cost less than 26¢ per kwh. Small-scale hydro power, a technology
that is old and obtainable "off the shelf," already is well below
comparable costs for oil-generated electricity.[23] Biomass generation
already is widely used in the Third World and can be supplied in many
countries at well below the equivalent energy cost of fossil fuels. (Often
the price will vary greatly, depending on remoteness, on whether the
power is subsidized, and on whether it is connected to an existing grid.)
We can expect fossil fuel and nuclear plant costs to increase over time.

The most significant fact about the potential use of solar energy in
the developing countries is that it appears to be moving on a downward
cost curve while conventional sources are in a generally upward-moving
cycle. Further, certain conventional energy sources do not typically take
into consideration many important external costs to society. Looking at
the comparative costs of energy on a global basis it is likely that global
petroleum scarcities, anticipated before the end of this century, will
make the development of safe, reliable, and economic alternatives to
petroleum fuels an urgent priority for all nations.

Looking at the larger global energy situation and its future
development there are important economic, technological, and political
factors which appear to support the argument for a greater expansion in

---

*Electricity prices are often quoted either as the cost of the installed capacity
(watt peak) or as operating costs as kilowatt-hours. In many developing countries
electricity costs are hard to determine since prices are subsidized by the
government.

the use of solar and other reasonable energy technologies. These include:

—Looking at the global market for solar energy we find many solar technologies (PVCs, solar-powered heat engines, wind generators, small hydro turbines and generators) are posed for cost reductions, some significantly, with the establishment of a market that will support mass-scale production.
—Another key factor is that energy costs are presently highest in remote rural areas of the Third World.
—Many developing countries, especially the poor tier, have natural advantages in the availability of most solar resources (insolation, hydro potential, and biomass) and in their relative lack of the massive petroleum-oriented infrastructures that characterize the industrial countries, which will allow them to avoid unnecessary dependence on depleting fossil fuel energy systems. This fact is especially true of rural areas of developing countries where little modern energy of any kind has yet been introduced, but where a majority of the world's population lives.

A new combined solar heating/electric generation system being developed by scientists at MIT could result in significant savings. One cost estimate holds that over a ten-year period with a $100 billion public investment enough such solar systems could be installed to provide 80 percent of required heat and a considerable fraction of the electric power in 75 percent or more of the single-family dwellings and all of the commercial establishments in the United States. At the end of ten years the fuel saved could be as much as 58 percent of our oil imports. The annual fuel saving would be about $21 billion. Therefore, the initial $100 billion investment could be paid back in five years.[24] One estimate is that by the year 2000, the United States could satisfy 17–20 percent of its total energy demands through solar power.

The total amount of energy which reaches the Earth from the sun is estimated to be about 750,000 million (7.5×10^{17}) kilowatt-hours of solar energy annually. As an example of how powerful the sun's energy is, only ten minutes of the sun's rays are equal to the total energy the entire world consumes in a year. Thus the total usable solar energy is far greater than that required by the present or foreseeable world's population. If the sun's rays were equally distributed throughout the world, it is theoretically possible for solar energy to replace all conventional sources of power.

The problem with solar energy has been that the total level of research over the last decade has been almost infinitesimal compared with research expenditures for conventional (i.e., oil) or nuclear energy. Part of the reason was its costs comparative to relatively cheap conventional fuels. Yet over the long run the sun's energy has far greater potential for many countries because of its renewability, low or nonexistent environmental effects, and its constant supply. As conventional fuels increase in price, more and more private and public funds will be directed towards the new solar technology. Undeniably even more probably should and can be done. So far, much of this research has been directed towards very specialized uses.

Solar energy research, unfortunately, has been given a very low priority in the past. For example, in the United States, fiscal year 1975's Federal budget for fission nuclear research amounted to $678 million; for fusion it was $174 million, for fossil fuel research it was $253 million, while solar research was $25 million. The year earlier it was only $9 million. For fiscal year 1978 it is estimated to be $389.2 million, a significant increase but still well below research and development for nuclear power.

While solar energy has different applications, it is only realistic to point out that it may be generations before the majority of our energy comes from direct solar energy. Solar energy, despite its very promising elements, is not the only answer to the world's increasing needs for economic energy. Some energy experts believe that even in a country well suited for the use of solar energy, such as Australia, only some 15 percent of that country's total energy needs will come from solar power by the year 2000.[25]

Inherent Advantages

The most important advantage of solar energy is that it can avoid the worst type of pollution of the world's ecology. It is available in abundance and is especially useful therefore in areas poor in other forms of energy. With the use of small household or village devices, there is no need for expensive networks of high-tension transmission lines. It also is a cost free source of energy once the (now relatively high cost) initial capital investment is made. Further, maintenance costs are very low compared with most other energy sources. In addition, smaller units can be employed and used even for individuals and they can be made in portable forms. Finally, they hold special promise for the developing world since they can preserve scarce foreign exchange spent on the importation of oil and they can be adapted for use in villages for heating, water pumping, and even electricity production.

It is obvious that countries need to concentrate a far greater proportion of their resources, knowledge, and money towards renewable and environmentally safer energy sources than has been the case. It is the only solution over the long run, and the earlier we reach this goal the better. For the present not only direct solar power, but also geothermal, wind, fusion, and ocean power sources must be expanded rapidly for the development, environmental protection, and security of the entire global community.[26]

TOWARDS A GLOBAL ENERGY STRATEGY: INTERNATIONAL ENERGY COOPERATION

The energy crisis poses a fundamental challenge to the capabilities of nations and their international institutions to meet the security, the technological, and the economic risks of our age. The energy crisis has an impact on employment and on economic growth in many countries, both rich and poor. It has caused serious dislocations in developed and developing countries. Just as the industrialized countries are vulnerable to increases in oil prices, so are the poorer developing countries of the world. Most countries—rich and poor—are far more dependent on oil imports than the United States. These countries have a strong interest in cooperation with each other to overcome their common vulnerability.

No individual country can, even through conservation and the creation of additional alternative resources, create a new balance in the world petroleum market. Further, no country alone can successfully defend itself against a new embargo or massive shifts in petro dollars. No single country can carry out all the research and development and invest the necessary capital required to put in place new energy sources to substitute for fossil fuels when they are finally exhausted.

It is clear that the industrial countries have suffered from their failure to restore competitive conditions in the global petroleum market. A degree of national freedom has, in fact, been permanently lost. There is always now the danger that the industrial countries could be split from one another as other countries with rich petroleum reserves offer or threaten to use those resources for strategic or political ends.

Because of the 1973 energy crisis the United States was first moved to convene the Washington Energy Conference in February of 1974. From this meeting, an agenda of cooperative action among the key industrialized oil-consuming countries was developed which finally led to the formation in November, 1974, of the International Energy Agency (IEA). The main objectives of the IEA are:

—To provide security against a new oil embargo by a cooperative program to build oil stocks and to share available petroleum in an emergency;
—To share equitably among industrialized countries the burden of energy conservation; and

—To coordinate cooperative measures to stimulate development of alternative energy sources.

Since the forming of the International Energy Agency, a program of emergency cooperation and planning has been initiated. On the basis of a detailed agreement the IEA has the necessary planning and machinery in a state of readiness which could be activated if we are confronted with a new embargo situation. Each country, in order to make this effective, would need to have the authority to implement quick-acting conservation measures on a coordinated emergency basis and to raise emergency oil stocks in all countries from the present minimum of sixty days of imports to an agreed-level of ninety days. Both emergency conservation powers and more storage are necessary for any effective response to a new embargo.

Conservation also is an important element in international cooperation. While it is sometimes painful and costly to restrain demand for oil, it is a matter of long-term planning and defensive politics to do so. Unless the industrialized countries join together in such an effort, it will be impossible to moderate market conditions.

The other members of the IEA have already taken action to decrease oil demand by passing through increased crude oil costs to the end user, by new taxation, or by such specific conservation measures as fuel switching and lighting and heating regulations. The United States, on the other hand, has lagged behind in this conservation effort. Here we see how greatly the success of an international effort depends on the success of domestic action and policy of individual states.

In addition to conservation, the third major goal is the development of alternative resources. While basic actions to stimulate the development of new energy resources must primarily be national, there are also important contributions which can be made internationally. One example is by finding ways to cooperate in energy research and development. It is clear that no country has a monopoly on scientific knowledge and technological innovation. Even the United States cannot, by itself, do all that is necessary to bring new energy technology to fruition. Further, much can be gained by avoiding duplication through the sharing of costs and scientific cross-fertilization. We can also add to our energy resources through the flow of foreign capital to areas of new energy development, where it is needed most and where the supplies would be available without restriction to the consumer countries.

Looking at the oil market structure over the last few years we have seen that the world economic slowdown has resulted in a temporary oil surplus while the OPEC countries themselves have decreased their output of oil in order to assure high prices. In May, 1976, OPEC produced 27 million barrels daily as against 32.8 million barrels in September of 1973 just before the energy crisis. Despite the soft market, over the last several years, the OPEC price structure has come through largely intact despite some efforts to undercut the agreed-upon price through quality differentials or the lengthening of credit terms. The decision of OPEC in December, 1976, to raise prices, but with a split between Saudi Arabia and the United Arab Emirates and the other member states on how much, reflects both the pressures of increasing demand for more oil stimulated by economic recovery and the intervention of political goals on the price decision.

Overall, the decision resulted in an increase of about 8 or 9 percent over 1976 prices.

In the early '80s prices, if left to market forces, could fall as North Sea, Alaskan, Mexican, and perhaps Chinese oil comes into the market in very large quantities. On the other hand in the long term with population increase and future economic resurgence, demand will firm and we could see a quickening of activities which will lead to the inevitable increase in oil prices on the part of OPEC. In the absence of serious conservation measures or the availability of alternative sources the OPEC countries can probably raise considerably the price of oil.

Looking at the OPEC countries, we see great differences among them. Some are rich and have large monetary reserves, such as Saudi Arabia and some of the Gulf states. On the other hand, some of the OPEC countries have already gone into balance of payment deficit positions starting in 1975. Algeria is already in deficit and so is Libya. And Venezuela and Iran are shortly approaching that limit. Thus the pressures will intensify within OPEC as their market shrinks, and when most other producers except for Saudi Arabia and Kuwait go into balance of payments deficit. Also some of these countries will be seeing their oil reserves shrink.

The industrial (IEA) countries' best strategy under those circumstances would be to first develop a 4-million barrel conservation program in order both to intensify the pressures on the OPEC cartel and to lower energy costs. Yet, it is not certain by any means that such a conservation program would suffice to bring prices down. In order to put sufficient pressure on the OPEC market for them to lower prices in response to reduced demand, consumer countries would have to compress or lower the OPEC market to somewhat over 20 million barrels daily. This can only be done within the next decade by large-scale development of new energy resources, including development within the United States and elsewhere of fossil fuels. To achieve this goal, the United States would have to import at a level of only 3 to 5 million barrels daily in the mid-1980s. This is unlikely to take place without large new energy investments.

While the industrialized countries will need to work together in order to establish a firm bargaining position, it is also necessary for the consuming countries to reach out to the developing countries to see whether a cooperative energy program might be possible. Several efforts in the past have already been made to establish a multilateral energy dialogue. In May, 1975, former Secretary of State Kissinger proposed a new approach, the launching of a dialogue between producers and consumers and broadening it to include a whole range of relations between the industrialized and developing countries. This effort was called the Conference on International Economic Cooperation or CIEC. But it did not result in much progress. In the future the international community will need to create some global mechanism for meaningful cooperation between the rich and poor consumer countries and the OPEC and other oil producers. Such a forum would seek solutions to global energy needs that are fair to all sides.

Yet a point might come when each group of countries believes that its major goals cannot be achieved either through confrontation on the one side or narrow nationalistic action on the other. At this point, they might be moved to realize that only through a truly global approach can their national and regional problems be solved. We are still far away from that era of global cooperation and we are just building instead the prerequisites for approaching the negotiating table. It is very difficult to achieve a lasting solution until both sides realize that they alone cannot dictate their own solution at the expense of another group. At the moment, the consuming countries are particularly vulnerable and the producers feel a sense of power. This will change, but not to a point where the consumers will be able to dictate terms of surrender to the producers. We should make a major effort to come to some kind of global bargain between these groups of countries unless we wish to see a constant struggle, with one group or another always seeking supremacy rather than a mutual accommodation.

Going beyond the short term the international community must see energy as part of a large global economic structure in which all countries are interdependent. Energy also is only one factor in this larger picture along with minerals, agricultural production, and technology. As it would be foolish for the United States to use its dominant agricultural production as a major tool of its political or security interests, it is dangerous for other countries to use their resources in the same narrow way. The end result is inevitably conflict rather than cooperation and mutual benefit.

In examining the future energy market we can only come to the conclusion that oil cannot play the same dominant role in the future that it plays today. This can be seen simply by noting that beyond the year 2000, synthetic fuels from coal, solar power, and perhaps fusion power will probably be the favored and predominant sources for the world's energy needs. This means that oil-rich Arab countries, in forcing up the price of oil, probably are hastening the replacement of oil as the main energy source and thereby decreasing their own leverage.

Another factor which the global community must consider is the relative long-term worth of crude oil. By burning for energy production large amounts of petroleum in this generation we are foreclosing the use by the oncoming generations of much of this valuable feedstock needed in the petrochemical industry. The burning of this declining and finite resource is probably wasteful when looked upon from a long-term perspective. Already some world leaders have recognized this fundamental fact. (The Shah of Iran, among others, believes we should use other sources of energy such as nuclear since oil is too valuable just to be burned.) This is but one example of how we have not yet factored long-term global considerations and values into our still nationalistic and short-term decision-making perspective. Neither OPEC nor IEA has developed a management plan for the rational use of energy on a global scale. These organizations and their member countries are still responding to their own crisis of the moment rather than the common energy dilemma which the follow-on generations in all parts of the world will face.

To move from risk reduction to contributing towards global well-being requires not just cooperation of the industrialized countries but also those of the newly rich oil producers and the population-laden countries of the Third and so-called "Fourth World." Unless countries rich in technology and certain newer energy sources can work together with countries rich in new surplus monetary reserves from oil exports, there is a good chance that both groups will face alone increasing economic problems. What good will empty oil reserves do the oil producers beyond the year 2000 unless the money can be invested to produce goods and services for future generations? What safety is there for the industrialized countries if the world is filled with nations seeking nuclear technology for both peaceful and military purposes? How much better both groups would be if the poorer countries could obtain low cost electricity and energy for their development purposes so that they could contribute to the growth of global trade which benefits all groups of nations.

It is clear that we have now or will have very shortly the technology to create a globe of energy abundance. There is no physical or resource reason why our world cannot ensure that by the end of this century almost every household, no matter how poor, has access to electricity and the many benefits that it brings. To meet this goal requires expanding the use and development of energy resources that already exist in the developing world. Further, the industrialized countries will need to provide the necessary energy technology on a massive scale if the shared risks of a world of energy imbalances are not to bring serious dangers to all. We have already noted the increased danger of the spread of nuclear weapons along with a very large proportion of the world's population continuing in a state of poverty and social unrest. A "technological fix" in energy will not solve our problems, but without the wise application of available technology, it is unlikely that many of our needs will be met. Even if they are, it will be with application of technological fixes which only increase our risks.

The capability of the globe to carry out a program of widespread and safe energy abundance exists but the forces working against such a course of action are formidable. Rampant nationalism, economic distress, poor communications, and narrow or short-term perceptions of interest all conspire against the necessary decisions and commitments of resources which could accomplish a significant sharing of energy on a worldwide scale. Perhaps, again, the moving force must be some deepening crisis or terrible event which can force men and nations to reappraise their interests. This could set the stage for a transformation of resources and institutions towards solving common problems.

CHAPTER VI

Mass Destruction Risks-Nuclear Weapons Proliferation and Terrorism

Introduction

One of the most salient characteristics of our modern age is the possibility—indeed even the likelihood—of the use of modern technology for purposes of mass destruction. By now, we are all familiar with the nuclear balance of terror which exists between the United States and the Soviet Union. It has been, perhaps, the most distinguishing and at the same time most frightening accompanying condition of the generation which has grown up since World War II. In more recent times the inherent horror of this "mutually assured destruction" situation has been somewhat muted by the acknowledgment on both sides that the employment of nuclear weapons by either side would amount to instant suicide for all. There has been some comfort in the recognition of this mutual assurance and in the implicit assumption that both sides will act in a rational way. But the problem with this assumption is that we are living in a different world from the simple bipolar nuclear weapon state situation. Indeed the recent trend has been away from this relatively simple world and towards a far more dangerous condition in which the proliferation of nuclear and other weapons of mass destruction seem to bring mankind closer and closer to ultimate catastrophe.

Along with this trend towards the proliferation of nuclear weapons, which is part and parcel of the spread of technology throughout the world—for good and evil purposes—is a similar trend towards the use of the new technology and its weapons by-products to carry out acts of terrorism. While terrorism can be carried out by legitimate governments it has become more and more the method of choice among elements of the world's disaffected peoples. The possession and use of sophisticated technology increase the ability of the weak to appear strong and able to humble the powerful. The spread of terrorism and its use of such technology will become more and more an uneasy part of life in the last quarter of the twentieth century.

Nuclear Weapons Proliferation

Until 1974 the world had only five nuclear weapon states; all of these were highly industrialized and relatively "responsible" about the control exercised over nuclear weapons. Further, there was some hope that the Nuclear Non-Proliferation Treaty (NPT) would be able to halt, in large measure, the spread of weapons beyond these limited powers. With the growth in détente between the two super powers there was even some hope that the existing weapons states themselves might increasingly limit the total amount of such weapons deployed and thus slowly bring about effective arms control and movement towards disarmament.

India's nuclear explosion in May, 1974, signaled the most serious breach in the wall that heretofore had prevented the spread of nuclear weapons beyond the members of the United Nations Security Council and moved this problem into the strife and conflict of the Third World. Beyond the symbolism of this event and the impetus it gives to other developing and developed countries to follow in the Indian path, there is the growth and spread of nuclear power plants and their accompanying associated technology, a growth accelerated by the worldwide energy crisis and the relatively high price of oil.

The increased use of nuclear energy and the spread of fissionable material will bring new dangers for the decades ahead. Here again we see how technology has become the master of man's fate by a combination of unforeseen changes in global politics and the seemingly inexorable march of modern technology. The desire of many countries to obtain energy independence from imported, high-priced oil, their general wish to be modern through the use of the latest technology, and the temptation to enter big power politics are all working towards a world in which there will be literally dozens of nations with nuclear weapons.

As a result of the proliferation of nuclear weapons among states there is an important and dangerous side effect—namely the increased possibility of these weapons falling into the hands of terrorists. This problem will be discussed in more detail later, but suffice to say here that the consequent instability and insecurity for the global system has a profound impact upon the way individuals view their long-term security and well-being. The possession of nuclear weapons by terrorist or criminal groups is the one contingency that no government has fully faced up to or prepared for effectively.

We have already noted that the use of nuclear energy accelerated as a result of the energy crisis. The larger political and economic aspects of this crisis have been discussed in the preceding chapter. Here we will concentrate on the potential of nuclear technology to create a world in which madmen can blackmail nations by the threat to obliterate cities. In order to cope with such problems in the coming decades, the world must understand some of the basic elements of nuclear power and how its associated technology is so closely related to the capability of building a nuclear explosive device or weapon.

The majority of nuclear reactors (light-water types) now use uranium enriched with U-235, the fissionable isotope from which weapons can be made. However, the quality of enrichment is to a maximum of about 3.5 percent which is well below the percentage needed for weapons-grade material. Therefore, by itself, the existence of this low quality material in many reactors does not constitute a major threat should it be diverted to terrorists or secret government use. What is a threat is the capability of terrorists or governments to further enrich this material up to weapons-grade or to have the capability of extracting plutonium (also a material from which nuclear weapons can be made) from spent nuclear reactor fuel. There are also certain reactors (mostly gas cooled) which require a higher level of enrichment for efficient operation, and another category of new nuclear reactors (fast breeders) which produce an even larger amount of fissionable plutonium. These types are more dangerous but they also have some advantages with regard to the provision of energy.

The enrichment process, an associated technology of the nuclear power industry, is the key which transforms basically normal natural uranium into enriched uranium with a higher percentage of U-235. Basically the enrichment objective, regardless of the different technologies available, is to increase the concentration of fissionable U-235 in natural uranium (which is mostly nonfissionable U-238), for use either in nuclear reactors or weapons. Only two enrichment methods have proven economical: the most important and oldest is gaseous diffusion, the more recently developed process is the gas centrifuge. The gaseous diffusion process requires very complex technology and engineering skill and large power supplies—all very costly. This technology has been limited to a very few major industrialized nations which also have been, until recently, nuclear-weapons countries. The gas centrifuge process was developed mostly in Europe and to some extent in the United States and the Soviet Union. It is now reaching a commercial stage and is largely favored by a multinational European group called EURENCO which includes Holland, Germany, and Great Britain.

There is another new technology called the nozzle or aerodynamic process which is being developed privately in West Germany. This is believed to be the basic approach used by South Africa to develop independently their own enrichment facilities and eventually to have the entire package of nuclear fuel and power facilities. The nozzle process could prove to be economically competitive but above all it is technologically simpler than either gaseous diffusion or gas centrifuge and thus more attractive to smaller or less developed countries (and potentially to private groups) that might want to manufacture nuclear weapons for use in terrorism or criminal acts.[1] The process, however, does consume very large amounts of electric power (twice as much as gaseous diffusion and twenty times that of an equivalent gas centrifuge plant) which means it would be most attractive to countries with cheap electric power. Brazil and South Africa would be in this category, for example. This technology was first invented by Erwin-Willy Becker at the Karlsruhe Nuclear Research Center and is being developed by the West German firm of STEAG, AG in Essen. There also are reports of discussions going on for international cooperation to develop the separation nozzle process.[2]

The mere existence of such enrichment facilities creates additional dangers for proliferation of weapons-grade materials and their diversion. This peril could increase with the discovery of some new and even more simplified method. There have been some reports that a laser technique could be applied to this process but little is known about its efficiency, and its application on a large scale may only be in the very distant future. Nevertheless the possibility that some private group or small country could clandestinely build an enrichment plant and manufacture the resulting material into weapons is a possibility the world community must take seriously in the next decade and deal with as a question of great moment.[3]

The other most dangerous technology associated with nuclear power is fuel reprocessing and fabrication. This is a process in which spent fuel, which is still largely U-238 but with reduced amounts of U-235 and containing significant quantities of weapons-grade plutonium, is utilized. Such a spent fuel, however, is highly radioactive and it is difficult to handle. The spent fuel from the reactor requires treatment in special reprocessing plants to extract the vital and dangerous plutonium. The separation of the uranium from the plutonium is not technically difficult but there are some real dangers due to the highly radioactive waste residue. This requires special remote control and shielded facilities. Such reprocessing facilities are expensive but this technology is far easier to obtain than building an enrichment plant. A country desiring to build weapons from spent fuel with waste plutonium from its reactors must have a fuel reprocessing facility.

There are a number of nonnuclear weapons states which have built such reprocessing facilities while other countries have plans to build plants in the near future. For example, India took spent fuel from a Canadian-supplied research reactor and built a small chemical reprocessing facility which extracted the necessary plutonium for its nuclear weapons. This reactor, unfortunately, was not under International Atomic Energy Agency (IAEA) safeguards, and Canada was unable to stop the diversion to explosive use of the plutonium resulting from the use of the reactor.

While much of the spent fuel from reactors is not now reprocessed into new fuel using plutonium as a key energy generating element, there have been studies looking towards this eventuality. If utilization of this waste plutonium becomes feasible, it could lead to a vast expansion of reprocessing facilities. So far only a small number of new fuel bundles have been manufactured using mixtures of recycled plutonium and uranium. and these have been largely for demonstration purposes.[4]

The real problem with reprocessing plants is that they present the most dangerous phase in the entire fuel cycle where there is the greatest potential for diversion. The International Atomic Energy Agency, which has responsibility under the Non-Proliferation Treaty for inspecting nuclear facilities for possible diversion of nuclear materials, concentrates much of its inspection force, its energy, and time to the reprocessing phase, especially when large quantities of plutonium or highly enriched uranium are being processed. The other phases of the fuel cycle offer fewer opportunities for diversion, especially during the operation of the reactor itself or in the earlier fuel fabrication phase when the uranium is formed into pellets and placed in tubing to form the final fuel assemblies used in reactors. At this stage the uranium cannot be separated easily between the fissionable U-235 and other types of uranium nuclei.

One additional hazard is that of possible loss of fissionable material through hijacking as it is being transported. This is not a major problem at present since spent fuel from reactors is very dangerous to handle due to radioactivity and is shipped in very large casks (some 30–100 tons). In the future there might be greater problems in transportation of materials if the number of gas-cooled reactors using highly enriched uranium increase, if plutonium recycling is widely utilized, or if the fast breeder reactor becomes a common technology.

It is this last problem which poses serious questions for the entire global community as choices are made about the form future energy supplies will take. The most advanced countries with research programs in the fast breeder area must make a most significant decision about the degree of commitment to a reactor type with both nuclear weapons proliferation problems and a number of environmental difficulties. Yet the problem of providing sufficient energy for the world's growing population and economy must be faced up to and the various trade-offs seriously examined, especially the external costs of proliferation of weapons and potential environmental contamination.

Some experts believe that the nuclear fission fast breeder reactor represents the best technology for significant increases in the world's energy in the period 1985–2000 until alternative technology such as fusion or solar energy becomes practical. However, as we have noted, the fast breeder reactor has many serious difficulties including diversion of fissile material, accidents, waste disposal, reactor safety, and routine radioactive emissions.[5]

One characteristic of the plutonium-based liquid metal fast breeder reactor (LMFBR) is that it breeds its own fuel by producing additional plutonium as it generates power. This leads to an almost inexhaustible fuel supply but it also produces huge amounts of fissionable material in the form of plutonium. This plutonium 239, a by-product of the fast breeder, has a half-life of some 24,000 years. Further, one must understand that it takes only about five to ten kilograms to build a bomb. Estimates have been made that one day we might have from 400 to 20,000 breeders, each producing very large quantities of radioactive fission products.[6] These high estimates may be unrealistic since they are based upon a world population level of 15–20 billion people. However, even given the low assumption, the amounts of plutonim in inventory or in shipment would be very large, with all the implications for accidents, clandestine diversions, and bookkeeping errors. We must ask if increased energy to fulfill man's needs is indeed worth the inherent dangers of this most imperfect technology just on security grounds, let alone the other accompanying problems.

The immediate question is whether we can identify methods by which this intrinsically dangerous technology can be lived with until other forms of energy are available. The response probably would be that we could formulate a system in which we could live in relative safety with the breeder reactor, but this presupposes so many drastic changes in how we use, control, and administer this technology, along with adjustment to changes in our national and international institutions, that it is highly unlikely a really safe method could be found. It would require a system of multinational nuclear centers under strong internal and IAEA safeguards with associated reprocessing chemical plants all needing specialized siting in very safe areas free, for example, from either earthquakes or civil strife. Perhaps they might be sited in the oceans. This would provide a number of advantages including a heat sink and an easily identified international area which would not be under the control of any single country. But there is also the problem of the long life of the radioactive waste which results from these reactors. How can we develop institutions which will look after huge amounts of very dangerous plutonium and other radioactive products with a half-life of centuries? We have not to this date found any method which completely and satisfactorily deals with radioactive waste disposal.

Given these difficulties we should ask ourselves again whether we really must go down the fast breeder path. If we decide, even partially, to do so we must be prepared to go to extraordinary lengths to ensure global safety from every viewpoint until less dangerous technologies become feasible. We would need to agree in advance that very rigid controls will be put over this technology and that it will be eventually phased out. Further these reactors should probably not be given to any nation or private body to own or completely control. One possibility is that they could be owned and operated by an independent competent international body possibly related to IAEA and under its safeguards. But to move to this solution will require more than a decision by the United States since fast breeder technology is not an American monopoly.

One of the key questions for our global political system over the next decade or two will be the extent to which the proliferation of nuclear weapons will be furthered by the specific action of those few countries which already have the necessary nuclear know-how and are now looking to other nations to sell such technology at a profit. This technology includes the already mentioned power reactors and enrichment plants, and a whole list of so-called trigger items which are required for a nation desiring to develop its own nuclear weapons capability. It is clear that without some kind of self-regulation or internationally agreed-upon guidelines among the exporters of nuclear technology, including stringent safeguards and international inspection, there will be a rapid spread of atomic weapons.

There are now about eight or nine countries able to export nuclear power technology. They include the United States, Great Britain, the Soviet Union, France, Canada, West Germany, Japan, and Italy. These and a few other countries have the ability to either speed up or slow down the proliferation of weapons. If they can cooperate and develop strict basic rules for the control of all nuclear technology and materials sold to other nations, there is some hope we can buy some time and perhaps find newer and better ways to limit weapons proliferation and obtain needed energy.

Perhaps the greatest danger is the effort of some countries to buy, for themselves, a whole nuclear package of technology including reactor, enrichment plant, and chemical reprocessing facilities. This kind of package, in addition to giving a country an independent nuclear power capability (especially if it has natural uranium of its own), gives it a full weapons capability at the same time.[7] More deals such as the one between Brazil and Germany may be in the offing if urgent action is not taken. The Shah of Iran has indicated that if twenty or thirty "silly, ridiculous little countries try to develop it [nuclear capability] what is going to happen? Will I have to revise my policy? They are talking about it. Even Libya is trying to manufacture or get an atomic bomb, God knows for what purpose."[8]

Nuclear plants can be purchased from a number of countries and from a number of firms. Already there are some 430 reactors planned or operating in about thirty-eight nations outside of the United States. Many more will be built over the next two decades and this spread of nuclear technology will largely take place without truly adequate international control despite the NPT and IAEA safeguards. There are already about 50 to 80 nuclear plants of a million kilowatts each planned and coming up for bids around the world over the next five or so years. Many of these countries will want not only the power reactor but also a whole nuclear package. This factor only strengthens the absolute need for close cooperation among the supplier countries.

Already far too many critical countries have not signed the NPT but have made efforts to develop their own nuclear technology capabilities. Iran, for example, a non-signatory to the NPT, with delusions of great power grandeur, is seeking from a number of countries a national nuclear technology capability to replace its fast-depleting oil reserves. France, also not an NPT signer, is likely to be a major supplier.[9] Argentina is another country seeking a nuclear capability that has not signed the NPT. Some thirty-six or more United Nations members have failed to sign the NPT and a number who have signed have failed to ratify. One major problem is the question of competition between countries which contributes to a sense of increased momentum or escalation. The fact that Brazil seeks a nuclear capacity speeds Argentina towards its own nuclear efforts. Further, while a nation initially may have no intention of acquiring nuclear weapons, it could eventually conclude that it is forced to do so by the actions of others. The maintenance of international stability in such a context would be incalculably hard and dangerous. For each local or regional conflict the risks would be much greater than ever before with possible tragedy for all mankind a result.

Another danger is that some signatories of the NPT might break the treaty or abrogate it. The penalties are rather mild sanctions by the IAEA, such as expelling a member and finally calling violations to the attention of the United Nations Security Council. Basically the IAEA can only warn the world community of some act of evasion or diversion of bomb material. This can, itself, discourage some diversion from taking place, but it cannot prevent it. Thus, there is some danger that the NPT might be weakened or breached over time through the increase of new nuclear weapons states, the foolish exporting of dangerous technology to nations which really intend to use it for weapons purposes, and finally, due to lack of progress towards arms control and disarmament, by existing nuclear weapons states.

Each one of these elements could help to plunge our Earth into a very dangerous situation of nuclear anarchy. Increased tension in the Third World could also prompt some countries in this area to start a nuclear weapons program or at least start building the necessary technological infrastructure so that weapons could eventually result from an ostensibly civilian power program. This is what happened in the Indian situation. Despite the fact that India said its device was developed only for peaceful purposes most other countries now assume a weapons capability on the part of India and this event will probably demonstrate to others the advantages of imitating India in this respect.[10]

If the manufacturers of nuclear power plants and associated technology are too eager to sell this equipment, the proliferation problem will grow and pose a major threat, through commercial competition, to the integrity of the Non-Proliferation Treaty. The Europeans, in particular, seem most bent on selling their technology without truly adequate conditions or safeguards. But it is also vital that other countries, particularly the United States and the Soviet Union, take a strong stand on the sale of their technology. The United States especially should make clear to its industry that foreign sales are in a very special category and relate to vital national security concerns. Sometimes firms put pressure on the American government to permit sales abroad when they may not be in our national interests.[11]

Peaceful Nuclear Explosions (PNEs)

One additional factor in the overall nuclear weapons proliferation problem area is so-called Peaceful Nuclear Explosions (PNEs). These devices, which are indistinguishable from weapons except for their supposed peaceful use, more often than not constitute an excuse for nonnuclear weapon states to justify acquiring nuclear weapons without publicly admitting their real purpose.

India justified its nuclear explosion program on the basis that it would contribute to its development projects. Yet these PNEs are known to be largely too expensive and dangerous for their intended purposes. The United States has studied PNEs carefully and has found them to be not cost-effective and also liable to create increased atmospheric exposure to radioactivity, which is banned under the existing partial test ban treaties. There are, however, provisions in the NPT for the use of PNEs, supplied by the original nuclear weapons states to nonnuclear weapons states when their use is required for peaceful purposes and when there is assurance that the devices will not be used for military purposes. In fact, however, the inherent dangers of PNEs are such that there is little justification for their use given the almost impossible difficulties they present in keeping the lid on testing of weapons and further proliferation.[12]

The main uses for which PNEs might be justified are: (1) creating underground storage caverns for natural gas and oil; (2) preparing oil shale for *in situ* retorting; (3) stimulating the flow of natural gas on tight rock formations; (4) excavating canals and diversion of rivers. The American government has spent about $160 million on PNE experiments, most of it on earth-moving or cratering work with the rest aimed at stimulating the flow of natural gas. Recently, United States interest in the PNE program has fallen to a low level and no new tests are being planned.[13]

PNEs also have a negative influence on moves towards a comprehensive test ban treaty which would cover explosions not now limited in the existing partial test ban agreements. Thus, PNEs militate against broader acceptance of the NPT. Such countries as Argentina, Brazil, and already cited India have justified their nonadherence to the NPT on the basis of the potential usefulness of PNEs. There are a number of possible approaches which might solve this continuing problem. One would be to have the IAEA carry out a long-term study of the usefulness and application of PNEs, with the clear implication that the study would show that they are more a problem than a solution, especially if the world moves towards a comprehensive test ban treaty. As we have noted the United States already has largely lost faith in PNEs but the Soviet Union still is divided on this question. Clearly, however, the Soviets will eventually see the wisdom of banning the use of PNEs and realize their larger impact on weapons proliferation.[14]

One other alternative beyond the present possibility of nuclear weapon states providing PNE services to nonnuclear weapon states is the creation of a mechanism for the international control and use of such devices should they ever prove, in fact, useful. By giving exclusive use and control of PNEs over to an international body, most appropriately the IAEA, a number of problems contributing to the trend towards proliferation could be eased. As noted, present PNE services are now theoretically available from nuclear-weapon states through the cooperation of the IAEA, but in fact they are largely controlled by those states and not by the United Nations or IAEA. There have been a number of proposals for the internationalization of PNEs and there is some merit in a careful examination of this concept. While some skeptics of this concept call it giving a bomb to the United Nations, this is not necessarily the case given man's ingenuity in devising appropriate checks and balances in institutions, as well as in applying modern technology to ensure against accidental or other illegal uses.[15] Control, for example, over an international PNE services organization could be exercised through a board of nuclear weapon states and nonnuclear weapon states working together to make decisions about the policy and use of PNEs in specific cases. Through the intelligent application of security and institutional precautions the provision and exclusive control of PNEs through an appropriate United Nations body could be far less dangerous than the continued spread of nuclear weapon states, which now justify their views and behavior on the basis of developing a national PNE capability. These states now claim that begging the great powers for PNE services is demeaning, but they would not, at least, have this excuse if such service could be primarily provided through a United Nations body. Again a competent, well-controlled and dedicated United Nations body is probably far safer with some access to PNEs under restricted circumstances than are a dozen small countries, each with internal stability problems, regional and local conflicts with other states, and each with only a rudimentary ability to provide control and security over the devices it develops and owns. Building a safer world does not mean abolishing all risks. It does mean reducing these risks to the minimum and to a level where there is at least a high expectation we can survive. Moving from national control over PNEs and towards responsible international control over these devices may be a move towards greater security and sanity.

Terrorism

International terrorism has already become a fact of life for many people and governments, and the trend is towards an increasing number of terrorist acts with international ramifications. Most importantly for our future perspective is the increasing vulnerability of our societies to terrorist action, as our lives become more and more complex and interdependent and as the technology of weapons and other tools of terrorism advances. Even more dangerous for international peace and stability is the possibility of terrorists' obtaining weapons of mass destruction such as nuclear explosives or highly toxic chemicals including plutonium.

Terrorism, particularly its widespread use in conflicts between groups and governments, has a great impact on international politics and global order and requires new attention by governments and international organizations. This is clearly seen as government after government has given in to the demands of terrorist groups. While terrorism so far has not yet had an unacceptable impact on international order, it has brought sufficient destruction and loss of life to cause even stable Western democracies to weaken their resolve, act sometimes like immobilized machines, and often to capitulate totally to terrorist threats.

Terrorism—defined as the use of often indiscriminate violence to coerce—is really a destructive form of psychological warfare. Its methods include bombings, the taking of hostages for ransom, and the killing of individuals and groups. Most often innocent civilians are its victims. It is the method used by the few and the relatively weak. It is the approach favored by the poor—in money, support, or power—against the "rich" who usually control "legitimate" power and wealth. Yet it can also be used openly or, more often, surreptitiously by governments against other governments and even against their own people. When practiced by governments or quasi-governmental bodies, terrorism can be particularly dangerous to international stability and peace. But, usually, terrorism is used by groups who lack other means of obtaining and using power.

Terrorism has contributed to increasing the level of violence in a number of local conflicts, often expanding them to larger areas or to previously uninvolved countries. It has also prolonged conflict and thereby increased the tension and bitterness of opposing sides. We see this, for example, in Northern Ireland and the Middle East. It has also weakened governments or contributed to their downfall.[16]

One specific characteristic of recent terrorism has been its international nature. Targets of terrorists are diplomats—often from opposing countries but just as likely from a neutral nation. Another favorite target has been aircraft in transit between countries and international airports. In these attacks the citizens of many countries are the victims—even individuals from the terrorists' own ethnic or religious group. Further, jet travel has made no area of the globe free from terrorist attack. Almost every country is vulnerable to terrorist action given the great mobility provided by international aircraft travel.

But of even more overall concern for the international community is the advance of technology which makes possible even higher levels of destruction and greater selection of targets. Terrorism is now more potent than ever before and will grow over time.[17] Because of the existence of new weapons of destruction, terrorism has become increasingly attractive to dissident groups. The use of powerful explosives, highly destructive weapons, and certain chemicals and electronic devices has increased the impact a small group of terrorists can make on the average citizen and his institutions. For example, the introduction of the Soviet-made hand-held, heat-seeking ground-to-air missiles into the inventory of terrorist groups' armories creates for all nations increased dangers for their aircraft along with the possibility of large loss of life. A single terrorist using a relatively cheap but sophisticated weapon can in a few seconds, from a place of relative safety, destroy an aircraft carrying hundreds of people and worth several million dollars. This is but one example of the increased vulnerability of our modern society to destructive acts of individuals using new technology.

One further element at work in this context is the availability of mass media as a means to disseminate information about the actions of terrorists. Through radio, television, and the use of communications satellites, terrorists and their actions can have worldwide exposure for their causes. Terrorists seek publicity, and now can find it almost instantly through modern mass communications media. Such publicity probably encourages acts of terrorism and makes acts of terrorism more attractive. The combination of a greater capacity for destruction along with large public exposure gives to very small groups a power over society that did not exist in earlier periods. (See Figure VI-1.)

Beyond the so-called conventional weaponry, which modern technology has made even more destructive, are weapons or other means of mass destruction. It is hard, sometimes, to distinguish in an advanced technological age between conventional and mass destruction weapons. It is even harder when so-called conventional weapons can destroy hundreds of lives. Yet some distinction can be made when we speak about nuclear or biological weapons since their capacity for widespread and almost total destruction is so great.

As we have noted, the proliferation of nuclear power facilities and the spread of nuclear weapons states increase the chances that fissionable material or the actual weapons might fall into the hands of terrorist groups who might use them to further their ends. The use of nuclear explosives is not the only or major danger since nuclear power also creates dangerous and deadly radioactive waste material that can be disseminated simply and with great impact in modern urban areas, causing both panic and death.

We have already seen a few examples of terrorists who have directed their efforts at nuclear facilities and we can expect to see this again in the future as nuclear power plants become more common. There will be increasing possibilities to steal fissionable or other radioactive material or nuclear weapons in the future. This is a fact we must live with. We should, however, do something to mitigate its dangers. The increasing

Figure VI-1. International terrorist incidents, 1968-77.

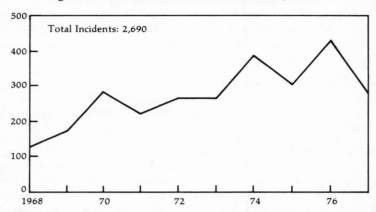

Source: *International Terrorism In 1977, A Research Paper*, National Foreign Assessment Center, Central Intelligence Center (Photoduplication Service, Library of Congress, Washington, D.C., August 1978), Figure 2, p. 1.

traffic in plutonium, enriched uranium, and other radioactive material increases the overall possibility of terrorist action directed towards nuclear facilities. Also there are more and more people familiar with the manufacture, shipment, and use of nuclear technology and weapons and these numbers will increase over the years.[18] Part of the problem is that the technical expertise required to manufacture a crude nuclear device is not all that great, given possession of the required fissionable nuclear materials. It is the lack of the required fissionable material which prevents small groups from manufacturing a bomb. They do not have the capacity to either steal a weapon from a storage site or achieve access to the required reprocessing or shipment facilities, which are the only points of the fuel cycle where such materials can be diverted. While most of these sites are guarded, many experts believe present security measures to be inadequate. With the increased capability of terrorist groups, such sites may become even more vulnerable unless extraordinary measures are taken by individual governments and the appropriate international organizations. It is even likely that we will see the threat of a nuclear attack by terrorists before we see the use of a nuclear weapon by hostile governments against each other.

There are a number of attractive incentives for terrorists to attempt nuclear action. First, is the association in the public's mind of nuclear weapons as the ultimate in danger and destruction. This gives to the terrorist an added impetus to move into this area. The second element is the desire of some terrorist groups to take action against nuclear facilities for their own sake, in opposition to nuclear power and all its implications. The added leverage of using a nuclear threat over and against a hated society also could have some appeal beyond politically oriented groups to the deranged individual who personally feels the need to destroy.

In fact it may be less likely that an ideologically motivated group would actually use or perhaps even threaten the use of nuclear materials. Such action might prove counter-productive since it would alienate the terrorist group from potentially sympathetic sectors in the society. It could also result in governments taking much more effective action against the terrorist group than otherwise would be the case since there would be greater justification for the use of force and extraordinary actions to control or destroy the terrorist group and its supporters if a nuclear threat were employed.

One additional problem would be to have criminals and not political terrorists attempt nuclear extortion or to steal fissionable materials which in turn could be sold either to political terrorist groups or back to the government from which it had been stolen. The involvement of criminals in any illegal effort of a nuclear nature poses a grave threat of both national and international dimensions equivalent to that of political terrorists except that it is likely their demands will be more of a monetary nature.[19]

The most likely danger to international stability from terrorism may come from a fairly well organized, disciplined group with political motivation. Examples of such groups include the various Palestinian organizations (like the Black September), the Baader-Meinhof gang, the Japanese Red Army, etc. It is possible that any one of these groups may one day use the threat of nuclear, chemical, or bacteriological destruction as part of their terrorist campaign. The responsible governments and concerned international bodies at that time will need not only to determine the authenticity of the threat but also how to respond with the strategy least likely to provoke the actual employment of such weapons. Very hard and difficult decisions will have to be made which will have serious implications for future threats and the subsequent behavior of other terrorist organizations. There is a real difference between the consequences of terrorism directed only at a few diplomats or even one plane and the possibility of a whole city being subject to a nuclear explosion or to having its water supply poisoned.

Political terrorists with a real nuclear weapon or even a hoax threat of the use of such a device would attempt to gain more by the use of such a terrible weapon. Their demands are more likely to be greater than, for example, the release of a few prisoners. They are more likely to require a change in policy or even the resignation or fall of a government. Some of the demands are likely to be relatively unrealistic and perhaps even beyond the ability of a government to deliver even if it wanted to. Also there is the very great problem of the follow-up to the terrorist demands and the problem of how to ensure that once the demand is agreed to that the device is made safe and there are not repeated demands.

The problems of nuclear terrorism are great but cannot here be discussed in great depth. Simply one must note that there are a great number of serious implications and complications to any terrorist nuclear or mass destruction action which take it beyond a normal terrorist activity. We cannot therefore respond to such an event in the way we have done in the past. The stakes are just too high. There is the danger of panic, there may be the question of associated radioactivity, and of the threat of external hostile action by a country while undergoing a nuclear threat. There is also the question of what action a government can legitimately take domestically to capture terrorists or prevent a nuclear device from being used, as well as the problem of who has final responsibility for deciding on the ultimate response to the threat.

There are important international implications of such a threat. What if a nuclear threat were made against the United Nations? Or if the terrorists were to demand a major change in a country's foreign policy? With the increase in the number of countries possessing nuclear weapons there is an increased possibility that third country nationals might attempt to steal these weapons for their own use or to embarrass the local government. The theft of a nuclear weapon which has fallen into the hands of an unknown terrorist group would itself bring a sense of panic to many countries and peoples and all, regardless of nationality, would and should share in a common sense of great danger.

It is for this reason that we should look more seriously into a stronger program of national and international action against both nuclear weapons proliferation and the thoughtless expansion of nuclear power and its associated technology and materials. Certain other actions appear called for. There should be some kind of international cooperation among nations to strengthen the security of fissionable materials including an exchange of technology and methodology regarding the protection and safeguarding of materials. Also, as noted elsewhere, consideration should be given to multinational or international facilities for storage, processing, and transportation of fissionable and other dangerous materials. International agreements should be developed which would increase the cooperation among nations in case a nuclear threat by terrorists with international implications takes place.

Special attention must particularly be paid to the few known terrorist groups which might be able to build or steal nuclear weapons or fissionable materials. International cooperation against such groups to prevent them from traveling across international borders or obtaining weapons which could be used against a nuclear facility appears called for.

Finally, the prospects of the world seeing increased terrorism and its consequent destruction is in many cases directly related to the repression of dissident groups by authoritarian regimes. As long as such dictatorial governments suppress different viewpoints and disaffected elements in the population, not permitting open political debate or participation in the legitimate governmental process, then there will likely be fertile ground for terrorist activity. Minority or majority groups desiring greater social and economic equality, when frustrated in advocating their legitimate rights through legal means, will inevitably use illegal means to obtain their demands. Thus, central to any change of the current trends towards increased terrorist activity is movement towards a greater degree of political liberty and economic and social equality. Permitting opponents of a ruling government a chance to voice their views and a chance to share in decision making about their future may be the most effective overall action society can take to protect itself from much of modern terrorist activity.

Terrorism is therefore related to larger issues of our age, especially the question of the growing gap between the "haves" and the "have-nots" both in industrialized countries and in the poorer regions. We are still living with the legacy of the past—actions by our fathers' fathers which set in motion the causes of violence we see today. We have the difficult task of setting right these past mistakes and also ensuring that we do not bequeath to a future generation the disaffection of our own times. The needs of the deprived and frustrated peoples must be attended to on much larger grounds than the threat of terrorism, but we can never be free of such violence until we deal with its root causes.

A Strategy Towards Putting the Genie Back into the Bottle

Given these circumstances it is imperative that major innovative and effective measures are taken by the responsible members of the world community to develop a comprehensive system to limit the risks mankind must face in the nuclear age. We have up to now only prevented disaster through the initial limitation upon the number of countries possessing nuclear weapons: those countries also being highly industrialized and able to put in place relatively sophisticated control and safeguard systems against accidents and diversions. But this will not be the case as more and more countries possess nuclear technology.

Most knowledgeable observers believe a major first step towards putting the genie of nuclear weapons back into its bottle is increasing the present authority and capabilities of the International Atomic Energy Authority as mentioned earlier. First, their current inspection capability needs to be greatly strengthened not only to deal with the present technology and nuclear materials now in place but also to deal with the large increase in such materials now contemplated as nuclear power becomes more common. The IAEA Inspection Corps and its technique must be permitted to improve to keep abreast of their responsibilities and to provide assurance that there are no illegal diversions going on. It is vital that the credibility of the IAEA inspection system be maintained if any progress is to be made towards limiting further nuclear proliferation. This means that large increases in the IAEA budget must be assured. For example, the IAEA safeguard staff should be increased greatly in numbers. The increased cost would be very small compared to the total cost of the technology, materials, construction, and maintenance costs of the plants themselves. What such safeguards and inspection buys is a measure of safety which is very great compared to its very low cost.

However, over the long term its obtaining the necessary increased funds to assume an adequate safeguarding function is a difficulty which requires a rather innovative approach. The United Nations formula for the IAEA budget has serious problems since there is reluctance to increase contributions from many states. One suggestion which has been made is to permit the IAEA to collect a kind of tax or fee for its safeguarding function based on the nuclear energy capacity of each power reactor, and this fee would be paid by the country based on its installed capacity. In effect, under this system the IAEA safeguarding function could become, in time, self-financing.[20] Another approach might be to permit the IAEA to obtain significant additional funds through special voluntary contributions and to, in effect, build up a large "endowment" which could be invested and used to finance over time its growing safeguard functions. Because of the sensitivity of the safeguarding function the IAEA performs, it must also maintain and improve its overall image of competence, prestige, and professionalism. Those who work on the safeguard staffs should consider themselves true world civil servants and indeed first and foremost citizens and guardians of the interests of the larger global community.

The IAEA should also be able to call upon the knowledge and

expertise of private, academic, and research organizations and individuals for assistance in carrying out its responsibilities. It should, for example, be able to contract directly with such groups for services and advice as necessary and do so freely without political pressure. Indeed, the functions of the IAEA should not be subject to the political or economic pressure of any single nation or group of nations if it is to perform adequately its vital functions.

Probably the most important function which can be performed in the future by the IAEA or by a related body would be to take on the enormous task of providing nuclear energy and related service to nonnuclear weapon states primarily in the developing world. It could be part of a concentrated global effort to provide the poorer developing countries with the energy they need for their economic expansion but doing so in a context which will not contribute to nuclear weapons proliferation. A number of proposals have been advanced over the years to put nuclear power under the control of an international body which would assure both adequate energy for developing countries and a large measure of global safety against weapons use or diversion by governments or terrorists.[21]

In effect, this international body could be a kind of public multinational corporation which would act as a global utility providing nuclear energy in the form of electricity to those countries which did not have sufficient sources of energy of their own. The energy would be provided by nuclear power plants located in various regions or countries on specifically designated land, as is the case with a diplomatic mission or international organization headquarters—i.e., with the international facility having sovereignty over the land on which the nuclear facilities are located with diplomatic rights given to the site and the officials who run the facilities. These facilities might also be located in sites off the coast of one or more countries in international waters. The international plants could generate power for more than one country. These nuclear power reactors might also be sited in a larger international complex which could include other nuclear energy and research facilities. The site might have, for example, its own storage facilities for waste, its own reprocessing plant, and perhaps even an enrichment facility.

A proposal for the development of multinational regional reprocessing plants by the former American Secretary of State, Henry A. Kissinger, in his United Nations General Assembly speech on September 22, 1975, goes a long way towards this concept and provides a greater recognition on the part of the American government of the need to strengthen international cooperation in this field.[22] Yet this step is only a start since a total effort to put sanity back into its proper place in the area of global nuclear security matters means ensuring that all technology and materials capable of being used for the production of nuclear explosive devices are increasingly and firmly placed under international control. The first priority must be to stop immediately the spread of this technology and the weapons themselves. Efforts must be made to reduce the total number of facilities and materials now existing and not under international control or safeguards inspection. Over time, efforts must be made to do away with nuclear weapons stockpiles as completely as possible. Until we move away from nuclear power the long-range goal would be to place all significant elements of this dangerous technology under competent professional international control with advanced and sophisticated techniques against misuse or diversion which would give assurance to all nations and peoples that they no longer need to fear a genocidal holocaust.

A wide number of highly respected and thoughtful individuals have increasingly come to this conclusion as each in turn has calculated the relative risks and benefits the world is likely to face in the coming decades as atomic power and nuclear weapons spread to more and more countries. It is a frightening prospect to see individual high-technology firms which have dangerous nuclear technology attempt to sell it to every potential customer without regard for the total costs humanity might one day be asked to bear. Why this technology should have ever been permitted by any government to be placed in the private sector is almost beyond understanding given its inherent capacity to destroy all living things on this planet and the known rapacious instincts of man. It is of great importance that governmental control over this technology once more be strongly asserted and where it already is in private hands it should be taken back under direct control or close regulation by the responsible governments. This would be a vital first step towards increasing international control over this technology and its associated fissionable materials.

As a first move towards the creation of a comprehensive international system of nuclear technology control some immediate and practical actions appear critical for preventing further proliferation. Putting the most dangerous aspects of the nuclear technological cycle under international regulation ranks as the most important step for the international community. This means focusing primarily on the chemical reprocessing plants with the associated plutonium from reactors, secondly the whole enrichment technology area, and finally, fast breeder reactors when and if they are sold to nonnuclear weapon states. Each of these stages or technologies represents the greatest danger of diversion where the need exists for the most care in inspection and operation. Peaceful nuclear explosions as noted elsewhere in this chapter need special international attention.

Also a new and better system is required to ensure the safe shipment of spent fuel rods with a high content of weapons-grade plutonium as well as high plutonium content new fuel rods. There are some estimates that between 7,000 and 12,000 shipments annually of fuel rods are made between reactors and reprocessing plants. Also by the early 1980s present nonnuclear weapons countries will possess annually some 26,000 kilograms of plutonium 239 or about enough to make fifty atomic bombs a week. The reprocessing of spent fuel rods is the most likely source for diversion of plutonium and can be accomplished relatively easily as India has shown.[23] If reprocessing plants can be placed under international or multinational control by both nonnuclear weapons states and nuclear weapons states, then an important move will have been made towards greatly limiting for the world the danger of nuclear weapons spread for the immediate and intermediate term. So far the only real check on widespread reprocessing has been the American policy of having recipients of United States manufactured fissionable materials in spent fuel rods send them back to the United States (or sometimes a third country) for reprocessing. This has up to now covered the bulk of nuclear fuels since the United States is the world's largest exporter and manufacturer of nuclear fuels.[24]

The United States government in 1977 took the important step of initiating a global study of nuclear technology problems called the International Nuclear Fuel Cycle Study. This effort is aimed at developing a global community consensus on the safest and most efficient means of controlling or developing nuclear power. The success of this two-year effort may determine the course of future proliferation of this technology. In 1978 Congress passed the Nuclear Nonproliferation Act which requires that all countries to whom we send nuclear materials and related equipment accept IAEA safeguards and inspection on all their nuclear activities and materials. In addition it includes a section which encourages cooperation between the United States and developing countries in nonnuclear sources of energy such as solar and biomass, etc. This legislation is an important symbol of the significance of this problem and a demonstration by Congress of its desire for strong leadership by the United States in this field.

Over the long run it will probably be necessary for the collective world community to control all fissionable materials except for existing stockpiles of nuclear weapons (stockpiles which it is hoped would be progressively decreased and the material contained therein reprocessed into peaceful fuel for energy generation). If uranium enrichment plants could be owned by international or multinational groups, these same groups could also retain title over the fuel rods, and just rent them to individual countries or utilities with the understanding that they would be returned for reprocessing after use. Older nuclear materials could eventually be sold to the international body which would control the enriched materials and would also buy all available natural uranium worldwide. The organization carrying out these activities (perhaps part of the IAEA) might be called the International Nuclear Materials and Services Corporation (INMSC). The INMSC could be responsible for the provision of electricity from nuclear power plants to requesting nations, the funding and control of critical research and development in the nuclear energy field, and the licensing of possession of natural uranium up to a certain stage of refinement. It might also be the sole buyer of natural and processed uranium fuels. It would provide storage of processed uranium fuels and fissionable materials including plutonium and waste radioactive materials. The ownership or management over all multinational or international reprocessing facilities and ownership or control and management over all nuclear enrichment plants, including exclusive right to control all future new enrichment research and development, could be part of its authority. Finally, it would have the sole responsibility for shipment of fissionable materials and related sensitive goods.

However, the inspection function over these facilities controlled or owned by the proposed INMSC could continue to be in the hands of an autonomous inspection and safeguards organization which would remain as part of the existing IAEA. In this way there would be created a checks and balance system which would ensure the objectivity and integrity of the inspecting function even for international facilities.

Individual power plants could, in some cases—especially in existing nuclear weapons states—be owned by national or local governments or private firms, but they would be licensed for the use of internationally controlled materials and would be therefore subject to required international safeguard inspection. Over time all nuclear power reactors in all countries would be subject to international inspection.

In order to obtain widespread acceptance of such far-reaching and even drastic measures there would have to be a major breakthrough among the nuclear weapons states to move towards significant measures of arms control. Only this would provide the proper context in which the "have not" states would be willing to forgo nationalistic nuclear technology efforts and eventually the development of their own bombs. The nuclear weapon states would have to start a real reduction in the absolute levels or numbers of their weapons, and as the materials in these weapons are dismantled they should be reprocessed for peaceful use. Further, as a first step, all plants producing fissionable materials for weapons purposes would be dismantled or converted, thereby cutting off the production of all weapons-grade material.

To carry out any such a complex and innovative approach would require the cooperation of the major nuclear weapons and high-energy-technology states including the United States and the Soviet Union. It is highly doubtful that such a move will be taken in the near future, except perhaps in partial efforts at solutions for specific and narrow problem areas, before the catalyst of a catastrophe such as a terrorist possession of a nuclear weapon or of sufficient plutonium to poison a whole city. This is in itself a sad commentary on the state of man's global perceptions of reality and of the state of mankind's global institutions. Is the destruction of a whole city required, despite foreknowledge of the danger, before mankind can take effective action?

In the final analysis, however, the necessary motivation to move in the right direction does not require all countries to agree but rather the participation of the most powerful and technologically advanced. To ensure, however, even wider support and participation, such an internationalization of nuclear energy technology and materials must be accompanied by concrete offers to ensure to all countries, especially to those in the developing world, cheap and abundant energy from whatever sources or technologies.

Finally, all our know-how should also be directed at finding safer energy sources than nuclear ones. It is important that we accelerate our efforts to develop nonnuclear energy technology so that over the median and long term we can offer to other countries alternatives to either dangerous nuclear facilities or increasingly high cost imported oil. Thus our domestic energy programs in solar energy or coal gasification, etc., can serve important international economic and security goals. If these countries can be assured over the long term that their needs for energy can be fully and reasonably provided for as their economies and populations grow then they will not have any economic or other reasonable excuse for not forgoing the nationalistic nuclear energy/explosive device option.

Such an effort by the "have" countries would be costly, but not over the long run more costly than fighting nuclear wars or facing the possibility of a nuclear device in the hands of terrorists placed in the center of New York, London, or Moscow. Nor would it be that expensive in economic terms since the provision of energy to the poorer countries could be paid for slowly at first and completely later by the using countries as their economies grow. Further, mass production of generating plants, solar cells, etc., would cut unit costs significantly, thereby lowering overall electric generating costs. The resulting increased economic activity due to the availability of relatively cheap power in the poorer regions would also give a significant boost to overall economic growth, food production, and world trade with a positive impact on per capita income.

Action that at first may appear too idealistic is really based on rather hard calculation of possible relative dangers and relative costs. Progress towards the suggestions given above may provide a far better chance for mankind surviving without a horrendous catastrophe. The dark alternative is to watch hopelessly as the world marches each day closer and closer to the increased threat of a nuclear cataclysm.

CHAPTER VII

Information
and Communications

A popular government, without popular information or the means of acquiring it, is but a prologue to a farce or a tragedy or perhaps both. Knowledge will forever govern ignorance, a people who mean to be their own governors must arm themselves with the power which knowledge gives. —James Madison

Introduction

There is a great risk to the world community in human ignorance. A person who is uninformed and illiterate is also less productive, less innovative and more narrow in his value system than a person who has the ability to learn about modern technology and has access to the world's literature. Ignorance is not bliss, but rather more akin to physical poverty. Notwithstanding the trendy popularization of the joys of simple savagehood, the person locked into ignorance is a prisoner far more than a man in a cell who can read a book.

Today great efforts are being made to expand knowledge, the information base and the communicative ability of those who have the least opportunity to share in the fruits of modern society. New educational efforts are being undertaken both at the local community level, nationally, and internationally to reach the world's poorest with information that can lengthen horizons, increase productivity, and provide a higher quality of life. New advanced technology is being employed in this effort, making possibly a major impact on all cultures and on the daily lives of millions.

Even as this expansion is taking place, however, new threats to man's knowledge and freedom of communication are increasing almost everywhere. A great struggle is taking place between, on the one side, those who would limit, prohibit, or censor the information received by the individual, and on the other side, those who believe in the maximum freedom of the flow of knowledge, ideas, and data. Basic principles of government and of human liberty are involved. The outcome will in large measure determine the kind of global society we will have.

There is also another risk for the modern world and that is the misuse of control over information and its associated technology to keep man a slave of one political or economic system. By controlling information a government can limit free inquiry and the discussion of alternative methods of organizing society. This has sometimes been called "thought control." This kind of world has been most vividly depicted by such writers as Aldous Huxley in his *Brave New World* and by George Orwell in *Nineteen Eighty-Four*. Technology can make possible the enslavement of man as much as it can also assist in his liberation. "Newspeak," the "feelies" or the "Ministry of Truth," all have their nonliterary reality. Thus it will be an important struggle for each man and for each nation to seek to maximize the access to all information and ideas.

Information and Social Change

The "word" has had a far more profound impact on the world's civilizations than wars or armies. It has been the men of ideas who have conquered the world. Plato, Christ, Newton, Darwin, and Einstein have shaped our modern world more than any general or warrior. It is also the technology associated with ideas and communications that has most advanced man's capabilities: the printing press, movable type, telegraph, radio, television, and now satellite communications. The value structure and behavior of almost all societies are influenced by these innovations in the communication of ideas.

There is a vast literature by anthropologists about how modernization or acculturation changes the social structure of past or traditional societies.[1] In very brief time periods, whole cultures have been radically altered—for the better or worse—by the influx of new and often different information. The pace of this change has quickened with the development of new technologies for the dissemination of information. Now rural Nigerian villagers can listen to broadcasts from a central city providing news and information unobtainable in the past and linking that remote village to the larger national community. Other African villages and towns are provided with local newspapers, again with news and information previously unavailable. Even the nomadic herdsman can listen to the events of the entire world through his transistor radio. To think these new technologies will not change the minds of those exposed is foolish, as foolish as those who would deny these traditional or primitive peoples this new knowledge of the outside world.

One result of the modernization process, in particular Western education and the availability of books and the media, has been the creation of a secular intelligentsia and related elites who have been trained to use modern technology and to profit from the world's resource of knowledge. They are not confined by either the limited information or the value systems of the older traditional society. They have become engines of change in their societies since they play the most active parts in the process of modernization. Further, this group—the modernized sector—has almost a complete monopoly on control over the main institutions of society, thereby controlling that entire society. Together the modernized military, intelligentsia, bureaucratic and business leadership dominate social change and power in the developing countries. From time to time, one of these groups rebels against the other (student riots, military coup d'état, etc.) but each group usually needs the others to keep the modern sector of society moving forward, usually leaving the rural, uneducated, and poor sectors of society behind.

Most writers on development believe that a basic prerequisite of modernization is the existence of a technologically advanced sector or intelligentsia. To create this reforming sector requires universities, a secondary educational system, a press, and supporting cultural and scientific institutions. This also means the creation of the bureaucratic function since a modern sector cannot exist without laws, rules, and order. These institutions create a revolution in ideas and values via-à-vis the traditional order. The result is often conflict and alienation for both the modernized and traditional sectors.

This conflict is more likely to increase rather than diminish in the future. Some observers in the past have wrongly equated the modernization process with the orderly development of democratic institutions. We have come to know better through experience that this rather naive viewpoint does not correspond to reality. Modernization can bring with it strong forces of authoritarianism as much as forces working towards democratic processes. Repressive regimes frequently identify with the modernization process and often justify their harsh methods in the name of development and technological advancement.

One of the tragic elements of our world today is that these knowledge and power gaps between the modernized and the traditional sectors of society are growing. Some 700 million adults are illiterate and thus unable to express themselves beyond their local community or to learn much beyond the knowledge handed down from father to son. For this large group of people the most fundamental facts of modern science, health, nutrition, and industry are unknown. Such an individual is a prisoner of his own time and place, of the values of his immediate society or group. The local cultural prejudices and limiting myths are all that he can compare life with. He has little communication with or understanding of the larger world and its resources.

The problem is made more serious by the contempt that the college-educated urban elite often feel towards the poor illiterate villager. This attitude will make more difficult the process of integrating the poorer and rural areas of a developing country into the total fabric of a developing society.

A main obstacle, however, to the growth of per capita income and modernization in many countries is the continued high rate of illiteracy. Worldwide it now amounts to about 39 percent and while proportionally it is generally falling, it is not in absolute numbers.

Most of this illiteracy is concentrated in the Third World. In many Asian, Latin American, or African countries illiterates make up one-half to three-fourths of the population. Illiteracy severely handicaps these societies in trying to increase the productivity of their people and limits the extent to which these countries can fully share in the benefits and decisions of a modern world.

The United Nations Educational, Scientific and Cultural Organization (UNESCO) estimated in 1963 that it would cost about $5 to $8 per person to attain literacy. With inflation since that time it would probably be more like $10 to $16 per person today. The costs would be lower for adults and higher for children. More and more countries are investing a large proportion of their funds in education and combating illiteracy. While most have utilized traditional schooling, others have emphasized new approaches outside of the formal education system. In some countries like Iran, for example, young educated individuals are sent into rural areas to teach the basic elements of literacy. Also private or political groups have enlisted themselves in the drive towards assisting people to read basic texts.

Just as is the case with basic health and family planning services, the utilization of local paraprofessional personnel will be required if illiteracy is to be overcome in a relatively short period of time. It will be necessary for those who have the traditional education to help in the teaching of reading and for those who have learned to read and write outside of the formal educational institutions to share their knowledge with others through a concerted program of literacy for the rural poor and urban masses.

Another important result of higher levels of literacy will be to increase the extent of participation by the masses of a given country in the governmental decision-making structure. A literate person will be able better to articulate his or her needs and to distinguish between different political options. While one must be careful in not assuming that literacy itself can assure democracy (we all should know better given the history of this century), we should also know that democracy is unlikely to flourish long or well without a high proportion of literate and informed citizens. Literacy provides a means by which complex ideas and communications between the country's leaders and their people is made possible.

One additional point needs to be made: this problem of illiteracy is not one confined alone to the developing countries. Within many advanced countries there are large numbers of people, mostly those economically, culturally, or racially disadvantaged by the society, who functionally are illiterate. This means that they cannot write effectively and have very poor written and oral abilities to the point of being almost unintelligible in terms of the basic communications required in modern sector jobs. As jobs become more complex, requiring even greater skills, those unable to learn effectively because they cannot read difficult texts will fall even further behind those with more advanced education and skills.

The Computer and Global Communications

Since 1950 the computer and its storehouse of information, with the capability to transfer that information almost instantaneously anywhere in the world, have revolutionized the availability of knowledge and made a tremendous impact upon institutions in every country. Once the bulk of the knowledge and information of modern society is accessible to any literate individual, to small towns in India or the cities of Africa, there will be a dramatic change in the perception and value of those who have obtained admittance to this global bank of mankind's knowledge.

The computer is the basis for much of modern society's industrial advance and its influence on future innovation is likely to be even greater than it is today. The day is not far off when global computerized information systems will be available to every nation and to a large number of highly educated and technically advanced individuals. Such global computer systems when combined with advanced satellite communications will enable a person to tap into a worldwide pool of data stored in national and specialized libraries, private institutions, hospitals, banks, universities, and government agencies. The day will not be far away when a person with access to a computer terminal will have available almost all of the information stored in computers anywhere.

The developing world will have access to the same information that, until recently, was only easily available within the industrialized countries. The poor of the world could thus obtain a key tool for improving their capability, understanding, and agricultural and industrial productivity. Today, more than ever before, knowledge is the most important input into an economy, a business, or a government. A country with a high rate of literacy and access to knowledge even if poor in natural resources can develop at a high rate compared with countries with very low literacy levels. A report from the Bellagio Conference said it this way: "In a capital short world, the most powerful sources of productivity increases are new technologies, and the effective engagement of well-trained people. Research, education, and engineering are major sources of these productivity enhancing capabilities."[2]

Another impact of a global information system will be on the individual with access to it. Those who can tap in to a global information system will gain advantages over those who cannot. Such access will produce new values and perceptions about oneself, about the world, and about the kinds of institutions that should serve mankind. Further, when one realizes that knowledge is not a local or even national prerogative or resource but rather an international phenomenon, individuals will become less willing to accept narrow interpretations of "the truth" or the easy assumption that one's national leaders are all wise. The diversity of the world's data will indicate to any intelligent observer the importance of an open and sharing global community.

To some extent a world information system helps to create a global community. One should be careful, however, and not assume that building such a community will, by itself, also prevent wars or other conflicts. It may even increase the chances of certain types of conflict. What is created is a new kind of interdependence. Hospitals in one country become dependent on the medical information stored in a distant computer linked through communications satellites with hospitals around the world. TV stations will increasingly depend on an international string of TV networks for filmed and live programs showing events thousands of miles away. Newspapers can be automatically printed in one continent using the material and words sent from another. A unified global financial information system will be possible with instantaneous readouts of data from stock exchanges throughout the world and vital economic statistics. One important test of this electronic information system is its ability to reduce the costs of obtaining and disseminating information. Only by so doing will it be useful to the poorer sections of the world.

Knowledge for the Third World

There is one major and tragic fact of which all of us who live in the modern industrialized world must be ashamed—that the fruits of our high level of technology and science have not been effectively applied to the problems of those who are the poorest of this world. We have solved the problem of the space traveler, we have solved the problem of the businessman who wants to fly between London and Washington in less than six hours, or the needs of our TV networks for instantaneous images of some new human disaster. But we have not gotten electricity into the far rural villages of the subcontinent, or vaccinated the children of West Africa against common disease, or provided literacy to the poor of the large urban slums of the world's fastest growing cities or family planning to the Mexican rural village. Yet for each of these needs, some relevant technology exists which can help solve the specific need and at relatively low costs.

Knowledge alone, even without hardware, can be of immense difference to the quality of life and the productivity of those who live within a society which is economically poor and traditional. To know how to utilize water, to have the basics of hygiene or what mix of foods would give better nutrition, is to be centuries ahead and to go from a marginal impoverished subsistence life to significant improvements in well-being and health—a move away from oppressing poverty.

Much of what has previously been discussed indicates the wide range of "technologies" or just information which can contribute towards a better life for the world's poor. There has been a lot written about appropriate technology for the developing world. Appropriate technology basically means technology which fits into the specific needs of the poorer communities and is not high in cost or too complex for easy maintenance. It must be cost/efficient for the economy in which it is used and should not disrupt the local productive system. Thus a labor-saving device in an area which has abundant low cost labor would not be appropriate technology. Whatever phrase is used the main requirement is for technology that can be easily utilized by the poor and not just useful to the modernized and rich sectors of developing countries.

Yet there also are a number of advanced technologies which are very efficient in providing information to developing countries which can assist in economic growth and modernization. Some of this technology has global significance. A few examples are given below.

Advance Technology and Global Problem Solving

Technology can provide a means for the international community to predict food production for the entire globe. This capability together with the necessary political and economic decision-making mechanisms can bring, in the near future, mankind closer to preventing starvation and food supply imbalances. The technology is now in an experimental state (known as Large Area Crop Inventory Experiment, LACIE) which, by utilizing space satellites, can estimate the amount of grain that will be harvested in any given area of the world. A prototype effort is under way on the part of the United States government and eventually it could become the basis for a global food watch.

The basic method is to have a satellite scan a given area measuring the light reflected from a growing crop at different wavelengths. The satellite studies each stage of growth through a scanning spectrometer. The multispectral images are then telemetered to ground stations and are put into a computer which is programmed to estimate the acreage planted and then to combine this estimate with meteorological information to predict eventual yields.

This technology can give to international organizations and individual governments warnings about damage from droughts, floods, and other disasters. This knowledge can help to prevent shortages and provide early warning for governments in their plans for storage, sales, and shipments of food. At present there do not exist accurate and regular reports on future food production, and forecasts of production on a global scale are now almost impossible to make. The developments of this technology could make possible rational management of food and feed grains.

Landsat satellites of the National Aeronautics and Space Administration (NASA) are the only experimental effort in this direction. The National Oceanic and Atmospheric Administration (NOAA) and the United States Department of Agriculture are cooperating in this program which covers the wheat crop in the Great Plains of the United States. Other areas will follow as will other crops. Already the technique is being used in Latin America. While much still remains to be perfected in this technology, there is little doubt that, in time, it will work. As the technology of remote sensing develops and can provide automated data of almost day-to-day changes in a given crop, the international community will have a tool which will make possible strengthening the total capability of countries and international organizations. It will thereby bring closer the time when effective global management organizations will exist to gather the necessary data, predict future food demand and supply, and provide for the necessary funding and logistical support to ensure sufficient food supplies to everyone.[3]

Yet even this technology which promises to bring so many benefits has its political problems. Some countries have expressed opposition or concern that commercial organizations would make use of the resulting information about their crops so as to adversely affect their interests. Also some countries may be fearful that this same technology is related to intelligence uses apart from just crop forecasting. So, as with communications satellites, there will be some controversy over the worldwide introduction of this useful technology.

As with other kinds of new technology with global implications there are major questions about how the technology is to be used and for whose benefit. The developing countries, poor in scientific know-how, especially feel that new and very complex technology will benefit them very little and the industrialized countries far more, thereby increasing the gap between them even farther.

The response to this concern must be an international system for crop forecasting which includes the developing countries and from which they can concretely benefit. Through such participation and elaborate safeguards against premature disclosure of information there can be developed over time confidence in the integrity of the system. What is needed—and what is lacking now—is not access to the raw data but rather the ability to analyze it and apply it usefully to national decision making. It is this gap which the industrialized countries should find a way of filling so that the majority of the world's population can have a sense of participation in this new applied technology. Perhaps, the best way of doing so would be through some kind of world food organization, most likely the United Nations Food and Agriculture Organization. This will be necessary since it is highly doubtful that many small developing countries will be able, even in several decades, to develop on their own the necessary technical and scientific infrastructure to do independent analysis and interpretation. (This important lack of capability holds true not only in this area but also in many other high-technology sectors.) The choice is simple: either international bodies provide new advanced technology to developing countries or the developing countries will continue to fall behind in the utilization of knowledge and consequently remain nonparticipants in the modern world.

The challenge will not, however, be in knowledge about this new technology but, as seen in so many other sectors, in the political and institutional capabilities of participating nations. Here is a new technology which can bring great benefits, with little or no environmental risks, yet we have not found the necessary institutional framework in which it can bring its many benefits to the entire globe. There is also a certain irony at work, since it is likely to be the developing countries, with the most ultimately to gain, who will probably be the most cautious about the widespread introduction of this technology.

One area where the combined technology of photography and space satellites can help to solve a serious global problem is in examining the cause and the impact of the spread of arid or desert lands. Images from the United States Landsat satellite can show how wind affects the growth of desert areas and thereby open the way for corrective action. Deserts now cover some one-fifth of the land surface of the Earth and are growing. Tunisia, for example, has lost about half of its arable land.[4]

Basically, satellites through broad coverage of orbital photographs are able to provide scientists with new information on deserts by showing features that cannot be recognized from any other position including an airplane. Through the use of color which enhances certain desert features, new meaningful aspects of the deserts can be ascertained and studied. Satellite photographs were able to outline an arable zone some ten to twenty miles wide along the African coast of the Mediterranean west of the Nile Delta, where fir trees could grow and where soil is reclaimable from the desert. These photos, however, also indicated the danger of shifting sands which could harm fertile soil on the banks of the Nile.

Photos have shown that African dunes have migrated southward an average of two feet each day in the direction of the prevailing wind. The result has been the encroachment on fertile soil. The ecological and food impact is especially dangerous for a nation like Egypt that has a growing population in need of more and more food.

Once knowledge is gained about the movement of sand dunes, science can also be of some help in stopping further encroachment. Saudi Arabia has sprayed the sands with a grain-cementing agent that halts the dune in its tracks. Another alternative is to plant eucalyptus trees in the path of sand-carrying winds. These trees grow to heights of up to 300 feet in desert environments. They can affect the advancing winds and cause them to deposit the sand. This technique is now being used to help stop the desertification of arable land in a 900-mile belt of the Algerian Sahara called the Great Barrier.

Despite these efforts, much of Sub-Saharan Africa is becoming desert. This process is continuing over a 4,100-mile belt from one side of the African continent to the other. The reasons for this movement include lack of rain, uncontrolled grazing, slash and burn agriculture, and shifting sands coming from the North. These factors together are creating desertification of previously fertile soils and pasture lands. Clearly, greater knowledge of the deserts, their growth and the location of their reclaimable parts will be of benefit to the entire world community.

These are but a few examples of how even the most advanced technology can be of service to the developing world. The question is whether the advanced industrialized countries will invest in the specific application of this advanced know-how to the problems of the poor. The computer, the satellite, new telecommunication methods, all can be applied to solving global problems. Indeed for many of these problems only such technology can do the job. The poorer countries cannot often afford to develop, own, or even operate much of this new technology. Only the advanced countries have this capability. Yet, some means must be found to disseminate to the poor the knowledge of the world in ways that are truly useful. Most likely this must be done by new institutions that can help act as a bridge between those who are information poor and those who are information rich.

The Communications Media

In both the industrialized nations and in the developing countries, the role of radio and television has become of overriding importance. Television now takes as much if not more of the time of a child in a modern society as does formal schooling. In many developing countries TV reaches into their urban areas. Radio has become a key medium for disseminating information. Even in very poor villages, the transistor radio provides a link with the outside and thereby supplies information on the modern world to the village. The media is the key instrument by which a government informs its people about new laws, weather, crop conditions, and changes in government policy. It has become such a vital link to the people that when a revolution or coup d'état takes place, the national broadcasting station seems to be taken over even before other such key locations as the army headquarters or the Ministry of Interior. That fact alone signifies the importance of the media in the social fabric of a nation.

Today modern communications media can transmit over great distances and provide instant news coverage of major global events. All can share in the triumphs and the tragedy of the Earth's people from remote Asian towns to world centers of industry and commerce. In this special way, both the rich and the poor can share the same knowledge of ongoing history. (For growth rate of telephones in use, see Figure VII-1.)

The media takes many forms both printed (newspapers, magazines, books) and audio-visual (TV, radio, recordings). Each type of media has undergone major changes in the last few decades. Today, there are hundreds of separate rural newspapers where none had existed before. Such rural newspapers help to extend and support literacy training programs in the developing world. Africa is a special focus for rural local language newspapers which perform important functions of communication between the people and local governmental, social, and cultural organizations.

On the other hand, in the developed countries, a danger exists that there will be fewer newspapers and a greater conformity of views. The existence of a free and diverse press is one of the most important factors

Figure VII-1.   Telephones in use

MILLIONS

REGION	1960	1965	1970	1975	Growth Rate 1965-75 % PA
World	139.5	195.0	272.7	379.5	6.89
Africa	2.0	2.5	3.3	4.6	6.29
America, North	80.9	102.4	132.8	166.9	5.01
America, South	3.3	4.2	6.1	9.2	8.16
Asia	7.7	18.2	33.2	57.4	12.17
Europe	39.2	55.6	80.8	118.2	7.83
Oceania	2.9	4.3	5.4	7.1	5.14
USSR	3.5a	7.7	11.0	16.9	8.18

a) 1963

Source: *World Statistics in Brief,* United Nations, N.Y., 1977, p. 227.

in the strength of democratic governmental institutions. Yet the trend towards fewer newspapers in some of the industrialized democracies poses a risk which needs evaluation and certainly concern. Many of the newspapers of the authoritarian developing and advanced countries have become instruments of oppression and help to enforce a dull conformity on the part of the local inhabitants.[5] In this case the availability of a free, if foreign, press can help to ensure that the people living under dictatorships can have some alternative source of information beyond that handed out by a restricted and controlled press.

We should also not forget the role that is now being played by highly specialized journals and magazines in providing not only useful technical information but also a diversity of viewpoints. Often it is these specialized publications which can provide depth of analysis and information that cannot be obtained from a newspaper. They also are a vital link between the professionals in given fields and especially provide a means by which trained personnel in the developing world can keep up with the latest methods and discoveries in all countries.

The existence of a free worldwide TV and radio media almost by itself ensures that the truth will in fact come out in time. A free media can only exist as long as it reports objectively and fairly the events of the world. If it does it will have a worldwide audience even in the most despotic of countries. Thus in Eastern Europe, Western journals and radio programs are widely followed in order to obtain information not otherwise available even about the local country. It was the Western press that first informed the people of the Soviet Union about the invasion of Czechoslovakia and about the fall of Khrushchev.

In short, a key role of the free international or foreign media is to keep the local press in an authoritarian country somewhat more honest than might otherwise be the case. It can provide a point of diversity of views which can encourage internal debate and thereby strengthen the movement towards a more open society. For the same reason it is important also to have a flow of media materials from, for example, the Soviet Union to the United States. Americans should never fear the penetration of Soviet ideas so long as a free society exists and has a strong independent press. Increased cross-cultural communication is more vital today than ever before just because of the growth of so many global risks we face and the need for common notions about them.

An important role of media in the Third World is to bring new ideas and aspirations to those experiencing rapid development. The media provides a context in which individuals can prepare themselves and their children for change. It can help change traditional society into a modern society and help unify a nation in the process. Tribal ties are extended through media coverage of an entire country. Media can mobilize the whole populace towards economic development goals including improving public health, increased agricultural efficiency, and especially education.

Changing technology related to the media can significantly increase the amount and diversity of information available to an individual and to a whole society. A generation ago we could only receive a few TV channels, then UHF channels became available, increasing greatly the possible number of programs available. Soon, with the technology of cable TV systems, literally hundreds of channels are possible, some with two-way capabilities. One important political implication will be the possibility of offering minority or dissident groups the opportunity to broadcast their views. Also a much wider choice of cultural programs will be available, broadening our taste and appreciation. This will increase the diversity and richness of our life, helping us to understand the world and make wise choices. It means that groups or individuals with less resources—the poorer elements of society—can have better access to the public. No longer will such access be a prerogative of the rich and the powerful. This added flexibility and diversity will be helpful in debating choices on how to deal with new changes in society and in the world.

This can also be true on a global scale. New technology—especially the communications satellite—can increase the flow of information between the various countries of the world. Live and filmed broadcasts between one country and another have become cheaper due to this technology. Most importantly it could increase the flow of news from the poorer countries into the richer countries. This is a problem which has attracted increased interest in the last decade and promises to continue to be debated in the United Nations long into the future.[6] Basically, many of the leaders of developing and nonaligned countries believe that there is largely a one-way flow from the richer countries to the poorer.

The report of the Symposium of Non-Aligned Countries on Communication, held in Tunis in March, 1976, stated that for the international news agencies information is "a commodity ... in whose processing and transmission intervene considerations which tend to perpetuate a system of domination in which the authentic interests of the developing countries are consistently ignored or misinterpreted."[7] The point made by many developing country leaders was that "most of the large Western news agencies consciously or unconsciously disseminate information which is fragmentary, schematic, and frequently distorted concerning the complex realities of the developing countries."[8] This viewpoint has two main thrusts. One is to strengthen developing country news media and perhaps create a Third World news agency. The other is towards attempting to limit the dissemination of news from the developed world.

Democracy and Information Dissemination

What is not fully appreciated by many individuals and groups is the important role the media plays in both developed and developing countries in the preservation of human liberty and human rights in general. Elections are more likely to be conducted honestly if domestic and foreign media widely cover balloting. They can attest to whether it was undertaken in a fair and democratic manner. That the world is watching could help guarantee a fair political process. The presence of hundreds of foreign correspondents and photographers can be a powerful force against widespread corruption and arbitrary rule. Certainly the press has had this role in the Soviet dissident and Jewish immigration issue. It has also had an impact in India during the "Emergency." South Africa has modified somewhat its racist actions because of the presence of a free media.

The greatest hope for democracy in this world of growing authoritarianism is the free flow of information and ideas. It is for this very reason that many governments are trying to prevent such exchanges and have taken drastic steps to control the quantity and kind of information received by their citizens. There are few countries in the world today where newspapers are not government controlled, where radio and TV are not under direct government management, or where the importation of newspapers, books, or magazines is not limited or censored by official bodies.

The costs are very great for any society which limits the free flow of information to its citizens. Beyond its direct implications for democratic institutions, the lack of free access to the world's storehouse of data means backwardness and narrowness on the part of the entire society compared with those nations which open their borders to all sources of information. This can have an indirect impact on the growth and strength of the active participation of the individual in the collective decisions of a society. Science is retarded. Technology does not reflect the state of the art. Cultural expression also becomes stagnant. The ultimate result is that the entire country becomes less able to deal with its real problems or to face the global risks shared by all nations. This disfunction harms the entire global community.

There appears to be increasing hostility towards a free press on the part of many Third World governments. Often press representatives are deported from a country for reporting unfavorably on events or personalities in that country. Typical examples include the treatment of the press in India during the "Emergency" period. In another case, at the July, 1977, meeting of the Organization of African Unity, held in Libreville, Gabon, the OAU Secretariat's official spokesman tried to have Agence France-Presse banned from the conference for reporting on ideological differences among member states. Another reporter was detained by Gabonese security officials who found him talking to OAU delegates.[9]

One of the great risks of the next decade will be whether there will be a strong and free press to serve an open world community where diversity will be encouraged; or whether the world will destroy media freedom in the name of one kind of ideology or another, with the result that truth will be the chief victim of a rigid and controlled media system monopolized by governments.

For Americans and others with liberal democratic traditions, freedom of the press or indeed of communication is the key to the maintenance of democratic institutions and indeed even to the social and economic advancement of any culture. Yet the majority of people live in countries without a free press, where information is regulated by the state. The control by the government of the press and media has enabled an elite— rich, educated, and powerful—to suppress the poor, often rural illiterate masses in most developing countries. In the industrialized authoritarian countries (such as the Soviet Union, South Africa, or in Eastern Europe), control over the press has been an effective tool to repress dissent, new ideas, and possible opposition leaders. Even where newspapers are not owned by the state or ruling party, censorship by the government can destroy criticism by the people and prevent redress of injustices.

The attack on the free media has become more and more ominous. In Africa, for example, governments exercise so much control over Western news agencies and correspondents in general that the truth of what is happening on that continent is not getting out. These news agencies have become veritable captives of local governments, publishing mostly favorable news and, in the words of one respected American correspondent covering the area: "Steering away from controversial local issues."[10] This trend is dangerous, for its implications are that even a free press can be intimidated by petty dictators from reporting the truth, especially human rights violations.

In addition to restrictions that are placed on the press in individual countries, there is a movement to "legislate" controls through various international organizations. The United Nations Educational, Scientific and Cultural Organization (UNESCO) has become the focus for debate on this issue as well as providing assistance to developing countries for media facilities. The problem is that UNESCO and the majority of its member countries appear to see the balance of the flow of information and the dominance of the Western media as the key international media problem rather than the freedom of the media and of journalists. With a majority of UNESCO member governments being either at least suspicious and, more likely, hostile towards a free press, it is not surprising that UNESCO's focus of action is more towards the control of the media than that of supporting its freedom.

One such move took place within UNESCO at its October, 1976, meeting in Nairobi. On the agenda for that conference was consideration of proposals to set a communications policy program to remedy what UNESCO describes as an unjust, largely one-way flow of information from the developed to developing countries. The basic thrust of a number of these proposals is to try to create, in effect, a Third World press agency, which could enjoy governmental backing and possibly prevent criticism or frank reporting of Third World events and official actions.

In addition, UNESCO has proposed the establishment of a Latin American news agency and the formation of national news agencies where none exist. Other items on the agenda were calls for the study of a mandatory international right of reply and long-range legal studies on the "right to mass communications." While some of these proposals sound moderate or innocuous they are seen by many as an attack on the existing independent press and an effort by governments to expand their control over international journalism. Already these UNESCO proposals have been opposed by such media groups as the Inter-American Press Association and the American Newspaper Publishers Association.[11]

It is now more and more commonplace for individual governments to ban the publication of news stories which are critical and, indeed, to ban altogether magazines or newspapers that do not conform to the dictates of the group in power. In addition to the Soviet bloc, with its comprehensive control over all information, this is a growing trend in developing countries. It is not necessary to take over a newspaper physically to gain control over what it publishes. An example of a somewhat more subtle approach is seen in South Africa, which keeps its press under wraps by merely threatening a new press law which would make it possible to destroy a newspaper which publishes items which might undermine confidence in the government. Thus we find a press which conducts self-censorship and accomplishes for the government the same purpose as a direct government control. Another mechanism of such control has been to kill, imprison, or threaten individual writers or editors such as in Argentina or Nicaragua. Economic pressure is yet another way effectively to silence a free press. All that is needed is to impose special taxes, or prevent the importation of newsprint, or to threaten advertisers with reprisals. Many of these techniques are now commonplace in the majority of countries of the world. Only in a limited number of countries is it possible to find a truly free press and even in some of these countries the press is largely controlled by the few and the rich and thus represents only a narrow spectrum of the society. In even fewer nations do we find a news media reflecting the full spectrum of views, parties, and philosophies truly free of arbitrary constraints.

It is upon this relatively free press that not only the citizens of the host country depend for the facts of major events, but also many others around the world. They look to a free press for both objective reporting and information and a forum to present views and information that cannot or will not be reported in their own news media. Thus we can read the work of Soviet dissidents in *The New York Times* or the London *Observer*, or can read about opposition actions in Uganda in *Newsweek* or the London *Times*.

There are a number of areas where new technology or the advance of science interacts with the question of the limitation on the free flow of information. One area is in direct TV broadcasting from satellites into home receivers and the other is the increased restrictions placed on marine scientific research. Both these case studies deserve thought and concern not only for their own intrinsic merit but also as illustrations of a larger problem which needs the attention of those who support democracy and freedom in the exchange of ideas.

Man's advance upward from primitive times has been the story of the advance of scientific knowledge. Without cumulative knowledge about the behavior of nature and its laws mankind would have remained as little more than cavemen in a world without history or learning. Societies that fostered learning, experimentation, research, and the publication of new ideas and discoveries prospered and became the centers of progress, personal well-being, and often power. Societies that discouraged new discoveries or closed their borders to the learning of the outside fell into dark ages, often experienced poor economic development, and generally came to be dominated, in one way or other, by more advanced and powerful nations.

In the advanced modern era it is even more vital than in earlier times to be open to scientific knowledge and to encourage its development. In large measure the ability of a nation to utilize wisely the fruits of scientific and technological work will determine how fast and how well that society will advance and be able to give to its citizens many of the benefits of modern society.

Unfortunately we have seen that many of the countries which can most benefit by the spread of scientific information and especially by research by foreign scientists of natural phenomena within or near the country often attempt to prevent scientists from carrying out their inquiry and thereby retard the development of new knowledge. The following examples provide some case histories of the problem.

The Case of Direct Broadcast Satellites (DBS)

On the horizon is a new technology which makes it possible to broadcast TV programs directly from satellites into individual home TV receivers on the ground. Already, we have the capability of broadcasting from satellites to community antennas in remote areas to provide a wide range of informational and cultural programs. Since it is possible for the satellites of one country to broadcast to the TV sets of another country, there is concern on the part of individual governments and international organizations about the implications of this new technology. The main problem appears to be the desire of many governments, especially those controlled by authoritarian regimes, to restrict the information available to its people.

The main focus of this debate has centered in the deliberations of the United Nations Committee on the Peaceful Uses of Outer Space. This committee is engaged in developing draft principles to govern direct television broadcasting by satellite. Since 1963 there has been considerable controversy over this subject within various international organizations interested in this matter.

Most governments appear to want to control such broadcasts. They are seeking within the United Nations to obtain agreement to a regime of prior consent, through which they would be able to control completely the content of all programs and thus control the information available to their citizens. From the very start these governments have favored an international agreement to prohibit certain kinds of programs and to require the prior consent of the authorities in the receiving country.

At stake in this debate is the basic principle of the free flow of information across international boundaries. This principle was affirmed by United Nations countries in Article 19 of the Universal Declaration of Human Rights: "to receive and impart information and ideas through any media regardless of frontiers." So far the United States and certain other countries have maintained that the right must not be impaired and indeed that the world community should encourage the free and open exchange of information and ideas.

One way that restrictions might be put upon the broadcasts from satellites is through the allocation of frequencies assigned to Direct Broadcast Satellites (DBS) by the International Telecommunication Union (ITU) and specifically by that organization's World Administrative Radio Conference (WARC). The ITU's aim is to ensure technical protection and efficient management of radio frequencies. The ITU's WARC, in January, 1977, agreed on the allocation of frequencies and orbital positions for DBS in the European, Asian, and African regions. Under this agreement countries in these regions may object to DBS use by others at frequencies assigned to them if such use causes technical interference with domestic systems in use. It is hoped that these technical agreements will not in the future become the basis for political decisions to keep out foreign broadcasts.

Should the principle of prior consent be adopted by the United Nations for DBS there is a real danger that it could be the opening wedge to other, much broader, restrictions against foreign broadcasting and the free flow of communications. Recent experience has shown that the voices are many in opposition to a free exchange of information and specifically a free media. We can, for this reason, expect increased attacks on the flow of information in the future either by restrictive broad political resolutions or through more subtle technical provisions which can have the same effect. DBS will be only one of many battlegrounds on which the struggle for the freedom of the press will be fought.

The Cases of Remote Sensing Satellites
and Coastal Scientific Research

For example, some countries are objecting to the free publication of data from the Landsat satellites which provide information and pictures of geological formations over most of the globe. Some countries object to the overflight of those satellites even though national sovereignty does not extend to outer space. They particularly fear dissemination of information about their countries' geological features, air pollution, water systems, agricultural crops, etc.

The same is true with respect to research conducted off coastal waters of many nations. Together such restrictions, if implemented or extended, could put a halt to obtaining vital information that would be in the interest of all mankind. A few illustrations will show how interdependent we are with respect to obtaining scientific knowledge of phenomena which ignore artificial national frontiers.

The opportunity for more useful forecasts about the weather would be possible if we could understand the timing and intensity of monsoon conditions over India and Pakistan and their relationship to the water temperature in the Arabian Sea which, in turn, is controlled by ocean currents along the east coast of Africa. Subcontinent agriculture is dominated by the timing and rain content of the southwest monsoon. Successful forecasting of the monsoon requires an understanding of the ocean-atmosphere interaction including monitoring of the ocean and atmosphere over much of the Arabian Sea. Achievement of the necessary understanding will require research and monitoring of ocean temperatures and currents off the coasts of Africa, the Subcontinent, and the Arabian peninsula involving a number of countries. To the extent that undue restrictions are applied to marine scientific research in the western Arabian Sea, achievement of the capability to forecast the monsoon could be correspondingly delayed.

Yet another area where new knowledge could help many nations is the study of the most productive fishery in the world off Peru extending to Ecuador and Chile. Periodically the oceanographic conditions that maintain this rich fishery change; cold, nutrient rich water is no longer brought up from below and warm water moves in from the north. This condition is referred to as *El Nino*. A major *El Nino* such as occurred off Peru in 1972 resulted in a drastic reduction of the fisheries and concurrent economic loss. The ability to predict ahead and to prepare for a major *El Nino* is of great economic importance to Peru and to other nations. Studies to date suggest that *El Nino* is not an isolated phenomenon, but is closely linked to changing wind patterns and ocean currents in the tropical Pacific. Thus the ability to develop a successful forecast of *El Nino* requires access to weather and oceanographic observations from the entire South Pacific area. In particular, it will require oceanographic observation from the Economic Zones of Colombia, Ecuador, and Chile, as well as Peru.[12]

The debate in the Law of the Sea Conference illustrates the nature of the opposition to freedom of scientific inquiry, specifically the attack by many countries on freedom of such research within the proposed 200-mile Economic Zone being negotiated at the conference sessions. The issue was most clearly stated by the Ocean Policy Committee of the Commission on International Relations of the United States National Academy of Sciences National Research Council in 1977 in a "special statement":

> In the Law of the Sea negotiations, which began in 1973, delegates have been more concerned with national pride, national rights, and national resources, than the "common heritage" concept. The most notable effect of the negotiations so far, after five long and difficult sessions, has been the movement towards increased coastal state jurisdiction through the very considerable extension of national boundaries seaward. Swept up in this move to a 200-mile "Economic Zone" is the question of jurisdiction over scientific research. Customary law clearly supports complete freedom for scientific research in the water column beyond the territorial sea. In the current Law of the Sea negotiations, however, proponents of the economic resource zone concept argue that authorization for all scientific research must go along with the regulation of the exploitation of fisheries and mineral resources from the zone.[13]

In that statement the National Academy of Sciences (NAS) argued that nature knows no artificial boundaries and that ocean phenomena do not stop at national boundaries. It went on to state:

> The importance of scientific research to a better understanding of the marine environment is axiomatic. Since marine scientific research yields knowledge of social utility, it is difficult to understand how any state can erect barriers that restrict mankind from learning what must be known about the ocean in order to optimize its use for the benefit of all.
>
> Because ocean phenomena do not respect national boundaries, if an individual coastal State has control over marine scientific research projects in its zone, it can control the flow of benefits of that proposed research to neighboring States. Thus, the refusal of one State can deny the benefits of new knowledge to others.[14]

This issue is being fought out at the United Nations Law of the Sea Conference. At that conference the majority of developing coastal countries support a LOS Convention text which would require prior consent of the coastal state for scientific research carried out by another state or its nationals within the 200-mile Economic Zone. Even some Western and democratic countries such as New Zealand support a consent regime. Present international law permits freedom of scientific research outside of the normally accepted limits of the territorial sea. The only exception is research carried out on the continental shelf which requires the consent of the coastal or "shelf" state.[15]

This new limitation on scientific research within the proposed 200-mile Economic Zones is serious since about 80 to 90 percent of all marine scientific research is conducted within 200 miles of the coastline. Unless some changes are made in this very restrictive approach the cost to the world's scientific community could be great. It could also be the start of a general attack on freedom of scientific research and restrictions on the dissemination of information flowing from such research.

One possible compromise of the marine scientific research issue would be to have a "consent" regime for scientific research directly related to the exploitation of resources in the Economic Zone, but for all other marine research there would only be required advance notification to the coastal state without the right of prior consent. Under this approach, the researching state would provide to the coastal state all necessary information about the kind of research being done, would make all data gathered available, would assist in interpreting the information and would offer the opportunity to the coastal state to participate in the research project, including permitting coastal state scientists to be aboard the research ship. But even this rather reasonable approach is unlikely to be agreed upon, with most developing countries, the Soviet bloc, and even many "democratic" countries favoring full coastal state control over all marine research.

There are other examples of restrictions on scientific research and the free exchange and publication of scientific data. These restrictions are a part of larger trends seen in the whole information or knowledge sector. The basic problem for both the media and for science is that rulers fear the truth. This fear comes from the realization that truth can indeed set men free, the opposite of the intention of many governments.

Yet the struggle for freedom is also not without its allies. Technology itself often demands for its effective functioning the free flow of information. But perhaps the greatest force in this struggle is man's own innate curiosity.

CHAPTER VIII

Future Patterns of Global Cooperation

Introduction

Our examination of global risks has indicated that present international institutions do not always serve the world's new needs or act to prevent new disasters. The world lacks effective organizations to manage change, to help its members adapt to new circumstances, and to decrease the risks of a modern society faced by the world community as a whole or by its individual citizens. The organizations of the past have not adapted well to new circumstances and attendant risks. They reflect the weakness of their members who equally are unable to understand or to adapt to a changing reality.

We have already seen a number of critical gaps in the world's institutional system through the examination of specific problems. In essence we are using primitive social and political mechanisms to cope with a world of high technology. The serious gaps in international institutions include the management of world food supplies or reserves, regulation of multinational corporations, the sharing of safe energy technology, development of cooperation between oil producers and consumers, and the monitoring and control of global environmental threats. Of particular importance is the effective handling of global economic factors including adequate resources for development. International trade/promotion and protection, as well as the effective supervision of balance of payments surpluses and deficits, require more innovative approaches in light of the important role they play in the world economy, especially for the expansion of opportunity among the world's poor. The reform of the world's economic institutions must therefore be a high priority in any overall restructuring of the mechanisms by which the nations of the world make decisions about their collective community.

In examining the changing nature of our global challenges and their concomitant risks, it is clear that the most overriding characteristic of that system is the great gap which exists between the very poor and the very rich both among nations and among groups within nations. We have seen this time and time again as we examined such problems as the spread of nuclear weapons, global energy needs, environmental decay, or the allocation of the world's food resources. In each of these areas the impact of the poor majority on the rich minority and vice versa has played an all important part in shaping the nature of both the problem itself and in the kinds of solutions which are possible.

Already it is clear to most observers that the developed countries cannot continue to exist in some kind of pristine isolation from the developing world which represents most of mankind. On the other side it is equally clear that much of the future and the well-being of the developing countries will depend upon changes taking place in the industrialized countries of the world, where now most of the world's technology, wealth, and managerial expertise are. However, a large proportion of the world's natural resources exists in the developing areas and those resources are vital to the industrialized countries.

In looking at global issues, we need first of all to admit that the rich and the poor have different problems that are not always shared or mutually understood. There are those who prefer to concentrate almost exclusively on the predicament of the developing world as if no other problems exist, and as if advanced societies had no difficulties or problems to which they might devote their resources, energy, and expertise. There are some who see an industrialized world in splendid isolation and concentrate only on the problems of "rich societies" such as auto pollution, suburban congestion, or the noise level of an SST. There is also a viewpoint that there is little the rich can do for the poor and therefore the best solution is to avoid any involvement in shaping the forces at work in the Third World. Finally, there are those who believe that in a high-risk world it is necessary to address not only problems that are close at hand but also those problems shared by all.

Each area's limited problems, together with the worldwide ones, will inevitably shape the ultimate nature of an ever evolving global society. In the end "regional" or even local problems will affect our shared environment and create dangers for all. In an interdependent world there is no salvation by mere self-protection. That route leads in the same direction as does "beggar-my-neighbor" trade and economic policies and practices: namely to depression and disaster. For this reason it is vitally important for all sides to acknowledge and share in the solution to problems that are both near and far. It would be tragic if both the world's technical capability and its natural resources could not or would not be used constructively in dealing with the problems of the developed and developing countries as well as the changing needs of the global society and its shared risks.

Further, we must not forget that we are living in a period in which there is a fundamental cleavage between the East and West, between the democratic industrialized societies with their economic flexibility and personal freedom and the Communist societies in Eastern Europe and in China with their orientation towards authoritarian rule and economic and ideological uniformity. Each is suspicious of the other, and in the case of the United States and the Soviet Union, there is the possibility of a nuclear holocaust which would be costly to all peoples and cannot be overlooked in any examination of the world's great risks.

Thus a major element in the global problem-solving framework is the relative separateness of the Eastern bloc countries from the rest of the world's political evolution and economy. There is little doubt that the cleavage between East and West is probably not being bridged effectively and that there is a continuing isolation which, if perpetuated, could exacerbate the existing ideological and political tensions and increase the risk of conflict. In the long run, it will be necessary, in order to reduce the number and variety of risks global society must face, for both the Soviet Union and China to be integrated more effectively and voluntarily into the global decision-making and problem-solving process than has heretofore been the case. It is particularly difficult for the Soviet bloc countries to participate in the organization of agreements which demand certain specific obligations which these countries would want to be free to determine on their own. They have an innate fear of any surrender of sovereignty and seek complete freedom of action. This attitude limits greatly the constructive participation of these countries in global problem-solving tasks with other nations.

Therefore up to now the Soviet Union and China have stood somewhat apart from the world's agonies. The Soviet Union is loath to acknowledge that the malnutrition and starvation of the world's developing countries are part of their concern or that they have a moral obligation to act along with the rest of the industrialized nations. China in its own way has isolated itself from the world's cares. It has largely pursued policies of ideological and political opposition to what it describes as the "great power hegemony." This narrow perspective has left China largely an irrelevant giant in the midst of a sea of troubles into which it ultimately will be engulfed if it does not join in devising common solutions. It would be a great tragedy if the third or more of the world's population that this group represents remained outside of the creative process of devising common solutions to the world's ills. It would be a tragedy for the rest of the world in that their resources and talents could not be utilized in this common enterprise, and a tragedy for the non-democratic "socialist camp" in that they could not participate in the most important and meaningful changes of the coming age.

For these reasons, one of the important world structural reforms of our global system will be to devise better means by which the industrialized democracies, the Eastern bloc, including China, and the developing world can act together to solve problems they all share in common. Obviously, the first step is to engage all of these nations in the process of analysis, evaluation, and examination. From that basic experience they must then go on to devise decision-making mechanisms and institutions, in which they all can fairly participate, aimed towards providing all societies with a greater measure of well-being, lower risks, and common technological and intellectual progress. In sum, it is fair to say that none of the individual problems we have examined such as global hunger, human health, the growth of population, or potential mass destruction will be finally solved without the full collaboration and cooperation of all relevant regional and ideological groups.

In a similar way, an effective global system, capable of coming to grips with the main global challenges of the future decades, cannot operate without providing a tangible means by which all nations can achieve a far more genuine sense of participation. This is true whether one wants to solve environmental problems or arms control. For example, nonnuclear weapons states must have a greater say over world energy and nuclear issues than is the case today if there is to be any serious hope of persuading them to forgo nuclear weapons and associated technology. The global system will need to assure them of competitive low cost energy and a say in the use of nuclear energy internationally. They do not want to be second-class citizens. One answer is to create an international institution or mechanism which will ensure that any future benefits of peaceful nuclear technology will be at the disposal of all countries—even if this technology is not directly controlled by the country obtaining the end product (energy) benefit.

Such institutions can be created on a global or regional basis and include centers for reprocessing of spent fuel and enrichment facilities. These institutions could be manned by international civil servants and controlled by boards of directors from the participating countries. It may be of even greater importance to develop organizations that will ensure the availability of new energy technologies which are nonnuclear. The above is only one example of how it may be possible to increase the practical participation by poorer or less powerful countries so that they can increase their stake in seeing that the world system is fairly and safely organized and managed.

In whatever field one examines, it will be necessary for the richer and more powerful countries to make significant contributions to assisting the poorer and less powerful to participate in a meaningful way in the system. A major contribution must not only be in money but more importantly in technology that can be usefully applied for developmental purposes.

The Technological Dimension of Global Cooperation

Almost all experts acknowledge the vital role technology and science play in providing instruments for social change and economic progress. Technology has the capacity to shape a more equitable and balanced global economy and social structure. The general belief has been that this can be accomplished by a massive program of technology transfer on behalf of the poorer nations. The belief is that by exporting technological hardware and supporting and strengthening the internal scientific and technological efforts of the developing countries there would take place a significant improvement in the productivity, competitiveness, and economic equity of these countries.

This rather simplistic assumption has proven to be only partially true. We have learned that highly complex and expensive technological goods are not always suitable for many developing countries which have large unemployed or underemployed work forces. Further, such high technology often benefits only the urban elites either in terms of return on capital or in providing for the consumer or other needs of the modern sector of the population.

Recent debate has focused on the concept of appropriate technology which usually is defined as being processes, techniques, or methods of production which are especially adaptable, suitable, and effective within the local context and which meet real needs of the poorer peoples. For example, one kind of modern energy technology might be suitable for a highly industrialized country or even a rich, low-population oil producing state, but it would not be efficient or practical for the poorer, more densely populated countries of the South.

While there is a growing consensus among development specialists that "appropriate technology" can be a vital element in uplifting the efficiency and individual well-being of the poor majority, there remains considerable debate on the best methods for developing such technology and applying it in the Third World. What is agreed is that such technology should be aimed at enhancing the inherent capabilities and resources existing in the local community.

Typically, while capital-intensive, large-scale technologies may be more efficient in the traditional economic sense, they are not often able to reach into the rural, usually non-cash-economy areas where the majority of people live and work. Further, much of the traditional large scale technologies of the industrialized countries are oriented towards the production of goods which often serve little purpose in societies where there is barely enough to eat.

The challenge is to develop technologies which can render and help the vast majority of the population which lives at subsistence levels in rural and small town areas. Only by reaching this segment of the Third World will it be possible to contribute to the development or even the survival of the world's poor majority. But from a practical standpoint there exists tremendous difficulty in identifying and developing, let alone disseminating and utilizing, appropriate technology. Success in this area undoubtedly will require support from both the industrialized countries and the strong leadership and internal resources of the developing countries themselves. There will have to be many different experiments and model programs, many of which will fail, before proven large-scale techniques or programs will emerge and affect the lives of the world's poorest peoples.

The 1979 United Nations Conference on Science and Technology for Development is an important milestone in the international debate on how technology can become a more effective instrument in improving the lives and productivity of the poorer countries. A main issue in the debate on this question is how to meet basic human needs with existing technology which can be adapted for use by the developing countries. Another question is whether and how all countries can increase their own research and development efforts towards the design of technology which could be especially helpful for the Third World nations.

For some developing countries a critical issue is the creation of an indigenous capability to either adapt technology originating in the more advanced countries or indeed create entirely new technology suitable for local circumstances and economics. This latter capability is most suitable for the larger and more advanced developing countries, but all nations will have to have the ability to modify the use of technology to suit local conditions. In the end the most important factor in either slowing or accelerating the importation, development, and use of technology in a developing country will be the host government's own policies and practices. If they provide incentives and welcome the introduction of new methods, ideas, and capital, there will be progress. The opposite will be true when governments impose overly restrictive controls or do not permit adequate incentives.

Some developing countries, however, have argued the position (as part of the Group of 77's "New International Economic Order") that the industrialized countries should provide, without charge, certain technology to speed their development. Arguments of equity apart it is unlikely that this will take place except in certain very specific sectors where governments have made considerable research and development efforts and therefore own or control specific useful know-how. The private sector has most of the useful technology and expects to obtain a profit from it no matter where it is used. There are certain incentives that advanced governments can establish, however, which can help the flow of technology to the poor and their problems, and it may be desirable to develop these in the name of both equity and the lowering of common risks.

Technological Change and International Institutions

Focusing on our global system, one basic factor of technology must be acknowledged: society's institutions must change to accommodate advancing technology. An important question is whether new technology will modify political systems before political leaders are able to manage such emerging technology. There usually is a large gap in the response of society's structures to already available technology, let alone to emerging or still experimental know-how. We are only now learning to live with technology which was first introduced some twenty years ago.

Systems analysts would call this situation a "delayed feedback loop." What we are seeing then is a twenty- to thirty-year time delay between the introduction of new technology and the establishment of effective political mechanisms to utilize or regulate such technology effectively and safely. In addition, most of our institutions are considerably behind the existing state of the art in the behaviorial sciences. Thus we are behind both in utilizing the most up-to-date technology for good ends and behind in controlling the bad consequences or high risks of technology run wild.

The point is that a number of new and effective institutional mechanisms probably need to be developed which will serve to bring the world's future problems to the attention of the global policy makers in a constructive way. Now may be a good moment for the world community to take affirmative action since there is increasing public awareness of these problems and a growing disenchantment with the way we have approached them in the past.

To move in this direction we need first of all to develop a much better global consensus about the nature and causes of our present and future problems. Essentially, this is an educational function as well as political function. It is educational in that it requires a certain basic common empirical methodology and data about what is really happening in the world. It is political in the sense that national and international leaders must articulate both to their followers and to each other their understanding of problems and of proposals to alleviate the world's common ills, develop cooperative mechanisms which can do the job, and ensure a fair distribution of responsibilities and benefits. Without these basic requirements there is little hope that real innovation or action will take place either to prevent "bad" technology and its consequences or the full utilization of "good" technology for the benefit of the world's poorest members.

One clear understanding emerges from an analysis of the predicaments of the modern age as it relates to international relations: we must find solutions which deal both with the social and political context as well as the technological. We must be equally or even more inventive with our social institutions as with our utilization of technology. The creation of social institutions is perhaps the more difficult of the two, but necessary if we are to cope with technology on any kind of effective basis. Does anyone today really claim that we can sit and do nothing with respect to international cooperative mechanisms while the consequence of population growth, pollution, resource scarcity, racialism, poverty, and spreading nuclear technology run their course uncontrolled by the collective wisdom and good intentions of most peoples on the globe?

In the search for solutions to individual global problems and in the process of generally structuring the world community to examine possible new problems emerging from rapid technological change, it is necessary to devise new approaches which can 1) reach across national borders, 2) utilize the most up-to-date state of the art methods of analysis and data gathering, and 3) at the same time effectively relate to the existing decision-making mechanisms. Certainly the first task would be for the governments themselves to start opening new areas of dialogue between them about the kinds of risks we will confront in the next decades and about the various forces and policies which will be needed to control the world's future, a future which is outside the power of any single actor in that system.

Already we have seen some emerging elements of new structures which have been devised to deal with specific global problems. One example has been the United Nations Environmental Program which emerged from the Stockholm Conference in 1972 and raised the consciousness of all countries with respect to the ecological dangers we now are facing. In the same way the world conference on population at Bucharest also stirred the world community to devise an action program with both national and international activities aimed at solving this serious problem. We now have within the United Nations system the United Nations Fund for Population Activities. In terms of global food needs there has been some structural progress resulting from the World Food Conference in Rome in 1974, with the establishment of a World Food Council and other related organizations. In addition, the world responded to the technological capabilities of the hour in the global communications field with the establishment of Intelsat when satellites provided new and exciting methods of contact between countries continents apart. In its own way each of these institutions was partially responsive to a given problem. The difficulty lies in that each of these institutions in its own way is limited. They have difficulties in raising sufficient resources to deal with their problem area and are largely dependent upon their member states for policy resources. Key to the relative lack of institutional capability in these areas is that many of the member states themselves do not have the necessary resources or at least are not willing to commit them in such a magnitude as to solve the problem that these institutions are addressing.

In one sense the institutions themselves have become barriers to finding answers to problems since many people assume that with the establishment of these institutions the problems themselves are solved. This is very far from the actual situation. It is clearly not enough to establish an institution with inadequate resources and staffing to remedy or solve massive global problems. Establishing an inadequate organization is in some ways almost a flight from true responsibility and accountability on the part of the world's decision makers.

Over the short-term it is very likely that most of the power to act on given problems will remain in the nation states. If this is so, then it seems encumbent upon all to expend a considerable amount of effort in increasing the capabilities of these governments to undertake major and effective activities in support of global goals within their own boundaries. The most serious dilemmas are obviously those of the developing countries with their limited ability to marshal resources, with little access to the most advanced technology, and with few financial resources or expertise. Further, in large part leaders of the developing countries are engulfed by their immediate problems which are all-pervasive and of the most serious nature. This leaves them with little time to focus attention on the larger world structure.

Another major block to their full participation in global analysis and decision making is the increasingly apparent orientation towards an extreme form of nationalism on the part of many of these countries. We appear to be living in an age of growing nationalism, while the relevance of such an ideology decreases and becomes even dangerous. While one might accept some demagoguery in the speeches of leaders of various nations as natural, such activity has acted to prevent the necessary examination of real and pressing common problems. It has turned our attention away from our real risks and towards isolationism, xenophobia, and acts of aggression or conflict over meaningless old wrongs or equally insignificant boundary lines. This myopic perspective refuses to acknowledge both a common humanity and shared risks. It emphasizes the power of the nation state at the time when such power is swiftly becoming more and more paralyzed before the force of modern technology. This characteristic is perhaps one of the most dangerous elements in our age since it could also frustrate an enlightened and forthcoming approach on the part of the industrialized countries.

In addition to the nationalistic orientation of many of the developing countries we also see the growth of regionalism and of bloc politics. These developments bode ill for the development of a global perspective and a sense of universal community. Bloc politics, particularly the split between the "Group of 77" (comprising almost all of the developing world) and the industrialized countries, most of which are members of the OECD, could in the end make impossible the process of common analysis and common problem solving. Should this be the case we are very likely to see a growth in our problems, a growth in the risks we all share—and ultimately common catastrophe.

In this context it is of the utmost importance that both the developing countries and the developed countries work together, particularly in the economic sector, to open their borders to the trade of other countries, to provide financial support, and to share resources. It is clear, in any case, that a prerequisite for global problem solving and global risk reduction must be the creation of an international, effectively functioning, and open economy in which both the developing and the developed countries gain through the exchange of trade, financial assistance, technological transfer, and resource sharing.

We have seen that attention of the developing countries to universal problems cannot take place unless they have a sense that their own problems are also shared and being supported by others and that a measure of progress can be seen. In the end there must be a bridging of the gap between the very poor and the very rich. It is clear that without the willing assumption on the part of the rich to share the burdens of the poor, no global problem can be fully solved. Insofar as this is not the case, there will be unnecessary and indeed frightening risks for all.

One of the major elements of any cooperation in the growth of world trade and the process of modernization is the assumption of mutual obligations between developed and developing countries. This is particularly true in the area of trade: in sharing technology and access to raw materials.[1] Access to developed markets by Third World countries and by industrialized nations to natural resources go hand-in-hand. An entirely one-way flow of benefits cannot sustain a stable system particularly during times of economic stress. For long periods in the past, the industrialized countries benefited greatly from raw materials and cheap labor in the developing, largely colonial, countries. This system did not work and was revised often, but not always, by revolution and conflict. Yet a reverse system of largely one-way flows in the other direction will also not work. The only way to sustain a continued and balanced interchange, in light of the spread of technology, is through mutual obligations and advantages which provide strong incentives for continued cooperation. Truly effective economic and technological sharing can only, in the last analysis, be carried out in a context of mutual benefit.

The cooperative search for shared solutions can only be accomplished if there also is recognition on the part of the developing countries that they must forgo a large measure of their cherished nationalism and their false sense of independence. Already the more intelligent and wiser leaders acknowledge, at least in private and some increasingly in public, the degree to which their own nation's economy, well-being, and safety rest upon decisions made outside their own borders. Whether or not they will search for solutions through confrontation rather than solutions in cooperation will depend first on the response of the developed world to the developing world's crises. Second, it will depend upon the willingness of the developing world itself to realize the needs of the larger community and to make the necessary sacrifices in their ideological and in some cases in their political objectives. They and the developed nations must see the world not as a zero sum game in which one group loses and the other gains, but rather as an interdependent community in which they must find shared solutions. In this group all the actors, on balance, gain by seeking not solutions at the expense of others but solutions which provide for the vital concerns of all major participants and which create an overall system that permits increased assistance and trade along with decreased vulnerability to global dangers.

Establishing Institutions of Common Analysis and Decision Making

In the effort at change and innovation in our international institutions, it is necessary to create some forum where the diverse issues of the world can be seen as a whole and integrated into some overall design. In particular, it is necessary to provide a mechanism whereby the conflicts between various goals and between various sectors are resolved. We too often experience individual organizations fighting with one another over "turf" or competence in a certain field. The result is overlapping and wasteful activities which are also counterproductive to the aims of those institutions. Yet the problem is not just a duplication of effort but rather the inability of the whole system to come to grips with reality and to act effectively. Time and time again we see these organizations shirking their responsibilities. The main reason for this deficiency is the values and the perceptions of the member states' governments. A secondary but still important reason is the antiquated structures of these organizations. A common problem in this respect is the tendency of these organizations and especially their secretariats to opt for the "lowest common denominator" solutions or recommendations in their proposals to member governments, and the willingness of the member governments to accept and even advocate such solutions to pressing problems that require imaginative and radical approaches.

At the very center of any restructuring of the global system must be the creation of mechanisms by which nations and their citizens can examine in a unified and comprehensive way the full scope of world problems, along with alternative solutions or ameliorative actions which might be taken. We need to apply the best professional analysis to the problems at hand or those which are on the horizon. It is necessary that such analysis take place well in advance of the problem before it becomes essentially unmanageable; or, to be more exact, before the risk becomes so great that the problem threatens major disaster no matter what reasonable actions are taken by the collective global community. Also it is necessary to provide enough advance time for the international community to debate widely the issues involved wherever possible and to apply solutions peaceably and, if possible, by consensus.

This function is still rarely performed on a national level and remains almost unheard of on an international level. Even in the United States there is no Federal governmental effort at technology assessment. There does exist within the United States a Congressional Office of Technology Assessment (OTA) but it has no control over the Federal government and merely provides advice to Congressional committees, mostly on request. This is a serious gap in our national governmental decision-making process and an even more serious gap in the global system.

One reason the Congressional Office of Technology Assessment is not effective is that it does not have direct and immediate access to the key governmental decision makers, especially the Cabinet members and the President. For the same reason, a global technology assessment or analysis function will not be potent unless it can have access to and directly influence the key global decision makers.

This is a serious problem for international institutions generally. Often the main meetings of these organizations are attended by permanent diplomatic representatives with little power in their home governments and this makes a sham of resolutions or decisions taken by these organizations since implementations by the governments concerned are lacking. Sometimes the meetings are attended by Foreign Ministers or even heads of governments but the actions taken are frequently structured in such a way as to be meaningless: little more than empty platitudes. Also many international meetings which are attended by Foreign Ministers raise issues needing action from the domestic sector, over which Foreign Ministers often have little control. On the other side of the equation, domestic affairs Cabinet Ministers often feel little responsibility for international problems even when they directly relate to their own areas of accountability. With this dilemma it is almost impossible to obtain effective action by nations collectively in solving major problems, especially those requiring the application of a considerable amount of resources.

The Scientific/Technological Link with Global Decision Making

We need to understand that science and its product technology cannot themselves be the source of economic and political decision making. At best they are simply inputs, like others, each having its impact and each having to be factored into the final equation which results in a decision. Unfortunately, both on a national and an international level we don't have a really successful switching mechanism which can communicate the evaluations and views of scientists and other experts to the political decision makers. Above all there is no institutional instrument which can look at longer range issues which lie beyond the perspective of political leaders, who necessarily are thinking within the boundaries of their time-limited political context to the next election or its political equivalent in authoritarian systems.

For example, one major area of great global concern is health. Almost any observer of this problem realizes that a better utilization and distribution of technology and manpower can be managed than we have at present. Clearly we also need to develop better global indicators of how the international community is progressing in this field. While the World Health Organization has done an excellent job in some areas it is evident that much more needs to be done which is presently beyond the resources, scope, and perspective of that organization as it is presently constituted.

In light of these deficiencies, it is necessary to either create new international institutions or radically reform those already existing. For international organizations to be effective, first, it is necessary that they contain a decision forum which can act effectively, especially in marshaling the necessary resources to do a particular job. This means that those who have the power over national resources—the only ones presently available—attend meetings that require their decisions. Second, it is necessary that the international bodies themselves examine problems realistically and completely and provide a range of possible actions in the form of options from which an action might be chosen by member states.

To formulate the nature of the problem effectively and to propose equally efficacious solutions require a radical change in the way international secretariats operate. To achieve these goals, it will be necessary to recruit the best talent available anywhere regardless of nationality. To be able to attract such talent will require worthwhile compensation scales. Experts of the highest quality in professional fields such as ecology, urban planning, international finance, and systems analysis command high salaries and other compensations. It is exceedingly short-sighted and "pound foolish" on the part of global organizations and their member states to expect first-class work while paying second-class salaries. Other more important attractions for high quality people are "psychic benefits," the opportunity for real accomplishment.

Beyond the attraction of high quality professionals to undertake the required examination of global problems, these organizations themselves may need, first, to engage in a radical restructuring of their decision-making process, second, expand their areas of competence, and third, increase their powers. In the first case, we have noted the importance of meetings attended by the real decision makers from national capitals. This, in part, is already increasingly taking place. (The model for this approach is the European Community.) These officials not only have command over resources but also bring important elements of expertise to the international decision-making process. The most significant stage in global problem solving is the follow-up action by the individual governments and the extent to which they support or do not support a given collective decision made at a particular meeting.

Another major related reason for the inability to deal effectively with our problems is the disparity between the structure, especially the form of decision making within most international organizations (especially the United Nations), and the reality of the world's distribution of overall power, including economic capability, population, and military might. In short, those without important responsibility or the ability to make a real contribution to global well-being and peace are often able to dominate international forums simply with their votes as sovereign independent nations. For example, the United Nations in its Assembly, with one-nation one-vote, does not represent the reality of world power. In any case, it is largely powerless. But the Security Council, as presently constituted, does not fairly represent the majority of the Third World and therefore it is mistrusted by them. The Security Council can work effectively only when the great powers can agree on a course of action, which is rare.

The specialized organizations of the United Nations have often done noble work but they are frequently narrowly focused, manned by poor staffs, and inadequate to deal with most of the really dangerous problems of the age. Further, they have sometimes become too "politicized" which impairs their effective global functioning and undercuts their impartiality and integrity. They are also short of sufficient funds to deal with most global problems. More important, collectively the United Nations system often cannot act independently of its member states and often must stand silent when wrong is done by one or more of its member nations.

Most of the regional organizations, inside and outside the United Nations system, suffer from many of the same faults. For example, the Organization for Economic Cooperation and Development (OECD), while useful as a forum for the exchange of views among the democratic industrialized countries, has not been able to address seriously, let alone solve, the many pressing maladies of advanced societies and their economic interactions. Inflation, high unemployment, low productivity, increasingly dangerous air and water pollution, lack of social mobility, inefficient and protectionist practices, continue and even increase among these countries despite the high goals and aims of the OECD and similar bodies.

There has, for example, been an increase in the number of "microstates" as members of the United Nations. We are likely to see nearly 100 additional new United Nations members before many more years, most of them with only a few hundred thousand or less inhabitants. It is estimated that at that point, nearly half of the world's nations would consist of islands and archipelagoes and 40 percent of the world's fully sovereign nations would have populations smaller than Norfolk, Virginia.[2] Even at present, of the more than 90 new nations the United Nations has admitted since 1945, half are less populous than North Carolina. More than half of the present membership of the United Nations individually contribute the minimum 0.02 percent of the budget, and collectively pay less than one-sixteenth of the share contributed by the United States. At present, this group, however, has a majority vote in the General Assembly.

With respect to changing the decision-making process of these organizations, it will be necessary to move from large unwieldy general debating bodies with one-nation one-vote towards smaller or specialized bodies making decisions on the basis of weighted voting or even consensus. In the long run, it will be necessary and helpful to establish bodies in which countries with larger populations, large gross national product, and significant elements of power are accorded greater say than nations with few people and little economic resources or potential. In the final analysis this is both fair and realistic.

The problem is not so much that these mini-states have a right to be independent and sovereign and to run their own affairs, but rather in an international structure that endorses a world system based on a false "equality," where China, India, the Soviet Union, and the United States are given the same weight as Djibouti and Fiji or Luxembourg. A hundred countries, all incapable of effective action, may produce a majority in a given meeting but will produce little in the way of solving worldwide problems. While this may sound somewhat harsh, it reflects a political and economic reality which would be foolhardy to ignore.

The simple fact is that there are but a handful of governments capable of acting on a global basis and only a few more that have the power to influence events within a given region. It is these powers which must be effectively engaged in international problem solving and especially risk reduction efforts.

Unless there is a reform of the international organizations so that decision making reflects the reality of responsibility and power, these organizations will count for less and less in international politics. The point is not that the mini-states should not have a voice in these organizations but rather that their voice should approximate the actual contribution they can make to the problems being addressed. In the real world of global politics, a majority vote by hundreds of countries cannot force large nations or the "superpowers" to act against their real interests. Too often empty votes or resolutions are passed by large majorities calling for sweeping changes. They are often ignored and thus bring into disrepute or scorn the concerned international organizations. This weakens these very valuable tools of diplomacy and reconciliation.

While it is necessary to develop decision-making mechanisms that more nearly reflect the reality of power, this does not mean that decisions about the future of the world community should be taken by a group of rich countries such as the OECD countries and the Eastern bloc. On the contrary, it is vital that the larger and more powerful developing countries participate more fully in the global decision-making process. For example, the newly rich OPEC countries should be given added weight in the key financial institutions such as the World Bank and the International Monetary Fund if they are prepared to play a constructive role in such organizations. But it is necessary that they enter these organizations with the aim of shouldering responsibilities in keeping with their newfound wealth. It makes no sense to include nations in important, even vital, organizations if those governments play either a passive or negative role—despite their great wealth or power. As we have noted earlier the same criteria should also apply to the Eastern bloc or countries led by the Soviet Union. Thus a vital element of global reform must be increased effective participation and burden sharing on a universal basis.

New Capabilites for Problem Solving

Yet another element is the "qualitative" structuring of international organizations. In order to accomplish major tasks in risk reduction and in assisting the development process for the poorest countries, there must be an ability to obtain and manage resources and to be able to act independently on behalf of the common world community.

First, let's look at the need for greater independence or opportunity for initiative on the part of these organizations to carry out their tasks subject to the original decisions by the qualified authoritative body. This independence is not a quality without limit or review but there is a need for international bodies to act on behalf of the collective good and not to be restrained by the influence of various national or regional interest groups who would like to see action biased towards their narrow goals.

This kind of independence must include integrity, impartiality, and fairness. If these qualities do not exist, the system will break down and fail since it will not be trusted by any rational government. Thus reform must mean a greater degree of loyalty to the collective interest of the global community and a very strong aversion to taking up the cause of any single group within that community.

International civil servants who run these institutions must have these qualities of independence, integrity, and impartiality if these organizations are to be looked upon by all their members as the focus for fair and effective global or regional decision making and implementation. Once either the organization or its secretariat personnel are looked upon as sectarian partisans supporting only one group or one ideological bent, the organization loses its credibility and nations will not delegate important powers to it.

As noted earlier, it is necessary for international organizations to find global community solutions to common problems. To do so requires the creation of new centers of initiative on the part of these organizations. These initiatives must reflect the common good and not be directed at harming any particular country or group of countries. Rather, such initiatives or proposals need to be formulated in such a way that all nations will gain, although not always in the same way or proportion.

The European Community has developed this kind of approach through the creation of the European Commission, which is a body of prominent individuals from the member countries, nominated by the individual commissioner's government but appointed to act in the common good and not on behalf of any country, party, or government. Once appointed they are not removable by their governments and it is their collective and exclusive task to propose "initiatives to the Council of Ministers" of the European Community which is the body representing the member governments that can accept or reject the proposals or initiatives of the commission. The member governments may not revise the proposals or initiate new ones. They can, however, make their views known in the council and through this process the commission can revise rejected initiatives. Most major decisions are now taken by consensus within the Council, but voting is according to a weighted formula depending on the size of the country. Most importantly decisions of the Council are binding on member governments. (Decision making within the European Community is still evolving and is in an early stage of development.) This process results in a number of worthwhile improvements on the model of a United Nations General Assembly of one-nation one-vote and broad generalized resolutions which bind no one. In effect the European Community model, while not doing away with member country "sovereignty," does in actual fact delegate it, in part, to an extranational or even supranational institution, for designated and specified subjects or areas.

The European Community also contains a judicial system for the adjudication of disputes over the meaning of the various treaties which compose the European Community structure. There is a European Court and its decisions, within the competence of the applicable treaties, are binding not only on governments but also on persons natural and juridicial. This is a significant improvement over the World Court, which does not always have either compulsory jurisdiction or binding authority over international disputes, nor does it have direct authority over individuals or corporations.

Any reform of the international political structure must include improvement in the settlement of disputes and conflicts among nations. It must also go beyond jurisdiction over national governments and reach out towards some kind of role over the new transnational actors: multinational corporations, certain private international bodies, and international organizations themselves. Further, we need to examine ways in which individuals can gain status before international courts— standing which is now largely lacking under common international law.

Financing International Community Needs

Now let us look at the other key factor in developing effective international institutions: the obtaining of resources. In the future collective action will need to be far more specific and require the application of a larger scale of resources than has been the case in the past. The already noted cases of empty, very general resolutions have rarely had commitments of real resources along with the words. The result often is to increase the risks the world community faces by lulling it into a false sense that something is actually being done to solve the problem at issue. One of the most important requirements of any effective international community effort to reduce risks or to seek common or shared benefits is the ability to obtain the necessary resources (money, people, and technology) to carry out effective programs. At present most international organizations are dependent on two basic sources of funding: (1) assessed budgetary contributions from member states based on a predetermined "key" (i.e., a set percentage of the regular budget) and (2) voluntary contributions (i.e., monies individual states are willing to put up for a specific and agreed purpose). Unfortunately, both these sources of funds have important limitations which weaken the ability of international organizations to carry out large, long-term projects or programs.

A number of suggestions have been made with respect to developing new means of obtaining resources to deal with international community needs. A very high priority for the world's institutions in the next few decades will be examining different new methods which could provide those needed resources on a constant long-term basis. Among the ideas that have been suggested are: (1) taxing those that pollute "global commons" such as upper atmosphere or oceans, (2) taxing those who would exploit the resources of the "global commons" such as seabed minerals, offshore oil, fishing beyond 200 miles or in Antarctica, (3) taxing international trade or shipping or a portion of that trade, (4) taxing international travel or the sale of arms, and (5) raising money in the international private sector, perhaps in the way that the International Bank for Reconstruction and Development (IBRD) is able to float its bonds with the backing of member governments.[3]

Each of the above suggestions has certain problems. For example, a tax on international trade could hurt labor in poorer countries or inhibit efficient production. On the other hand if rates were set very low (as they are likely to be in any case) there should be no serious distortions to trade. Another related issue is whether such revenue should go to help solve problems in the sector that the money was obtained from or should it go into a global pot from which it can be drawn for any purpose. (For example, should revenue obtained from fishing in international waters be set aside only to maintain or protect those fish stocks?) If such an international tax were established it is more likely that it would be created for a specific, shared, and vital purpose than for general revenue, at least initially.

In any case it is necessary that the global community devise some mechanism for obtaining large-scale resources to deal with pressing problems and that such resources not be subject to the control or veto of a few states. A considerable base of common analysis, of acknowledgment of the shared risks, and of the actions required to deal with them may need to be first established before such a change will take place. We will next look at these vital prerequisites.

Global Institutional Tasks to Reduce
Common Community Risks

A responsive and relevant international institution must not only have an effective decision-making mechanism and sufficient resources. It also will need to be able to carry out effectively certain vital functions if it is to act to reduce the world's risks and to create greater overall well-being. Some of these functions have already been noted and they include: forecasting or analysis of trends, risk reduction through the widening of choices, and finally crisis management.

One way for the global community to reduce the overall possibility of risk would be through creation of new international centers for developing global indicators, forecasting, and analysis. These could be established using already existing organizations which partially perform similar functions or perhaps through creating from scratch whole new global think tanks. The global policy-making and resource allocation mechanisms can then request through task orders assessments of current problems, potential future difficulties, and also—and this is equally important—development of policy options in key areas. A massive mobilization of the best talent available—worldwide and without regard to "regional representation"—should be carried out to staff these centers of global indicators and analysis. The talent should be so good and so respected that it would be difficult for political leaders to ignore their findings or their recommendations.

The proposed "Global Indicators and Analysis Centers" would have full-time staffs, who would be able to lay out the nature of individual problems and provide expert advice, but the centers could also draw upon outside contributions since no single institution could possibly contain all of the best minds even in a single field. Above all, however, the centers should be interdisciplinary since few global problems will find their solutions in only one subject area. The world—as we have already seen—is far more complex than to allow this simplification. These centers would largely be for data gathering, analysis, synthesis or integration, and finally for development of suggested actions which would serve the whole global community. Their work would be to understand synergetic relationships between differing forces at work in the global community. The aim would be to ensure that, for example, we do not work against our other goals (environment, nuclear proliferation) in pursuit of only one goal (such as adequate energy). The systemization through analysis of the tasks that the world will face in the next few decades will be a major challenge itself. This must take place even before we are able to apply the creative political acts which are necessary for successfully achieving effective implementation of recommended solutions.

A key element in the success of building essentially a global consensus is ensuring that there is a close relationship between those who analyze and those who finally must make the decisions. The centers should not be narrow or overly technocratic in their perspective. They must take into consideration the realities of the present global system even as they look to changing patterns and new directions. They must know the concerns of the decision makers even if they are not blinded by their shorter time perspective. They must make practical suggestions, in effect, on how to get from here to there and not merely say we must go in a certain direction without providing a map showing how it can be done.

Widening Our Choices

A related element in managing risk is the creation of mechanisms which can provide a wide array of choices for the global society. It is dangerous to be caught with only a few, if any, options to certain events or problems. To choose between only one, two, or three alternative lines of action, all with serious unknowns or possibly dangerous side effects, is not desirable. Over the long run it would likely be ruinous.

We can illustrate this problem by examination of the energy problem. The extraordinary emphasis by the United States government on research and development of nuclear power reactors and associated technology and its almost complete neglect of solar and other renewable and innovative energy technologies left us with a serious imbalance in energy policy choices. This wrongheaded emphasis left us with little alternative in energy options once the Arab oil boycott and higher prices for OPEC crude brought home how precarious our energy situation was. We have only slowly learned that the heavy emphasis on nuclear technology, including fast breeder reactors and reprocessing plants, brings with it even more danger than the lack of inexpensive oil—the danger of the spread of nuclear weapons and the risk of increased threats of their use. We need to do better next time or there may not be a next time.

Using the same example, we could have considerably broadened our energy choices if we had made a large investment early in solar and other renewable energy technologies. In addition we could have put more effort into the more efficient and cleaner use of coal, a fossil energy resource we have in abundance. Only now are we shifting somewhat that original imbalance and thereby providing for this and future generations a choice of wider and hopefully safer options.

The same problem and the same opportunities exist in most of the other areas of global challenges. We need to examine very closely our risks and, if possible, create the basis for a number of possible solutions, rather than rely on just one approach to provide the answer. We are unlikely to know always in advance all the intermediate and final consequences of a single approach or solution. Also what appears the best option at one stage may not be the case later.

In part this relates to the importance of early planning and analysis. We need more and more lead time if we are to have in place solutions to growing global problems. Rarely will we be able to pluck off the shelf, as it were, solutions or new technologies to deal with massive global high risk situations. We need therefore to apply ourselves to the task of broadening our future on long-term choices so as to decrease our vulnerability to serious disruption.

There are a number of specific methods that might be used to broaden our choices and reduce our vulnerabilities to high risks. The first is early warning: i.e., careful examination of problem areas, emerging technology, new social trends. The second is the development of additional or different options for solving the problem at hand, and the third is creation of the required appropriate institutions for implementation and monitoring of the chosen solution(s) and its (their) impact. For example, one action might be the coordination of research and development activities among many countries aimed at discovering a number of alternative technologies to solve a given problem. In the end decreasing our risks can only be achieved if we have provided to present and future decision makers a wider set of options than would be the case if we simply let nature take its course.

Crisis Management Capability

Another great danger of our present global system is that it lacks a crisis management capability in a world where crisis is or will become endemic. This lack, on both a national and particularly on the international level, is a most dangerous weakness in the present nation-state system. Further, the difficulty is heightened by the fact that we have very limited capability on the national or international level of dealing with more than one crisis at a time. In the real world of the future we are likely to have to deal with several major crises simultaneously. Even at present, the United States government has a very difficult time in focusing on several major time-sensitive problems because of the way decisions are taken in a large and complex bureaucracy with final authority resting on one person.

There is a limit to the time and attention that a finite and small group of decision makers can give to any one problem when there are a large number of serious problems to be solved immediately. Often the result of trying to solve several problems at once is that some are given short shrift. Those that are may by pure luck still be satisfactorily resolved, or the results—even if negative and serious—are not catastrophic. What happens however when several crises come upon a government at once, all with the threat of a very serious catastrophe if they are not properly solved? There is little indication that we have within the United States fully thought out this kind of situation and no evidence that we have planned for it and put in place mechanisms to prepare ourselves for this eventuality.

The situation is far worse in most other countries, some of which have even more antiquated governing structures and analytical capability. But for the world community such a capability hardly exists for even one crisis area, let alone several simultaneously. Yet there is on both the national and on the international level the need to do many things well at the same time. Crises by their very definition cannot be put off. They require immediate action. This kind of response is almost unheard of within any international organization.

This absence of a crisis management capability goes hand-in-hand with the lack of a long-term analysis and planning competence. All of these functions are required to deal with massive high risk situations characteristic of a fast moving high technology world. Without them, man becomes powerless to deal with his own society.

The capacity to act effectively against major forces at work in the world is not easy to achieve in a universe of economic, political, and ideological diversity, if not outright national hostility. Certainly, the development of such a capability will require a greater degree of cooperation between normally antagonistic political entities than has been the case heretofore. But must we await the growth of greater trust or decreased antagonism for the creation of a better global system of crisis management? An even better question is whether a global crisis will await that day. Some action towards the implementation of the suggested reforms could set in motion even greater efforts at risk reduction cooperation.

There are some hopeful signs of growing awareness. The Soviet Union and the United States and Europe jointly cooperated in establishing the Institute of Advanced Systems Analysis located in Europe to examine major societal problems. China has criticized individual terrorism as being against mass revolutionary struggle. Finally, the Soviets have cooperated with other industrial states to help prevent the further spread of nuclear weapons through working towards common criteria on the transfer of sensitive nuclear power technology. In this last case the Soviets recognized that their own security was threatened by a world in which a great many countries have nuclear weapons. They have not yet recognized this fact in such areas as global food shortages, pollution, or population growth. The reasons may be similar to those that exist in many other developed countries—a too short-term political perspective, lack of adequate analysis, and especially a myopic perspective about their own self-interests and their attitudes towards world community responsibility.

Great efforts will need to be undertaken to engage the Communist bloc in a serious dialogue about global challenges and problems. In particular, communication with the professional and more educated younger generation would be helpful. In place of empty diatribes about the imperfections of Communism we would probably do better to engage, in our broadcasts to the Soviet Union and Eastern Europe and in our discussions otherwise, their interest in the future of the world community, their inexorable relationship to it and interdependence within it, and the extent to which they can be brought down by it every bit as much as any other nation or group in the world. This will be a slow, long process.

In the end, it may be necessary for the non-Communist world to proceed alone in developing new mechanisms of risk reduction and community well-being. It may even be necessary for the developed countries initially to work together to this end if the developing world is unwilling or unable to participate. In the end, however, it will be necessary for both the developing world and the Communist bloc to join in this effort. An acknowledgment of willingness to accept true responsibility for all the world's people and recognition by all of a wider burden sharing is the only effective means to reduce the massive global risks we have seen.

In sum, what can these described mechanisms of global community burden sharing and common action do to help us in a world of increasing high risks? First, they can give us a better fix on the broad dimensions of the risks we are likely to run given a certain set of events. They can warn us about potential long-term impacts, so-called secondary consequences of new technology, and new social patterns. Second, they can identify better the resources that are available to solve problems. Identification of contradictory trends, ameliorative factors, or amenable forces which could be employed to improve a dangerous trend or reverse it is required in any approach for recommending corrective action. Third and finally, such mechanisms can propose alternative courses of action and outline their relative costs, thereby providing some insight into probable benefits and the likelihood of final success.

This last function is crucial. It should also be part of any study or report to responsible decision-making bodies. These proposed reports would also, as a general rule, be public as a matter of principle since this will reinforce two important elements in moving towards responsible global management and decision making. First, it is required if the world is to move towards democratic institutions and free debate of various alternative choices. Second, an open global debate by the public, the media, and a larger group of informed experts would contribute to the probability that the final choices made by the responsible bodies will be not only more technically correct but also more likely to reflect some kind of normative consensus by the public of the direction they wish the world to go and of the risks they are willing to take.

Notes

Chapter I

1. For a discussion of the impact of technology on traditional society and the changes it brings, see Margaret Mead, ed., *Cultural Patterns and Technical Change* (New York, New American Library, 1955).

2. Kant's view was: "...reason comprehends only what it considers according to its own plan;...and that it must compel nature to answer the question rather than let itself be lead around by nature, as if on leading strings. But reason must not approach nature like a pupil who lets the teacher recite what he will, but like a duly appointed judge who compels the witness to answer the questions he puts to them."

3. See Ruth M. Davis, "Preventive Technology: A Cure for Scientific Ills," (editorial) *Science*, Vol. 188, No. 4185 (April 18, 1975), p. 213.

4. *Ibid.*

5. Wolf Hafele, "Hypotheticality and the New Challenges: The Pathfinder Role of Nuclear Energy," *Minerva*, Vol. X, No. 3 (July 1974).

6. Alvin Toffler, *Future Shock* (New York, Bantam Books, 1971), p. 372.

7. See among others Lester Brown, *World Without Borders* (New York, Random House, 1972); *The Planetary Bargain, Proposals for a New International Economic Order to Meet Human Needs* (New York, Aspen Institute for Humanistic Studies, 1975); and Mihajlo Mesarović and Eduard Pestel, *Mankind at the Turning Point, The Second Report to the Club of Rome* (New York, Reader's Digest Press, 1974).

8. Henry A. Kissinger, Text of speech to U.N. General Assembly, "Toward a New Understanding of Community," Washington, D.C., The Department of State *Bulletin*, Vol. LXXV, No. 1948 (October 25, 1976), p. 497.

9. See Donella H. Meadows, Dennis L. Meadows, Jorgan Randers,

and William W. Behrens III, *The Limits to Growth*, A Potomac Associates Book (New York, New American Library, 1972); and H. Cole, *et al.*, *Thinking About the Future: A Critique of the Limits to Growth*, University of Sussex (London, Chatto & Windus, 1973).

10. A more moderate follow-up to the "Limits" study is Mihajlo Mesarović and Eduard Pestel, *op. cit.*

11. See for example Wassily Leontief, *et al.*, *The Future of the World Economy; a United Nations Study* (New York, Oxford University Press, 1977).

Chapter II

1. Note that population grows exponentially. A 2.0 percent rate doubles a population in thirty-five years. The 2.5 percent growth rate of the developing countries doubles population in twenty-eight years. Developed countries are growing at between zero to 1.5 percent annually, while developing countries are growing at 2.0 to 3.5 percent. World population will double in less than fifty years at current growth rates.

2. Source, Population Reference Bureau, Inc. *Notes*, March, 1975.

3. See Michael S. Teitelbaum, "Population and Development: Is a Consensus Possible?" *Foreign Affairs*, Vol. 52, No. 4 (July 1974), p. 748.

4. For the United States position and unofficial text of "World Population Plan of Action" see Washington, D.C., Department of State *Bulletin*, September 30, 1974. Also see Philander P. Claxton, Jr. "The World Population Conference: An Assessment," Washington, D.C., Department of State *Bulletin*, November 11, 1974.

5. For a somewhat different and very optimistic viewpoint, see Howard M. Bahr, ed., *et al.*, *Population, Resources, and the Future: Non-Malthusian Perspectives* (Provo, Utah, Brigham Young University Press, 1972). For more pessimistic views, see Thomas W. Wilson, Jr., *World Population and a Global Emergency* (Washington, D.C., Aspen Institute for Humanistic Studies), and Paul R. Ehrlich and Ann H. Erhlich, *Population, Resources, Environment: Issues in Human Ecology* (San Francisco, W. H. Freeman & Co., 1970).

6. See "Concise Report on World Population Situation in 1970-75 and its Long-range Implications," United Nations document ST/ESA/ SER.A/56, 1974. The document defines urban population as each country's own definition of localities which contain 5,000 or more residents.

7. For a broad early discussion of some of these issues see M. C. Shelesnyak, *Growth of Population: Consequences and Controls* (New York, Gordon & Breach, Science Publishers, 1969).

8. See Teitlebaum, *op. cit.*, p. 755.

9. See findings of Bernard Berelson, "An evaluation of the effects of Population Control Programs," in H. B. Parry, ed., *Population and Its Problems* (London, Oxford University Press, 1974). For a study of the

health benefits of family planning see Erik Eckholm and Kathleen Hewland, "Health: The Family Planning Factor," *Worldwatch Paper 10* (Washington, D.C., Worldwatch Institute, 1977).

10. This basic concept was included in Secretary Kissinger's speech to the Seventh Special Session of the United Nations General Assembly, September 1, 1975; see speech text, United Nations, New York, Bureau of Public Affairs, Office of Media Services.

11. Speech of Dr. S. G. Srikantiah, Director, Indian National Institute of Nutrition, to Indian Council of Medical Research, reported by Agence France Presse, in *The Seattle Times*, April 24, 1977.

12. Source: U. S. Department of Agriculture.

13. See Lester Brown, "Increasingly, the U. S. Is Breadbasket to the World," *New York Times*, December 7, 1975.

14. See Lester Brown, *et al.*, *Worldwatch* Paper 5, 1976, pp. 28-29.

15. *The World Food Situation and Prospects to 1999* (Washington, D.C. Department of Agriculture), p. 35.

16. See *World, Food Production, Demand, and Trade*, Iowa State University Center for Agricultural and Rural Development (Ames, Iowa State University Press, 1973).

17. *The World Food Situation and Prospects to 1999*, USDA, *op. cit.*

18. *A Hungry World: The Challenge to Agriculture*, Berkeley, University of California, A Food Task Force, July 1974, p. 23.

19. See for a general discussion of the many factors affecting food: "Food: A Crisis for All," *New York Times*, September 19, 1974, p. 1.

20. Pierre R. Crosson, "Institutional Obstacles to Expansion of World Food Productions," *Science*, Vol. 188 (May 9, 1975), pp. 519-24.

21. See Jonathan Kendell, "Brazil Miracle Makes a Staple Scarce," *New York Times*, December 14, 1976, p. 3.

22. See William R. Cline, "Distribution and Development: A Survey of the Literature," *Journal of Development and Economics*, Vol. 1, 1975, pp. 359-400.

23. Allen Berg, *The Nutrition Factor: Its Role in National Development* (Washington, D.C., The Brookings Institution, 1973).

24. See for issues in this debate, Tenard Joy, "Food and Nutrition Planning," *Journal of Agricultural Economics*, January, 1973; and John W. Mellor, "Nutrition and Economic Growth," in Allen Berg, Melvin S. Crimshaw, and David Call, eds., *Nutrition, National Development and Planning* (Cambridge, The MIT Press, 1971).

25. See especially Johanna T. Dwyer and Jean Mayer, "Beyond Economics and Nutrition: The Complex Basis of Food Policy," *Science*, Vol. 188 (May 9, 1975), pp. 566-70.

26. See for discussion of this issue: David L. Call and F. James Levinson, "A Systematic Approach to Nutrition Intervention Programs," in *Nutrition, National Development and Planning*, edited by Berg, *et al.*, *op. cit.*

27. *Ibid.*, p. 565.

28. See for discussion of health care and nutrition, Michael C.

250

GLOBAL CHALLENGES

Latham, "Nutrition and Infection in National Development," *Science*, Vol. 188, No. 4188 (May 9, 1975), pp. 561–65.

29. *Ibid.*, p. 564.

30. See for discussion of these issues: Berg, *Nutrition, National Development and Planning, op. cit.*

31. "Vaccination Drive Set by UN Agency," *The Washington Post*, May 20, 1977, p. A-13.

32. Morton Minitz, "Polluted Ohio Waters Linked to Cancer," *The Washington Post*, September 20, 1976, p. A-24. For a general discussion of environmental aspects of disease see Erik P. Eckholm, *The Picture of Health, Environmental Sources of Disease* (New York, W. W. Norton & Co., 1977).

33. Lester Brown, *et al.*, *Worldwatch* Paper 5, *op. cit.*, p. 61–62.

34. See Sharon Rosenhause, "Dacca's Barefoot Doctors Have Family Planning Impact," *The Washington Post*, November 7, 1976, p. F-6.

Chapter III

1. See Samuel J. Williamson, *Fundamentals of Air Pollution* (Reading, Mass., Addison-Wesley, 1973), p. 46; and T. A. Hodgson, "Short Term Effects of Air Pollution on Mortality in New York City," *Environmental Science and Technology*, Vol. 4 (July 1970), p. 589; see Greenburg and Schimmel, "A Study of the Relation of Pollution to Mortality," *Journal of the Air Pollution Control Association*, Vol. 22 (August 1972), pp. 607 f; and John M. Fowler, *Energy and the Environment* (New York, McGraw-Hill, 1975), pp. 148–51.

2. See John M. Fowler, *op. cit.*, pp. 136–59.

3. *Ibid.*, p. 151.

4. "Acid Precipitation in Europe," *Environment*, Vol. 14, 1972, p. 36.

5. See Fowler, *op. cit.*, p. 153 and "Acid Rain," *EPA Journal*, June, 1977.

6. See "Science and Citizen," *Environment*, April, 1968, p. 72; and "The Automobile and Air Pollution," Part III (Washington, D.C., Department of Commerce, December, 1967).

7. See Fowler, *op. cit.*, p. 158.

8. See E. G. Walther, "Rating of the Major Air Pollutants and Their Sources by Effect," *Journal of Air Pollution Control Association*, May, 1972, p. 352.

9. *Ibid.*

10. The major reports dealing with the problem of the ozone layer and the impact from halocarbons include the following: (1) "IMOS Report," published as the "Inadvertent Modification of the Stratosphere (IMOS), Report on Fluorocarbons and the Environment," published by the Council on Environmental Quality and the Federal Council for Science and Technology, Washington, D.C., U.S.G.P.O., 1975; (2) "The National Research Council's Committee Report on Impacts of Stratospheric Changes," Washington, D.C., National Academy of Science, 1976; and (3) "Chlorofluorocarbons and Their Effects on Stratosphere Ozone," Department of Environment, Central Unit on Environmental Pollution, London, H.M.S.O., 1976.

11. "The Inadvertent Modification of the Stratosphere Report," *op. cit.*, 1975.

12. The National Research Council Report, *op. cit.*

13. "Chlorofluorocarbons and Their Effect on the Stratosphere Ozone," *op. cit.*, p. 6.

14. "Chlorofluorocarbons and Their Effect on the Stratosphere Ozone," *op. cit.*, p. 7.

15. See Mariana Gosnell, "Earth's Vulnerable Shield," *The Washington Post*, August 10, 1975, p. B-3.

16. See Lee Lascaze, "Changes in Earth's Weather Are Expected to Bring Trouble," *The Washington Post*, January 30, 1977, p. A-6.

17. See Walter Sullivan, "International Team of Specialists Finds No End in Sight to 30-Year Cooling Trend in Northern Hemisphere," *New York Times*, January 5, 1978, p. 51.

18. See "Why It's So Cold," *Newsweek*, January 31, 1977, p. 39.

19. Quoted in Lascaze, *op. cit.*

20. For various views on climate changes see: (1) *Inadvertent Climate Modification, Report of the Study of Man's Impact on Climate*, sponsored by M.I.T. (Cambridge, The M.I.T. Press, 1971); (2) *Understanding Climatic Change, A Program for Action*, U.S. Committee for the Global Atmospheric Research Program, National Research Council (Washington, D.C., National Academy of Sciences, 1975), and (3) *Living with Climate Change, Phase II*, Conference and proceedings, Mitre Corporation (the Aspen Institute for Humanistic Studies and the American Meteorological Society, 1976). Also see *Climate Research and National Climate Program* (December, 1976) and *Primer on Climate Variation and Change* prepared by the Congressional Research Service for the Sub-committee on Environment and the Atmosphere of the House Committee on Science and Technology.

21. See Erik P. Eckholm, *Losing Ground* (New York, W. W. Norton & Co., 1976), pp. 26–45.

22. William Nye Curry, "Farm County of 7,600 Loses Millions to Wind and Blizzard," *The Washington Post*, March 26, 1977, p. 1-F.

23. Lester Brown, Patricia L. McGrath, Bruce Stokes, "Twenty-two Dimensions of the Population Problem," *Worldwatch* Paper 5 (Washington, D.C., World Watch Institute, March, 1976), pp. 70–71.

24. For a general discussion of the global problem of pressures on renewable resources see (1) Erik P. Eckholm, *Losing Ground, op. cit.*, and (2) Lester Brown, *The Twenty-ninth Day* (New York, W. W. Norton & Co., 1978).

25. Brown, McGrath, Stokes, *op. cit.*, p. 65.

26. Boyce Rensberger, "Water Crisis Caused by Man and Nature to be Explored at U.N. Conference," *New York Times*, March 14, 1977, p. 12.

27. *Ibid.*

28. Harold Faber, "Deadly Rain Imperils Two Adirondacks Species," *New York Times*, March 28, 1977, p. 31.

29. Rensberger, *op. cit.*

30. "Iceberg Shortage Ahead?" Editorial, *New York Times*, November 11, 1976, p. 42.

31. Rensberger, *op. cit.*, p. 12.

32. *Ibid.*

33. See for a general discussion of environmental health problems: Erik P. Eckholm, *The Picture of Health, Environmental Sources of Disease* (New York, W. W. Norton & Co., 1977).

34. Peter and Katherin Montague, "Mercury: How Much Are We Eating?" *Saturday Review*, February 6, 1971, p. 51.

35. See "Secretary's Commission on Pesticides and Their Relationships to Environmental Health, Part I, Recommendations and Summaries," Washington, D.C., Department of Health, Education and Welfare, November, 1969.

36. Statement of Robert H. Finch, Secretary of Health, Education, and Welfare, November 12, 1969.

37. "The War on Pollution Spreads World-Wide," *Business Week*, September 27, 1976, p. 82.

38. For a discussion of "growth" issues see Mihajlo Mesarović and Eduard Pestel, *Mankind at the Turning Point, The Second Report to the Club of Rome* (New York, Reader's Digest Press, 1974).

39. Department of the Interior, *First Annual Report of the Secretary Under the Mining and Minerals Policy Act of 1970*, Washington, D.C., March, 1972, Table 9.

40. For a discussion of issues of growth, resource exploitation, and environment see Donella H. Meadows, Dennis L. Meadows, Jorgan Randers, William H. Behrens III, *The Limits to Growth*, A Potomac Associates Book (New York, New American Library, 1972); Erik P. Eckholm, *Losing Ground, op. cit.*, and Lester Brown, *The Twenty-ninth Day, op. cit.*

41. See Harry C. Blaney, "NATO's New Challenge to Problems of Modern Society," *The Atlantic Community Quarterly*, Summer 1973, pp. 236–47.

42. See for discussion of this subject mimeographed text: Address by Christian A. Herter, Jr., former Deputy Assistant Secretary of State for Environmental and Population Affairs, before the International Conference on Environmental Sensing and Assessment, Las Vegas, Nevada, September 17, 1975, pp. 14–17.

43. See "The War on Pollution Spreads World-wide," *Business Week*, September 27, 1976, pp. 82 and 86.

44. *Ibid.*, p. 82.

45. For discussion of funding global environmental needs see Chapter 4 in Eleanor B. Steinberg and Joseph A. Yager, *New Means of Financing International Needs* (Washington, D.C., The Brookings Institution, 1978).

46. See for discussion of legal and other issues involved in pollution and international law: Oscar S. Gray, "International Responsibility of State for Environmental Damage Arising from Non-navigational Uses of International Waters," a report to the U.S. Department of State Pursuant to Contract No. 1722-220055, April 1974, pp. 1–64.

Chapter IV

1. *Oil Transportation by Tankers: An Analysis of Marine Pollution and Safety Measures,* Congress of the United States, Office of Technology Assessment, Washington, D.C., U.S.G.P.O., 1975, p. 26.

2. *Chlorinated Hydrocarbons in the Marine Environment,* Washington, D.C., National Academy of Sciences, 1973.

3. See Douglas M. Johnston, "Marine Pollution Control: Law, Science and Politics," *International Journal,* Canadian Institute of International Affairs, Vol. XXIII, No. 1 (Winter 1972-73), p. 72.

4. See *Oil Transportation by Tankers: An Analysis of Marine Pollution and Safety Measures, op. cit.,* p. 28. See also statement by J. H. Kirby, Director of Shell International Marine, Ltd., quoted by J. R. Wiggins, *Washington Post,* March 15, 1970; also Scott Dillon, *Ship Construction and Operation Standards from Oil Pollution; Abatement,* paper for CCMS Conference on Oil Pollution, 1971; and see *Petroleum in the Marine Environment,* Washington, D.C., National Academy of Sciences, January, 1975.

5. See Max Blumer "Scientific Aspects of the Oil Pollution Problem," unpublished paper, Woods Hole, Mass., Woods Hole Oceanographic Institution, 1970, for the NATO Committee on the Challenges of Modern Society; and Max Blumer, "Oil Pollution of the Oceans," in *Oil on the Sea,* D. P. Hoult, ed., Plenum Press, 1960.

6. *Ibid.* and *Final Draft of the Task Force on Used Oil Disposal,* New York, American Petroleum Institute, 1970.

7. *Petroleum in the Marine Environment, op. cit.*

8. *Ibid.*

9. See Max Blumer, G. Souza, J. Sass, "Hydrocarbon Pollution of Edible Shellfish by an Oil Spill," *Marine Biology,* Vol. 5, 1970, pp. 195-202.

10. J. A. Murphy, *Environmental Effects of Oil Pollution,* paper presented to session on Oil Pollution Control, American Society of Civil Engineers, Boston, Mass., July 13, 1970.

11. *Pollution: An International Problem for Fisheries,* Rome, Food and Agriculture Organization of the U.N., 1971, pp. 15-36.

12. See S. O. Haway, "The Comparative Toxicities of Crude Oil, Field Studies," cited in *Oil Transportation by Tankers, op. cit.*

13. Blumer, "Scientific Aspects of the Oil Pollution Problem" *op. cit.,* pp. 5-6.

14. *Ibid.*

15. *Ibid.* p. 17.

16. *Ibid.* pp. 4-5.

17. See *Oil Transportation by Tankers, op. cit.,* p. 31.

18. See *Chlorinated Hydrocarbons in the Marine Environment, A Report Prepared by the Panel on Monitoring Persistent Pesticides in the Marine Environment of the Committee on Oceanography,* Washington, D.C., National Academy of Science, 1971.

19. *Ibid.* p. iv.

20. *Ibid.* pp. 8-13.

21. *Ibid.* p. 2.

22. *Ibid.* p. 2.

23. *Ibid.*

24. Thor Heyerdahl, "Man Against Nature," Speech text to joint Committee on Environment, Consultative Assembly of the Council of Europe, Strasbourg, 21 January 1972. Press Communiqué, D (72) 3, p. 7.

25. The earlier treaty was "The International Convention for the Prevention of Pollution of the Sea by Oil 1954" which was slightly amended in 1962 to strengthen it somewhat. However, these conventions did not really provide for strict discharge standards nor strong enforcement. The restrictions in the Amended Convention which still must be adopted by individual adhering parties include:

    (a) A limitation on the total quantity of oil which a tanker may discharge in any ballast voyage to 1/15,000 of the total cargo carrying capacity of the vessel.

    (b) A limit on the rate at which oil may be discharged to a maximum of 60 litres per mile traveled by the ship.

    (c) A prohibition on any discharge from the cargo spaces of a tanker within 50 miles of the nearest land.

26. IMCO Assembly approved a number of amendments to the International Convention for the Safety of Life at Sea of 1960. There was also drafted and approved the 1969 Intervention Convention and the 1969 Civil Liability Convention. Provisions included, for example, the mandatory carrying of certain navigational equipment.

27. See *Coastal Water Pollution: Pollution of the Sea by Oil Spills,* No. 1, Brussels, NATO, Committee on the Challenges of Modern Society. Note the relevant Resolution on oil spills was passed by the NATO Council on November 27, 1970.

28. This Convention was preceded by a regional effort, *The Convention on the Control of Marine Pollution by Dumping from Ships and Aircraft at Oslo,* signed in October, 1971, and opened for signature in February, 1972. This regional initiative of nations of the Northeast Atlantic included a "black list" and a "green list" of substances that may not be dumped at sea by contracting states except under extraordinary circumstances.

29. See Charles S. Pearson, "Environmental Policy and the Ocean," in *Perspective on Ocean Policy, Conference on Conflict and Order in Ocean Relations,* prepared for National Science Foundation, by Ocean Policy Project, the Johns Hopkins University, Washington, D.C., U.S.G.P.O., 1975, pp. 207-19; and Richard M. Cooper, "An Economist's View of the Oceans," in *Journal of World Trade Law,* Vol. 9, No. 4, 1975, pp. 357-77, and by Yale University Economic Growth Center, as *Center Paper No. 228,* 1975.

30. See John Temple Swing, "Who Will Own the Oceans," *Foreign Affairs,* April, 1976, pp. 527-46.

31. The LOS Treaty draft only provides for general principles, asking states to take action to reduce land-based pollution.

32. For economic analysis of global fishing and its management, see Richard M. Cooper, "An Economist's View of the Oceans," *op. cit.*

33. G. Saetersdal, *Assessment of Unexploited Resources,* Technical Conference on Fishery Management and Development, Vancouver, Canada, February 13–23, 1973, Food and Agriculture Organization of the U.N., Document FI:FMD/73/S-33, January, 1973.

34. G. Hempel, *Productivity of the Oceans,* Technical Conference on Fishery Management and Development, Vancouver, Canada, February 13–23, Food and Agriculture Organization of the U.N., Document FI: FMD/73/S-38, January, 1973.

35. *A Hungry World: The Challenge to Agriculture,* Berkeley, University of California, A Food Task Force, July 1974, p. 31.

36. In 1970, Peru took 18 percent, Japan 13 percent, U.S.S.R. 10 percent, China 9 percent, and the U.S. above 7 percent of the total.

37. The regional projections of consumption break down as follows: Western Europe, from 20 kilograms per capita to 26, U.S.S.R., 24 to 33; U.S., 15 to 17; Japan, 57 to 65; Latin America, 6.5 to 8; and Africa, 6.7 to 9.

38. See *ibid.,* p. 1; and Clarence P. Idyll, *The Sea Against Hunger* (New York, Thomas Y. Crowell Company, 1970), pp. 28–46.

39. See Figure 8, p. 47, and p. 46, Donella H. Meadows, *et al., The Limits to Growth,* A Potomac Associates Book (New York, New American Library, 1972).

40. *Ibid.*

41. FPC consists of about 80 percent protein and 13 percent ash (mostly minerals including calcium and phosphorus). FPC is highly nutritious; two ounces can contain as much protein as a twelve-ounce steak.

42. The U.S. Food and Drug Administration initially banned (a ruling since changed) the use of FPC made from whole fish for human use and this has been a barrier to its introduction both in the U.S. and abroad.

43. The utilization of blacksmelt, anchovettas, hake, squids, sardines, menhaden, and pilchard for FPC in place of fish meal is an alternative if a global economic market for FPC could be developed.

44. Idyll, *op. cit.,* pp. 142–3.

45. For a more detailed discussion of the potential contribution of FPC, see Frank E. Firth, ed., *Encyclopedia of Marine Resources* (New York, Van Nostrand, 1969), pp. 271–2.

46. Idyll, *op. cit.* pp. 70–71.

47. See Howard A. Wilcox, *The Ocean Food and Energy Farm Project,* paper for International Conference on Marine Technology Assessment, Man and the Oceans, October 29, 1975, Monaco; available from Naval Undersea Center, San Diego, California 92132.

48. See for an interesting but narrow economic perspective on this topic, Francis T. Christy, Jr., "Distribution Systems for World Fisheries: Problems and Principles," in *Perspective on Oceans Policy, op. cit.*

49. For a different concept, based on management of individual stocks and on purely economic principles, see Richard M. Cooper "An Economist's View of the Oceans," *op. cit.,* pp. 361–4.

50. Of special interest is the fact that some of these minerals,

existing as "nodules" on the deep seabed, are continually growing. (We are still not sure exactly how this happens.) It should be possible, when harvesting these minerals, to apply the theory of "maximum sustainable yield"—a "conservation/exploitation" principle for renewable living resources like fish. Thus, we can "mine" exactly the amount annually of seabed minerals replaced by nature over the same period.

51. See, for an optimistic assessment, David B. Johnson and Dennis E. Logue, "U.S. Economic Interests in Law of the Sea Issues," in *The Law of the Sea: U.S. Interests and Alternatives*, Ryan C. Amacher and Richard James Sweeney, eds., Washington, D.C., Enterprise Institute for Public Policy Research.

52. *Ibid.*, p. 39.

53. For various estimates of the potential of seabed mining see: *United Nations, Economic Implications of Seabed Mineral Development in the International Area; Report of the Secretary-General*, A/CONF. 62/65, May, 1974; Alvin Kaufman, "The Economics of Ocean Mining" in *Marine Technology Society Journal*, July/August 1970; Rebecca L. Wright, *Ocean Mining, An Economic Evaluation*, Washington, D.C., Ocean Mining Administration, Department of Interior, May, 1976; *Mineral Resources of the Deep Seabed*, U.S. Congress, Senate, Subcommittee on Minerals, Materials, and Fuels of the Committee on Interior and Insular Affairs, 93rd Congress, 2nd Session, March, 1974; and *Deep Seabed Minerals: Resources, Diplomacy, and Strategic Interest*, Subcommittee on International Organizations of the Committee on International Relations, House of Representatives, by the Congressional Research Service, Library of Congress, March 1, 1978, Washington, D.C., U.S.G.P.O.

54. See John L. Mero, *The Mineral Resources of the Sea* (New York, American Elsevier Publishing Co., Inc., 1965).

55. See Ambassador Arvid Pardo's memorandum of August, 1967, to the First Committee of the U.N. General Assembly.

56. Henry A. Kissinger, speech text, "International Law, World Order and Human Progress," August 11, 1975, No. 408, Washington, D.C., Department of State.

57. "Grabbing the Oceans," *The Economist*, May 13, 1978, pp. 86-7.

58. See for background: Ann L. Hollick and Robert E. Osgood, *New Era of Ocean Politics* (Baltimore, Johns Hopkins University Press, 1974).

59. See Richard M. Cooper, "An Economist's View of the Oceans," *op. cit.*, p. 367.

60. *Ibid.*

61. See: *Our Nation and the Sea: A Plan for National Action*, Report of the Commission on Marine Science, Engineering and Resources, Washington, D.C., U.S.G.P.O., January, 1969, p. 122.

Chapter V

1. Joel Darmstadter, *et al.*, *Energy in the World Economy: A statistical review of trends in output, trade, and consumption since 1925* (Baltimore, Johns Hopkins

University Press, 1971); and *World Energy Supplies: 1950–1974*, United Nations, New York, Department of Economic and Social Affairs, Statistical Papers, 1976.

2. John M. Fowler, *Energy and the Environment, op. cit.*, p. 99.

3. *World Energy Supplies: 1950–74, op. cit.*, and in Denis Hayes, *Rays of Hope: The Transition to a Post-Petroleum World* (New York, W. W. Norton & Co., 1977), p. 25.

4. *Energy Needs, Uses and Resources in Developing Countries*, Policy Analysis Division, National Center for Analysis of Energy Systems, Brookhaven National Laboratory, prepared for U.S. Agency for International Development and U.S. Department of Energy, Washington, D.C., March, 1978, p. 4.

5. Fowler, *op. cit.*, p. 9 and p. 95.

6. *Ibid.*, p. 96.

7. *Ibid.*, pp. 68–9.

8. See Joel Darmstadter, "Energy Consumption: Trends and Patterns," in Sam H. Schurr, *Energy, Economic Growth, and the Environment* (Baltimore, Johns Hopkins University Press, 1972).

9. Fowler, *op. cit.*, p. 290.

10. *International Energy Supply: A Perspective from the Industrial World*, New York, The Rockefeller Foundation, May, 1978, p. 27.

11. *Cooperative Approaches to World Energy Problems*, A tripartite report by *fifteen experts from the European community, Japan and North America* (Washington, D.C., The Brookings Institution, 1974), pp. 1–51.

12. *Energy Needs, Uses and Resources in Developing Countries, op. cit.*, p. XV.

13. *Ibid.*, p. XVI.

14. Lester Brown, *et al.*, "Twenty-two Dimensions of the Population Problem," *Worldwatch* Paper 5, Washington, D.C., World Watch Institute, March, 1976, pp. 74–5.

15. Neil H. Jacoby, *Multinational Oil: A Study in Industrial Dynamics*, (New York, Macmillan, 1974), p. 258.

16. Stephen D. Krasner, "The Great Oil Sheikdown," *Foreign Policy*, No. 13 (Winter, 1973–74), p. 136.

17. A "quad is a standard unit of measurement for energy. The quad is based upon the British Thermal Unit (BTU) which is defined as the amount of energy required to raise the temperature of one pound of water one degree Fahrenheit. It is a convenient measure of energy when dealing with large figures and many different types of energy used in a single country or worldwide. A "quad" is defined as one quadrillion BTU's or 10^{15} BTU's. For example, one quad per year is equal to 472 thousand barrels of oil per day. To give another example of the amount of energy in a quad, in 1973 the State of Iowa with a population of about 2.8 million people used one quad of energy for all purposes.

18. John M. Fowler, *Energy and the Environment* (New York, McGraw-Hill, 1975), p. 405; and Edward Teller, *Energy: A Plan for Action* (New York, Commission on Critical Choices for Americans, 1975), pp. 14–7.

19. This set of policy objectives was adopted and modified by the

author from: Robert B. Krueger, *The United States in International Oil, A Report for the Federal Energy Administration on U.S. Firms and Government Policies* (New York, Praeger Publishers, 1975), p. 10.

20. Since 1973 the price of oil has risen about 300 percent from $2.90 a barrel for Saudi Arabian light to $11.51 a barrel at the end of 1976 and after 1977 to $12.70.

21. James Tanner and Ray Vicker, "Cartel's Crossroads," *The Wall Street Journal*, June 16, 1978, pp. 1 and 20.

22. See Norman L. Brown and James W. Howe, "Solar Energy for Village Development," *Science*, February 10, 1978.

23. Typical electricity generating costs in kwhs in sample developing countries are: 95¢ for rural electricity using diesel engines in Senegal, with 25¢ for capital city electricity; a rural hospital in Upper Volta was $1.25, and a village in Mali 55¢.

24. Barry Commoner, "The Solar Solution," *Washington Post,* September 12, 1976, p. C5.

25. Muammer Cetincelik, "Is Solar Energy the Fuel of the Future?" *Impact of Science on Society*, Vol. XXIV, No. 3, 1974, pp. 261–6.

26. See for discussion of new energy technologies, Denis Hayes, *Rays of Hope: The Transition to a Post-Petroleum World* (New York, W. W. Norton & Co., 1977). Also see *Solar Energy, Progress and Promise*, Washington, D.C., Council on Environmental Quality, April, 1978.

Chapter VI

1. See Robert Gillette, "Nuclear Proliferation: India, Germany, May Accelerate the Process," *Science*, Vol. 188 (May 30, 1975), pp. 911–14.

2. See "Nozzle Enrichment for Sale," *Science*, Vol. 188 (May 30, 1975), p. 911.

3. See Victor Gilinsky, "The Military Potential of Civil Nuclear Power," in Mason Willrich, ed., *Civil Nuclear Power and International Security* (New York, Praeger Publishers, 1971), pp. 22–5.

4. William O. Doub and Joseph M. Dunkert, "Making Nuclear Energy Safe and Secure," *Foreign Affairs*, July, 1975, p. 762; and Victor Gilinsky, *op. cit.*, pp. 21–2.

5. See unpublished paper, Alvin M. Weinberg, "Can Man Live with Fission—A Prospectus," March 21, 1973; and Alvin M. Weinberg, "The Moral Imperatives of Nuclear Energy," *Nuclear News*, Vol. 14, No. 12 (December 1971), pp. 33–7.

6. Weinberg, "The Moral Imperatives of Nuclear Energy," *op. cit.*, p. 34.

7. For example, in 1975 West Germany agreed to sell to Brazil (an up-to-then nonnuclear weapon state) a whole technology package which, over the next fifteen years, will give Brazil the capability of building atomic weapons as well as nuclear electric power. Further Brazil has not signed the Nuclear Non-Proliferation Treaty by which nonnuclear weapons nations are prohibited from making nuclear explosives and

agree to submit to international inspection of nuclear facilities. See Bowen Northrup, "Unchained Atom?" *Wall Street Journal*, July 2, 1975, p. 1, f.

8. *New York Times*, September 24, 1975, p. 8.

9. France has stated, however, that she will act in her export policy as if she were a party to the NPT.

10. For a further discussion of the international implications of nuclear technology sales see James Reston, "The Nuclear Power Race," *New York Times*, June 4, 1975, p. 35.

11. All sales abroad of special nuclear material and associated technology must be approved by the U.S. government including the Nuclear Regulatory Commission (NRC) and the Department of State. The Ford Administration planned to encourage private ownership of all new enrichment plants (existing United States plants are owned by the Federal government) and this approach could create new pressures on the government to export enriched uranium to states with less than peaceful intentions or with weak safeguard arrangements. However, current government policy is firmly opposed to the spread of both enrichment and plutonium processing technology.

12. A number of studies were done within the United States on the PNE question and most have shown they are too expensive and/or too dangerous. One report is by Gulf Universities Research Consortium at Galveston, Texas, and was done for ACDA, a follow-up report was done by Professor Franklin A. Long at Cornell University, and both reports were largely skeptical of the use of PNEs.

13. See Luther J. Carter, "Peaceful Nuclear Explosions: Promises, Promises," *Science*, Vol. 188 (June 6, 1975), p. 996. There is one new concept called Project *Pacer*, which is thought to be a possible shortcut to fusion power. Through the use of thermonuclear devices, which would be fired inside of huge, partly water-filled cavities leached out of salt domes, this project hopes to produce electricity and breed fissionable material. The detonation of two 50 kiloton devices would produce heat steam which would also contain uranium 233 or plutonium 239 that could be taken out of the steam for later energy use. See William D. Metz, "Energy: Washington Gets A New Proposal for Using H-Bombs," *Science*, Vol. 188, No. 4184 (April 11, 1975), pp. 136–7. This concept, however, is rather visionary and has many major problems in theory and application.

14. The Soviets largely wish, they say, to use PNEs for rerouting of rivers, dredging of canals, and the moving of mountains.

15. See suggestion in Lincoln P. Bloomfield, "Nuclear Spread and World Power," *Foreign Affairs*, July 1975, pp. 748–54.

16. For a sociological and historical study of terrorism see Walter Laqueur, *Terrorism* (Boston, Little, Brown and Company, 1977). Another historical study is by Albert Parry, *Terrorism; from Robespierre to Arafat*, (New York, The Vanguard Press, 1976).

17. See Brian Jenkins, *International Terrorism: A New Mode of Conflict*,

260 GLOBAL CHALLENGES

California Seminar on Arms Control and Foreign Policy, Research Paper No. 48, Los Angeles, Crescent Publications, January, 1975.

18. See Theodore B. Taylor, "Nuclear Terrorism: A Threat of the Future," *Science Digest*, August, 1974, pp. 12–6, and Mason Willrich and Theodore B. Taylor, *Nuclear Theft: Risks and Safeguards* (Cambridge, Mass., Ballinger Publishing Company, 1974).

19. It is possible that criminals might traffic in plutonium with nations without an independent nuclear capability and this would pose very serious problems. However, there are a number of constraints on this kind of business which probably would make it unlikely to be a favored option of criminal groups.

20. See Doub and Dukert, "Making Nuclear Energy Safe and Secure," *op. cit.*, p. 764.

21. See Weinberg, "Can Man Live with Fission—A Prospectus," *op. cit.*, pp. 7–10; Harry C. Blaney, "The Energy Crisis: A Challenge to the International System," *World Affairs*, Vol. 136, No. 3 (Winter, 1973–4), pp. 204–6; Lincoln P. Bloomfield, "Nuclear Spread and World Order," *Foreign Affairs*, July, 1975, pp. 743–55; Mason Willrich, "Global Politics of Nuclear Energy," *op. cit.*, pp. 97–100 and pp. 179–86.

22. See speech text, Henry A. Kissinger, to United Nations General Assembly, September 22, 1975, Washington, D.C., Department of State.

23. Lincoln P. Bloomfield, *op. cit.*, p. 750.

24. It should be noted that there already exists a multinational reprocessing facility in Western Europe, EUROCHEMIQUE, which serves most of the countries in the region and is jointly owned and controlled. Thus the multinational concept already has a working model.

Chapter VII

1. Among the writers on this topic are Margaret Mead, Ruth Benedict, Geoffrey Gorer, David M. Potter and David Riesman.

2. *Science, Technology and Society—Prospective Look, Summary and Conclusions,* The Bellagio Conference, U.S. National Academy of Sciences, June 1976, p. 23.

3. Allen L. Hammond, "Crop Forecasting from Space—Toward a Global Food Watch," *Science*, Vol. 188 (May 2, 1975), pp. 434–6; and Craig Covault, "Remote Sensing Commitments Urged," *Aviation Week & Space Technology*, May 16, 1977, pp. 49–51.

4. Farowh El Baz, "Expanding Desert Creates Grim Beauty But Also Threatens Crucial Cropland," *Smithsonian*, Vol. 8, No. 3 (June, 1977), pp. 36–40.

5. Item: Prime Minister Sirmavo Bandaranaike closed down Sri Lanka's largest newspaper group five days before that nation's eighth general election in 1977 according to the *Washington Post*, July 17, 1977, p. A-18.

6. Ridha Najar, "Towards a New World Order of Information," The UNESCO *Courier*, April 1977, pp. 21–23.

7. *Ibid.*, p. 22.

8. *Ibid.*

9. Jonathan C. Randal, "Gabon's Mood Is Its Own But Its Muscle Is French," *Washington Post*, July 4, 1977, p. A-15.

10. David Ottaway, "Africa: Shutting the Door to the Press," *Washington Post*, July 23, 1977.

11. "Press Warned by Nairobi Peril," Associated Press Dispatch, *Richmond Times Dispatch*, October 14, 1976; and "UNESCO Resolution on News Softened," UPI report, *The Miami Herald*, January 21, 1978.

12. See "The Marine Scientific Research Issue in the Law of the Sea Negotiations"; Statement of the Ocean Policy Committee, Commission on International Relations, Washington, D.C., National Academy of Sciences, National Research Council, 1977.

13. *Ibid.*

14. *Ibid.* The difficulties of obtaining the cooperation of coastal states in permitting scientific marine research were further outlined in the cited NAS statement: "As the protracted Law of the Sea negotiations continue, more and more coastal States are adopting restrictive positions concerning scientific research. In the past year the records of the U.S. National University Oceanographic Laboratory System, which coordinates the activities of the academic fleet, indicate that about half of the scheduled cruises for work in waters over which other nations claim control have been cancelled because requests were denied, or have been hindered sufficiently to prevent the cruise taking place. Some requests were never acknowledged; sometimes approval came too late for the program to be successfully conducted. At least 18 nations were involved one way or another in inhibiting science in this way. It is believed that oceanographic vessels from other countries have suffered from a similar problem."

15. See relevant articles of the 1958 International Continental Shelf Convention.

Chapter VIII

1. See for discussion of this question: *The Plenary Bargain Proposals for a New International Economic Order to Meet Human Needs*. Report of an International Workshop convened in Aspen, Colorado, July 7–August 1, 1975; A Policy Paper of the Aspen Institute for Humanistic Studies, n.d.

2. See "March of the Lilliputians," Editorial, *Wall Street Journal*, June 11, 1977.

3. See Eleanor B. Steinberg and Joseph A. Yager, *New Means of Financing International Needs* (Washington, D.C., Brookings Institution, 1978).

Index